SOCIAL WORK PRACTICE

PRACTICE

A Radical Perspective

Jeffry Galper
Temple University

PRENTICE-HALL, INC., Englewood Cliffs, New Jersey 07632

Library of Congress Cataloging in Publication Data

Galper, Jeffry H
 Social work practice.

 Includes bibliographical references and index.
 1. Social service. 2. Social change. 3. Radicalism. I. Title.
HV41.G293   361   79-20800
ISBN 0-13-819508-0

As I wrote this book I had before me an image of those of you who are likely to be the majority of its readers. You are, I believe, people in the social service sector, including practicing social service workers, social welfare students, and social welfare faculty. Most of you do not consider yourselves to be radical, but you are frustrated and angered by the general conditions of the society and by the specific circumstances within which you practice in the social service sector. It is my intention to offer you a socialist perspective for analyzing and acting on that frustration and anger, in the belief that such a perspective will serve you and all of us. This book is dedicated to you. I present it with the hope that you will make it a useful tool in clarifying the nature of our common circumstances and subsequently in moving toward action to address the tasks we face.

Jeffry Galper

Printed in the United States of America

10 9 8 7 6 5 4 3 2 1

Editorial/Production supervision
 and interior design by Scott Amerman
Cover design by RL Communications
Manufacturing buyer: Ray Keating

PRENTICE-HALL INTERNATIONAL, INC., *London*
PRENTICE-HALL OF AUSTRALIA PTY. LIMITED, *Sydney*
PRENTICE-HALL OF CANADA, LTD., *Toronto*
PRENTICE-HALL OF INDIA PRIVATE LIMITED, *New Delihi*
PRENTICE-HALL OF JAPAN, INC., *Tokyo*
PRENTICE-HALL OF SOUTHEAST ASIA PTE. LTD., *Singapore*
WHITEHALL BOOKS LIMITED, WELLINGTON, *New Zealand*

3 6 1
G 178

Contents

1 1 6 33

Preface

This book presents the theory on which radical social work practice can be based. It develops, for a variety of specific practice arenas, some directions and guidelines for that practice. The rationale for such practice rests on a socialist critique of the society in general and of social work and social welfare institutions specifically. However, that critique is only reviewed and not developed extensively in these pages since a more thorough perspective was presented in my earlier book, *The Politics of Social Services* (Prentice-Hall, Inc. 1975). The theory that is elaborated here, and which constitutes Part I of the book, concerns the nature and process of social change from a socialist viewpoint. This theory then forms the basis for Part II of the book which addresses the particular contribution that can be made by progressive workers within the social services to the larger processes of change.

I have kept several guidelines in mind while preparing this material. First, I recognize the commitment of social service workers of various political persuasions to meeting the immediate needs of service users as well as they can, given the limitations under which they work. Therefore, in looking at the contribution social service workers can make to long-term processes of transformation, I have also been conscious of our short-term obligations to people in need. The focus of radical practice, as I develop it here, is on integrating the long-term commitments to social change with the short-term responsibility for crisis intervention.

Second, I have been conscious of the fact that a fully useful theoretical perspective for radical practice requires some serious thinking about fundamental social processes from a perspective with which most social service workers are not familiar. I have tried to address the basic questions to provide readers with a broader framework for developing theoretical sophistication about change processes than social work education usually offers. At the same time, I have minimized the use of unfamiliar leftist jargon and shorthand so that these ideas, and the social perspectives to which they refer, will be accessible to readers who do not have a history of study and practice from a radical perspective.

Finally, I have attempted to balance the larger theoretical framework with specific guidelines for intervention. There are dangers involved in overlooking either end of the spectrum. To develop theory without developing practice implications is to leave readers wiser, possibly, but surely more frustrated about the possibilities of their actually intervention to make a difference in the world. On the other hand, to move too far in the direction of a "how to do it" approach runs the risk of presenting radical practice as technique or method rather than as a comprehensive orientation to practice. With this in mind, I have not written a cookbook or provided a blueprint. I have developed what I consider to be relevant theory and I have offered practice guidelines, in the hope that this book will stimulate radical social work practice and further research and writing in this area.

Acknowledgments

Many people contributed to this book by reading and commenting on individual chapters, major sections, or the entire manuscript. Their assistance was invaluable. Particularly, my dear friends and political allies David Tobis of New York City and Peter Findlay of Ottawa, Canada, read through a complete early draft and commented and criticized thoroughly and thoughtfully. In addition, Carol Angell, John Romanyshyn and Edith Galper offered useful feedback on major parts of the book. A larger number of people than I can mention here read specific chapters in an earlier format and freely shared their reactions and insights with me. To all of you, my sincere thanks for your willingness to invest yourselves in this project. I know that you did so because of your commitment to the political tasks we share and because of the personal relationships we have developed and nurtured over the years.

A significant portion of the work on this book was undertaken during a study leave which was granted to me by the School of Social Administration, Temple University, Philadelphia. The award of that leave would not have been possible without the support and recommendation of a committee of my teaching colleagues and the willingness of still additional faculty to cover my assignments in my absence. While many of my colleagues do not share the political viewpoints presented here, they have consistently endorsed my right to pursue a socialist analysis in teaching and writing and have supported me in a variety of ways. I appreciate them keenly.

THEORETICAL
FOUNDATIONS

1

Orientation and Definitions

Introduction

Social work practitioners, students, and teachers share a growing interest in the relationship of radical ideas to social work theory and practice. This interest is a result of the increasingly difficult circumstances arising within Western capitalist countries and their effect on the people working within social service sectors of capitalist economies. It is becoming less and less possible to believe that the conventional processes of reform can create conditions in which the majority of people can have adequate access to the material necessities of life and can have reasonable opportunities for achievement, satisfaction, and personal growth. For social service workers particularly, a manifestation of the broader discontent is the growing recognition that the social services offer very limited and imperfect opportunities for service to others, and that they do not support a personally fulfilling and materially rewarding career.

This book is an effort to formulate an approach to social work practice and more generally, to work in the social service sector, by speaking to the underlying discontent. It does so by elaborating the theoretical underpinnings of what can be called radical social work and by suggesting the kind of practice that flows from such theoretical underpinnings. Specifically the analysis of the dilemmas facing social services and social service workers rests on a socialist perspective, both in the critique of the present system which it develops and in the alternative strategies and outcomes which it proposes.

Most of the people who are likely to read this material do not consider themselves socialists and in fact, may be largely unfamiliar with a socialist model of analysis. I know too that some readers will have more or less hostile, as well as an unformed, reaction to a socialist outlook. I am intentionally directing my writing to these people as well as to those who have thought through the issues and have concluded that a socialist perspective best expresses their desires, concerns, and analysis.

This book does not assume a great deal of prior political sophistication or a clear radical commitment on the part of its readers. It does assume a deep concern about the status quo, about conventional analyses of the status quo, and about the practice methods and strategies advanced by mainstream, conventional social work. It also assumes some willingness to explore new intellectual and political territory, even when that territory seems dangerous or tainted by virtue of its newness and by virtue of the fact that defenders of the status quo have tried so hard to discredit socialism. For readers willing to reexamine the political socialization they have received through years of one-sided and often misleading analysis and propaganda, this book will offer a beginning acquaintance with the basic ideas of socialism and with some of the major analytic tools that derive from a socialist perspective. Hopefully, these analytic tools will be of use in people's day-to-day lives and in their day-to-day work in the social service sector.

A socialist analysis and model for practice is not the only option available to those who are dissatisfied and disturbed by the status quo. In fact a wide variety of alternative forms of practice or of practice techniques exist, some of which identify themselves or are identified by others as radical. These approaches use the term radical to imply fundamental difference. This has been true of advocacy approaches, the creation of alternative or street agencies, behavior modification methodologies, non- or anti-Freudian casework, interest group organization and others. I do not regard these various techniques or approaches as radical, since they are not rooted in and directed toward a socialist commitment.[1] None the less there is good reason why such approaches do receive, and sometimes willingly adopt, the radical

---

[1] I have developed a critique of several of these alternatives in *The Politics of Social Services* (Englewood Cliffs, N.J.: Prentice-Hall, Inc., 1975), see Chapter 5, "Social Reform: The Liberal Response," pp. 73–87; Chapter 6, "Social Work as Conservative Politics," pp. 88–110; and Chapter 7, "Community Organization and Social Casework: The Containment of Change," pp. 111–139. See also David G. Gil, *The Challenge of Social Equality* (Cambridge, Mass.: Schenkman, 1976) especially Part I, "Contributions to Theory and Philosophy of Social Development," pp. 1–76.

label. In so doing, they speak to the need of social service workers, sometimes experienced more at an intuitive level than at a fully conscious level, for a fundamental alternative. At the same time, by continuing to operate within the larger framework of capitalist society, they do not force us to reconsider some of the most basic ideas we hold. They promise remedy without the hard work of transformation. Since the socialist approach goes deeper, in this sense, it is more frightening and alien and more exciting and promising.

There have been several periods in the history of social work when radical people associated with it have attempted to articulate the relationship between a socialist perspective and social work practice. Since there are varieties of socialist analysis and practice and since socialism is not a blueprint, but an approach to be applied in varying historical circumstances, the practice of socialist-oriented social workers has varied over the course of time. During the Progressive Era the relatively conservative socialism of the settlement house leaders led them to fight for what became the rudiments of welfare state measures. In Chapter 4, I will analyze and critique the welfare state approach because of the role it plays in helping to maintain the fundamental structures and ideology of capitalism. Despite the fact that socialists may now be critical of the conservative nature of current social welfare measures, we can acknowledge the progressive thrust these measures represented at the turn of the century and cannot dismiss the extent to which their advocates were forging new ground for social work practice.

In the 1930s leftist social workers helped to organize rank-and-file clubs among social workers in a number of cities across the United States. These clubs participated in creating militant worker-service user alliances and focused particularly on the problems created by unemployment during the Depression.[2] Leftist social workers, in contrast to Progressive Era social reformers, shared perspectives closer to those represented in this book.

In the 1960s some social workers, influenced by the civil rights movement and the New Left, became involved with progressive groups of service users, for example, the National Welfare Rights Organization and various tenant unions. Later they formed independent leftist social work organizations, such as the Social Welfare Worker's Movement.[3] In the 1980s radical

---

[2]For example, see *Social Work Today*, the journal of the rank and file social work groups of the 1930s and early 1940s. Also useful is Bertha Reynold's autobiography, *An Uncharted Journey* (New York: Citadel Press, 1963), see especially Chapter X, "Vitality," pp. 153–169 and Chapter XI, "Rethinking," pp. 170–188. See also Leslie Alexander, "Organizing the Professional Social Worker: Union Development in Voluntary Social Work, 1930–1950," (unpublished doctoral dissertation, School of Social Work and Social Research, Bryn Mawr College, August, 1976) and Leslie Leighninger and Robert Knickmeyer, "The Rank and File Movement: The Relevance of Radical Social Work Traditions to Modern Social Work Practice," *Journal of Sociology and Social Welfare*, 4(November, 1976), 166–177.

[3]Stanley Wenocur, "The Social Welfare Worker's Movement: A Case Study of New Left Thought in Practice," *Journal of Sociology and Social Welfare*, 3 (September. 1973), 3–10.

politics in social work has its own particular flavor and organizational forms, much of which will be discussed more fully in the following chapters. As we examine the current manifestations of radicalism in social work, however, let us do so with an awareness that we are exploring the relationship of social work to socialist thinking within the context of a long standing tradition.

Although the legacy of leftist thought in social work is notable, but not fully recorded or well understood, each successive period of political development has required new definitions, formulations, and understandings of the major political tasks facing leftist social workers. We are always both starting over and continuing. The conceptualization and practice of radical social work at any moment is related to the nature and level of radical activity in the society at large at that same moment. It is inevitable that the resurgence of a larger radical movement in the society will stimulate radical thought and organization within various subsectors of the society, including the social welfare sector. Similarly it is difficult for a well-formulated and organizationally developed radical presence to emerge within one sector, such as social work, in the absence of broader support and stimulation. Of course it is possible that the development of a radical perspective and radical activity within social work will lag behind similar developments in other sectors of the society, as it is possible that social work can be more advanced, at a given period, in generating a left wing than are other sectors. However the developments are likely to be roughly parallel. Therefore, to understand the possibilities and potential of radical social work practice, it is necessary to have a perspective on the larger political scene, particularly in terms of the stage of development of a radical movement.

I believe, as do many other North American leftists, that the present period is one of relatively rapid change in the political, social, and economic circumstances that influence the possibilities for radicalism. The period since the early 1970s has been marked by a deteriorating standard of living for a large proportion of people, by an increasing difficulty in state financing of public services, and by a growing loss of confidence in the idea of disinterested government service to all segments of society. It is not possible to point to a proportionately rapid increase in radical ideology and organization, but it is relatively easy to identify many signs that the present order is in a period of significant dislocation.

Recent political history can be characterized in terms of alternating cycles of quietude and activity. Seen in this light the lower keyed struggles of the 1950s gave way to the activism of the 1960s, with the emergence of the civil rights movement, the New Left, the antiwar movement, the women's movement, and others. The period from the mid-to-late 1970s once again was one of less widespread political struggle. The late 1970s, I believe, were the spawning grounds for another mobilization—the precursors of which are now to be found in the ongoing work of many of the groups and people active in the 1960s, as well as in the movements for sane natural resource use, antinuclear technology, and democracy in both the blue collar and white collar sectors of the labor force. There is also a small but growing interest in Marxist thought and methods of analysis, and an increasing willingness to investigate the meaning of and possibilities for socialism within a North American context.

Clearly this is a period of transition, and not the height of a cycle of radical activity. Those of us who feel the need to formulate and practice in a radical way within social work at present may well wish for a more overt and highly developed level of struggle. Rather than be discouraged, we can be more useful and can better sustain our energy and commitment, if we locate our particular sector and our piece of the action within a suitably larger framework and develop a radicalism within social work that is appropriate for the time and place in which we live. This does not imply that there is little we can do, because little is happening "out there." A great deal is happening out there. We will find it if we know what to look for. And there is a great deal we can do if we have the insight, theory, courage, and support to do it. However contemporary needs and abilities are not the same as they might have been in the 1930s or the 1960s or what they will be at some future point.

A Definition of Radical Social Work

There is by no means complete agreement among leftist social workers about the definition and nature of radical social work practice. To some extent this is desirable, since there is no single, clearly optimal direction for radical change efforts to take at present in the United States. On the other hand, there is need for more clarity, for greater codification of schools of thought, and for more open debate about the alternatives. We need to attempt to define and to formulate more specific principles of practice at the same time that we need to avoid sectarianism, that is, rigid adherence to a narrow "party line." In fact it seems quite likely that a larger number of formulations of radicalism within social work will be developed in the near future and that successive formulations will provide greater clarity for leftist practitioners.[4]

There have been a number of efforts in recent years to define radical social work and to clarify some of the principles on which such practice rests. One effort to develop a definition suggests that radical practice is "that practice which attempts to be of maximum service to people experiencing

---

[4]An explicit discussion of alternative analyses, within a socialist framework, can be found in Colin Pritchard and Richard Taylor, *Social Work: Reform or Revolution?* (London: Routledge and Kegan Paul, 1978).

problems in their daily lives and at the same time are informed by a commitment to radical social change."[5] This definition suggests both short-and long-term perspectives for radical social work and sees as the connecting link the effort "to define those small and simple changes we can make—not as marking time–but a seeding, a building of a foundation by our daily work."[6] Such practice is based on "understanding the nature of capitalism, its racism and imperialism and the pejorative theories of human nature which underlie and perpetuate these."[7]

Another effort at definition, oriented to the expression of radicalism in casework, but easily generalized to the notion of all radical social work practice, suggests that radical casework is casework which

> seeks to find ways in which the casework experience might help to directly encourage social, political and economic change. To a great extent, radical casework is consonant with a Marxist social vision. The starting point is historical materialism or the transcendence of the economic order over social behavior... The development of class consciousness or the desire to work collectively toward altering alienating conditions is the social-psychological process to be encouraged. The ideals of socialism are offered as an alternative to the ideals of capitalism.[8]

Here again, efforts are made to link the specifics of experience in immediate practice with a larger notion of change, in this case that particularly associated with the Marxist tradition.

Some efforts at definition build more fully on an underlying critique of capitalist society and the role of social work in that society and suggest larger goals toward which a radical social work practice might strive. For example, one radical social work collective suggested that the goal of radical practice is

> a humanistic and egalitarian society and to that end we see the abolition of classism, racism, and sexism as vitally necessary in our social work practice. We see traditional social work as counter productive to the attainment of these goals.... Radical social work, on the other hand, emphasizes the importance of the socio-economic system as a source of people's problems rather than looking

---

[5]Barbara Loundes Joseph, "Radical Perspectives in Our Field," in *The Social Service Alternative View*, Voice of the Radical Alliance of Social Service Workers, 1(January, 1975), 4. Available from the Radical Alliance of Social Service Workers, P.O. Box 40, Gracie Square Station, New York, N.Y. 10028.

[6]Ibid., p. 5.

[7]Ibid.

[8]John F. Longres, "Radical Social Casework," Paper Presented at the Council on Social Work Education, Annual Program Meeting, March 1977, Phoenix, Arizona, Mimeographed, p. 1.

solely to intrapsychic or interpersonal explanations. It emphasizes change instead of adjustment and to that end sees raising people's consciousness of the systemic sources of many of the tensions and problems which we experience as part of radical social work practice. Collective solutions to the problems are sought, not *for* others, but *with* them. . . . We are aware that the practice of social work, both radical and traditional, is a political act. The radical position threatens the status quo because it demystifies our role as 'professionals' and also because it challenges the present inegalitarian socioeconomic system and leads to basic redistribution of power and resources.[9]

The most explicitly socialist perspective on social work to appear to date in the journal of the mainstream National Association of Social Workers, *Social Work,* suggested that

The Marxist approach sees the social service institutions serving low-income people as an extension of the dominant political and economic forces that shape everyone's life. Therefore, the social worker's role is to apply the knowledge he [*sic*] has gained about the American community to educate and organize other social workers in the agency so that they have greater leverage and thus are in a better position to effect change. . . . The Marxist model presupposes that the struggle in the agency is just one of many struggles that must occur in every institution in society before significant reforms will occur. The Marxist approach asks fundamental questions about agency policies, involves fellow workers in the development of a change strategy, and coordinates its strategy with the recipient community.[10]

Here particularly note the emphasis on work within the community of social workers itself and the reference to the social service sector as one arena for political work, among many.

Finally in speaking to the question, Can there be a radical social work? two British leftists answered affirmatively, and suggested that

radical work . . . is essentially understanding the position of the oppressed in the context of the social and economic structure they live in. A socialist perspective is, for us, the most human approach for social workers. Our aim is not, for example, to eliminate casework, but to eliminate casework that supports ruling-class hegemony. To counteract the effects of oppression, the social

---

[9]The Radical Social Work Collective, "A Statement on Radical Social Work Practice," School of Social Work, University of Connecticut, 1975 mimeographed. Note in this discussion that forms of oppression based on class, race, and sex are specifically identified. As I will argue, capitalism is not the sole and exclusive root of these forms of oppression. It is, however, a powerful generator and sustainer of these forms of oppression. It also serves to divide us so that we cannot address these issues in a unified way. To this list, we might well add oppression based on age (agism), religion (i.e., anti-semitism), sexual preference (heterosexism), and physical difference (handicapism).

[10]Robert Knickmeyer, "A Marxist Approach to Social Work," *Social Work,* 17 (July, 1972), 63–64.

worker needs to innovate a dual process, assisting people to understand their alienation in terms of their oppression and building up their self esteem. . . . A radical form of social work must be developed. Social workers themselves suffer from economic exploitation (though far less severely than, for example, hospital workers), and development of a radical critique may mean their involvement in a programme of political action.[11]

Numerous other efforts have been made to define radical social work and to provide a theoretical underpinning for it.[12] This brief review was intended to introduce the range of thinking supporting the development of radical social work, and to give some of the flavor and some of the diversity within the tradition.

My own understanding of the most useful way to define radical social work in the context of present day Western monopoly capitalist societies is to suggest that *radical social work is social work that contributes to building a movement for the transformation to socialism by its efforts in and through the social services. Radical social work, in this understanding, is socialist social work. Those who practice radical social work are those who struggle for socialism from their position within the social services.*

It is the burden of the rest of this book to elaborate the meaning of this definition and to provide more specific suggestions for making that meaning more operational. Such elaboration is not only the work of this book; it must be the work of many other books by many other authors as well as the work of practice efforts and theoretical contributions by large numbers of people. Nevertheless some initial clarifying statements are in order.

This definition, like several of those presented earlier, identifies radical practice specifically as socialist practice and places radical social work clearly within a concern for the development of a socialist movement, building toward the creation of a socialist society. I am among those who believe that the theory of socialism can be "rescued" from the confusion and stigma which have surrounded it and that it is worthwhile to do so, for at least two reasons.

First, identifying ourselves as socialists provides access to a body of

---

[11]Roy Bailey and Mike Brake, "Introduction: Social Work in the Welfare State," in *Radical Social Work* eds. Roy Bailey and Mike Brake (New York: Pantheon 1975), p. 9.

[12]Some useful efforts are by Bertha Reynolds, *Social Work and Social Living* (Washington, D.C.: National Association of Social Workers, 1975); Richard Cloward and Frances Fox Piven, "Notes Toward a Radical Social Work," in *Radical Social Work*, eds. Roy Bailey and Mike Brake pp. vii–xlviii; Philip Lichtenberg, "Radicalism in Casework," *Journal of Sociology and Social Welfare*, 4 (November, 1976), 258–76; Peter Leonard, "Toward a Paradigm for Radical Practice," in *Radical Social Work*, eds. Roy Bailey and Mike Brake, pp. 46–61; Gil, *The Challenge of Social Equality*, see Chapter 13, "Practice in the Human Services as a Political Act," pp. 195–210; and Daphne Statham, *Radicals in Social Work* (London: Routledge and Kegan Paul, 1978).

theory, analysis, and strategy which is extremely useful in making sense of the world, in suggesting ways to change the world, and in providing some images of the kinds of changes we might find desirable. Key concepts central to the socialist mode of analysis include *materialist analysis* and *dialectical analysis*, which are found in Marxist methodology. Material analysis refers to the way in which any society organizes itself to fulfill the basic material requirements associated with physical survival and growth and occupies an important place in Leftist understanding of society. *Dialectic analysis*, refers to a model analyzing the nature, growth, and change of systems through the interplay of internal and opposing forces within those systems. Subsequent discussion will clarify the meaning of *dialectical materialism* and will make these concepts a powerful tool in analyzing our circumstances and in suggesting ways to proceed. I know of no competing framework that does the job as well.

Second, resting our analysis on an explicitly socialist perspective has the advantage of locating our efforts more clearly within the major dynamics of social change in the world at large. The struggle for socialism is one of the major forces for change throughout the world. It is true that no socialist society has perfectly achieved the ideals of socialism. It is also true that the understanding of socialism, as method and goal, varies widely throughout the world. None the less the struggle for human liberation within a socialist perspective is a struggle that is understood and valued by many people in every continent. To understand the issue before us as the task of creating a Socialist States of America suggests the commonality and unity of our struggle. It is useful to support language and strategy that make these linkages more explicit.

The definition of radical social work offered here also takes into account the fact that radical social workers are both radicals and social workers. Their political commitments are socialist and their specific occupational category is social worker. We must not accept the dead-end conventional understanding of the relationship of politics and social work practice in which it is argued that political work is something people do after working hours, not as an integral part of "professional" practice. The problem with this argument is that conventional practice is fully political, whether or not its politics are acknowledged. The ends it serves, however, are conservative ones. Radicals do not seek to introduce politics into an apolitical situation. Rather we mean to challenge the politics of compliance and to introduce the politics of resistance and change. But if we are to integrate radical politics and social work practice we must, among other things, find ways to bring that political commitment to bear on the daily events of our work. To do so means, in part, to pay full and serious attention to the immediate and pressing needs of those who come for our help and to constantly relate our efforts to the building of socialism.

Finally this definition does not specify a particular strategy or mode of practice, but focuses on definitions of larger political commitments and goals. Various strategies and practice approaches will be developed in the following chapters. To define radical social work, it seems desirable to address the overall process that is required, not the form that practice may take at a particular moment. *Radical social work is not technique, a practice modality, a fad, or even a particular strategy.* At any given moment, the creation of a movement for socialist transformation and the contribution that social workers can make to that movement may require certain techniques, particular forms of practice, or action within some particular guiding strategy. However the particulars of the struggle at any given moment do not define the struggle. The struggle is defined by its larger goals and by the theory that is applicable to the achievement of those goals. Radical social workers, to the extent that they practice radical social work, are not liberals whose practice of social work is radical. Rather, radical social workers are radicals who are social workers and who bring greater consistency to their lives by integrating their political commitments with their work—as they try to integrate their politics with other aspects of their lives.

What Radical Social Work Is Not

The concept of radical social work frequently conjures up a series of erroneous assumptions about what it means to be a radical and a social worker at the same time. Therefore, in addition to suggesting that radical social work is not defined by a particular technique or strategy, it may be useful to clarify several other things which radical social work is not.

Radical social work practice within our society is not based on the same principles as the practice of social work or social service delivery in existing socialist countries. There is much to learn from such countries and from an exploration of social work practice in them. However the tasks facing social workers in socialist countries are substantially different from those facing social workers in capitalist societies. In our case the important task is to find ways of integrating work within the social welfare sector into the broader struggle for socialist transformation. This is quite a different task from that of making social services as effective as possible within an existing socialist society.

Radical social work, as some detractors imply, does not ignore the immediate day-to-day survival needs of social service users for the sake of a distant, ultimate goal, that is, for the final revolution or a postrevolutionary utopia. If it did that, it would be guaranteed isolation on the grounds of irrelevance to people's immediate needs and on the grounds of sheer inhumanity. Rather radical social work is based on the point of view that the best way to help a user of social services to receive meaningful support and assistance is to connect the immediate problem facing that person with the larger changes that are required to bring about a decent life for all of us. If counselling is required, it must be provided. But if a counselling situation fails to link a specific and immediate problem with the social dynamics of which it is but one manifestation and if it fails to link the temporary and partial solutions with the larger social transformation that is required for realistic solutions, then it is extremely limited, at best, and deceptive and repressive, at worst. Radical practice is not juxtaposed on meeting immediate and pressing needs. It is another way to look at what it means to take our commitment to meeting those needs seriously.

Similarly radical practice is not practice that asks the practitioner to be self-sacrificing to the point of self-destruction. Practice which leads to unemployment on a regular basis or is adventuristic or militant beyond the understanding of most people is not radical. It may satisfy some psychological needs of an individual committed to that style of action, but its contribution to developing a socialist movement or to meeting the needs of anyone other than the practitioner is left strictly to chance. Radical practice will call on people to grow, to risk, to change, and to work hard. It is not defined by its commitment to dead-end adventures, one-shot acts of conscience, militant postures, and the like.

Radical social work is also not social work that tries to "make things worse" in the hope that stimulating social deterioration will hasten revolution. Our social condition is deteriorating, and our lives are becoming more difficult without any help from radicals. The irrationality and brutality of capitalism itself create the conditions that put revolutionary change on the agenda. We do not need to divert our energies assisting that process. Socialists need to be in the business of organizing people to meet their needs—not of making their lives worse. This is the basis on which people become mobilized for change.

Nor can we define radical social work practice as a practice that is indifferent to or that condemns struggles for partial victories and incremental gains, on the theory that nothing is worth doing until the climactic moment when the ultimate blow can be struck for the achievement of a socialist society. The radical critique of incrementalism and reformism is not that such change is piecemeal, or that it is slow. Rather the critique is based on the conviction that incremental and reformist change does not reform. The history of reformism in capitalist society has too often been a history of contradictory reform—of reform that does give minimal benefits, but that does so in a way that tightens the hold of destructive capitalist institutions and ideology.

And yet we must work in small ways, inasmuch as that is what is possible for us to do. We must find a way to work that avoids the dead end of reformism and builds toward a fundamental transformation. If we wait patiently, or impatiently, for the climactic moment, that moment is much less likely to arrive. And if it does arrive without our help, we will not have prepared ourselves to participate in its unfolding.

Finally, contrary to conservative and liberal interpretations of radicalism, radical practice in social work is not demagogic or dictatorial. Socialists do not have a single "answer" which they impose on an otherwise blind or misled populace. If this were the approach of socialists, and to the extent that it has informed some aspects of socialist practice historically, it is doomed to failure. It is true that socialist thought gives rise to perspectives on practice, possible outcomes, and strategies. However these components of socialism must speak to the needs of people in their everyday situations, or they will be ignored. We do not need to fear the imposition of radical thought. Approaches that are "imposed" will be rejected, as well they should. On the other hand, to the extent that a way of thinking about social issues and social change fits with any individual's and group's real life situation and helps advance that situation, it will be embraced as a better life choice and direction. If socialist thought more nearly expresses people's hopes for a decent and fulfilling life, as I believe it does, the issue of imposition will increasingly be seen as part of the propaganda of defenders of the status quo to obfuscate and to make more difficult a realistic assessment of the meaning and possibilities of socialism.

A Note on Criticism of Radical Social Work

A necessary part of a discussion of radical social work practice must be a frank and nondefensive assessment of the limitations of radical theory and action at any particular moment and place in history. Such assessment is undertaken in these pages. However the fact that there are constraints of many sorts on radical practice ought not prevent us from exploring what is possible and desirable.

Many, including the mainstream thinkers within the social services, assume that radical social work represents an impossible contradiction, a destructive mode of thought and action, possibly a desirable, but surely an unrealistic, approach, and so on. What perspective can guide our response to such assessments? We must and will acknowledge the limitations and what are conventionally called "the realities" that accompany radical social work. At the same time, we cannot allow our assessment of radical practice to be based on conventional political thought. It is necessary for us to develop an understanding and a critique from a radical perspective. To the extent that we accept liberal and conservative understandings of the possibilities of radical practice, we will be discouraged from pursuing legitimate and crucial paths. But after all, that is just the point of the liberal and conservative analyses—to rule out such explorations, to make them seem foolish, futile, irrelevant, or unnecessary. The liberal and/or conservative analysis of radicalism within social work serves the same purposes as liberal and/or conservative analysis elsewhere, namely, to legitimate the status quo. We cannot ignore this critique. We need to understand it. But we cannot take it on its own terms. It serves a historical purpose that differs from our own.

This is quite different from criticism that arises within the radical perspective. For example, we can acknowledge and address that point of view within the left that argues that much of Western radical thought has been couched in the language, analysis, and perspective of nineteenth-century European history and circumstance and has not and ought not be grafted onto the conditions of twentieth-century North American capitalism. We should listen to this criticism, analyze it, explore its utility and its limitations, and let it inform our work appropriately. But let us not follow the liberal and/or conservative understanding of this criticism, which leads to the denial and dismissal of the relevance of radical thought in general. The underlying assumptions of any criticism—in this case assumptions about the appropriateness of radical understandings of capitalist societies—must be as much the subject of our analysis as the criticism itself. This basis for responding to criticism is expecially important in a period, such as the present one, in which the legitimacy of a leftist perspective is still a major issue, at least in the United States. We are not at the point at which large numbers of people are prepared to debate alternative paths within a socialist perspective, and so we must be careful to distinguish between what can loosely be called friendly and unfriendly criticism.

2

The Socialist Approach

Socialism as Model and Method

In one sense what socialism is "all about" is simple and straightforward. In every society it takes the efforts of the majority of us, working with our hands and minds, to produce the goods and services on which the physical maintenance of life depends. Making society work is a collective effort. Socialism takes this obvious fact seriously, and pursues its implications. Without all our efforts, the soil on the planet's surface would not yield sufficient food to nourish us, the forests would not yield wood to make our homes, and the oil in the ground would not, of its own volition, warm those homes. A few of us working alone could not do this job. We must all do it if it is to get done and, for the most part, we all do pitch in when the structure of society offers us a chance to participate. It seems both logical and moral to socialists that we all should participate in determining what will happen with the products of our labor and that we all should benefit from that labor roughly according to the effort we expend.

In a capitalist society, however, a majority of the people who do the work of the society do not enjoy a level of material and psychological well-being commensurate with their effort. The really tremendous job we have all done does not create the kind of life for most of us that it could, given the level of our effort and the extent of our wealth. Many of us suffer from some form of material or psychological deprivation, despite the fact that the resources now exist to permit the satisfaction of basic needs for all.

Socialism is concerned with understanding why the people who live in capitalist societies, even in the wealthiest capitalist nations which have made tremendous advances toward solving the production problems historically associated with material scarcity, continue to experience problems associated with scarcity, such as malnutrition, poor housing, high infant mortality rates, and poverty. Socialism tries to learn why these same societies create conditions in which life is disproportionately concerned with the struggle against economic and psychological deprivation instead of being concerned with living itself as a creative enterprise. Most important, socialism is committed to analyzing and contributing to the forces and movements which can transform these unsensible and destructive ways of organizing our efforts into more rational and life-endorsing arrangements.

As a method of analysis, socialism ascribes dominant, and ultimately determining, significance to the material and economic base of the society, or to what are called the *means of production*, the *forces of production*, or the *infrastructure* of a society. Socialist analysis suggests that the most critical factor shaping a society is the way in which that society produces the concrete goods and services required for its maintenance and growth. It is this aspect of Marxist analysis that leads to its identification as a *materialist* form of analysis.

Socialist analysis also places great emphasis on examining the patterns of social organization which emerge as a result of particular production patterns. The network of social relations in a society is referred to as the *mode of production or the relations of production*. Social relations are shaped by the relationship which various groups or classes of people have to the wealth-producing capacity of the society, that is, to capital, or to the means of production. The owners of capital (the capitalists), and those who do not own capital but sell their labor power to capitalists (the working class, or proletariat), are the major classes created by capitalist economic arrangements. These classes are in conflict with each other since they compete for the wealth of the society. In fact it is the conflict of these classes, as I will elaborate in the following chapter, which creates the pressure for social change in capitalist society.

Socialist analysis also suggests that the material base of society is the principal factor shaping the values, culture, and social institutions, or what is identified as the *superstructure* of society. It explores economic determinants as the major, though not exclusive, source of religious values, relations between the sexes and races, family organization, beliefs, customs, and so on.

As we have seen, socialism starts with the basic condition of things—the planet Earth, the people on it, the natural resources to be worked, and the basic tasks of human maintenance. It looks at the ways in which we have organized ourselves to do our work within these concrete circumstances, and it looks at what we have made of the possibilities which life presents us. It concludes that we have made much of them to this point. At the same time, socialists see that we are selling ourselves far short of our potential for creating the fullest possible lives for ourselves. Socialism explains why and how we have sold ourselves short and what we can do about it. It suggests that changing the way in which we organize ourselves is, first, necessary for our continued survival; second, extremely difficult; and third, not only possible, but entirely likely.

If this is a quick overview of the concerns to which socialism addresses itself, the full story takes volumes. Socialist theory is indebted to the work of Karl Marx[1] but it is by no means exclusively reliant on, or limited and subservient to his insights and analysis. Socialism is an analysis of social and economic development in the world; that is, it categorizes and analyzes the nature of that development and suggests underlying dynamics responsible for it. It is a theory of planned as well as unplanned social change. It investigates the impersonal forces which underlie social change, and it points to ways in which human intention and self-conscious intervention have been and are crucial in shaping human society. It rests on strong moral commitments to the desirability and legitimacy of equality among people. It argues that people's lives should not be shaped to conform to the requirements of production, but, rather that production should be organized to meet people's needs for material, psychological, moral, and spiritual development.

Many people do not have experience in considering and analyzing these dimensions of their lives, particularly in political terms. These do not tend to be the issues addressed by most trade unions, newspaper editorials or conventional political speeches. As a result, understanding the socialist perspective can be difficult since it charts new and often threatening ground. At the same time, these issues speak to the basic conditions of our lives.

---

[1]Marx was born in Germany in 1818 and died in 1883. Marx was by no means the first socialist thinker and analyst on the world scene, though his theoretical work, particularly on the underlying dynamics of the capitalist system itself, most significantly represented in his major work, *Capital*, was, to that date, the most thorough and well-grounded analysis of capitalism the world had seen. While Marx was involved in the political currents of his day as theorist, strategist, and activist, his work is not as significant in understanding revolutionary practice as it is in understanding capitalism itself. It was left to Lenin, the great Russian revolutionary (1870–1923), to develop the fundamental application of Marx's "scientific" socialism to revolutionary practice. During and since those times, of course, a great deal of other important theoretical work has been accomplished by numerous socialist thinkers.

Exploring the socialist alternative is exciting because it views and speaks to the dilemmas of daily life in fresh ways and in ways that often make sense to people.

In this chapter and the two that follow, I will present some important aspects of socialist analysis. This chapter particularly has two foci. The first is the socialist understanding of the nature of capitalism. The second is the possibilities that might open for us as a people if we were to become socialist; it suggests some visions of a Socialist States of America.

Chapter 3 introduces the socialists' understanding of the roots, nature, and processes of social change as we work to replace a capitalist system with a socialist one.

Chapter 4 applies the socialist critique of capitalism to that segment of capitalist society that is concerned with social welfare services and policy and which is loosely called "the welfare state." Since the socialist analysis of the welfare state rests in large measure on its conception of the state, or government, a portion of Chapter 4 is concerned with presenting the socialist understanding of the nature and role of the state in capitalist societies.

The first half of the book concludes with a consideration of the relationship of the social service sector to the process of socialist transformation. This discussion of analytic tools and their applications is intended to establish a theoretical foundation as an introduction to specific approaches to radical social work practice, which comprise the second half of the book.

Weaknesses of Capitalism

Regardless of an individual's political commitment or degree of political sophistication, anyone familiar with the Western capitalist countries can easily point to a wide variety of social problems in those societies. Socialists do not have a unique ability to observe problems. Nor do they claim a monopoly on compassionate concern about them. However the socialist perspective and analysis of capitalist societies are distinguished from a non-socialist perspective in several ways.

The socialist analysis highlights the *systemic* nature of social problems, that is, their interconnectedness, and it emphasizes their roots in the way the society organizes itself to meet the requirements of production. In the case of the United States that form of organization is capitalist. A nonradical analysis, that is, an analysis which does not trace the roots of various social problems to the fundamental nature of the society itself, leads to the conclusion that the problems we experience are simply deviations from the potential capacity of the existing society. From that perspective, social problems are more likely to be seen as anomolies or as unfortunate transgressions from the norm. Problems are seen as exceptions to the general practice and not as products of the fundamental dynamics of the system. As a consequence, they are seen as potentially resolvable within the existing system.

Socialist analysis points to the way in which the basic structure of the existing system, the system of capitalism, gives rise to unresolvable problems as a result of its own internal dynamics. In Marxist terminology, socialist social theory rests on a dialectic mode of analysis. This mode of analysis will be presented more fully in Chapter 3. In brief dialectic analysis suggests that the natural internal dynamics of capitalism itself give rise to the problems of the society. Capitalism carries within itself contradictory, that is, opposing forces. These opposing forces are generated by and within capitalism. They must, and do, conflict with one another, and that makes the old system unworkable. They cannot be resolved within the framework of the existing system. Consequently the resolution of the struggle must eventually result in the creation of a new system.

Another important aspect of socialist analysis is the idea that radical transformation of societies is possible and likely. The socialist analysis, while not the only kind of radical critique, is distinguished by the links it uncovers between the internal dynamics of the old society and the processes necessary to advance us to a new set of arrangements. These processes will receive fuller attention shortly.

A full critique of capitalism is, of course, a very complex undertaking. I will illustrate the way in which socialist analysis highlights the problems of capitalism in four areas: the irrationality of production for profit, the necessity of inequality and exploitation, the distortion of the value and meaning of human life, and the inherently antidemocratic features of the system.[2]

irrational economics

In a capitalist society the primary motivation which underlies economic decision making and patterns of economic development is the drive for profit. Each capitalist enterprise must try to grow and to expand its profits. If

---

[2]A useful collection of essays on these themes is Richard C. Edwards, Michael Reich and Thomas E. Weisskopf, (eds.), *The Capitalist System* (Englewood Cliffs, N.J.: Prentice-Hall, Inc., 1972). Also useful in developing a socialist critique of capitalism are Michael P. Lerner, *The New Socialist Revolution* (New York: Dell Pub. Co. Inc., 1973); C. Wright Mills, *The Marxists* (New York: Dell Pub. Co. Inc., 1962); Howard Selsam, David Goldway and Harry Martel, eds., *Dynamics of Social Change: A Reader in Marxist Social Science* (New York: International Publishers, 1970); Irwin Silber, *Grasping Revolutionary Theory: A Guide for Marxist–Leninist Study Groups* (New York: Weekly Guardian Associates, 1977); Stephanie Coontz, *What Socialists Stand For* (New York: Pathfinder Press, 1973); *The Basic Political Education Course*, New American Movement, n.d., 3244 N. Clark St., Chicago, Illinois 60657; and Pierre Jalee, *How Capitalism Works* (New York: Monthly Review Press, 1977). Several of the books or pamphlets cited also list and annotate some of the historical and modern classics of Marxist analysis.

it does not do so, then another, more aggressive capitalist enterprise will take that company's share of the market, and will eventually buy up the smaller, less efficient unit. In practice, this happens constantly. As capitalism has continued to develop from its infancy to more advanced stages, the larger and stronger enterprises have continued to absorb the smaller and weaker ones so that fewer and fewer corporations own a larger proportion of the productive capacity. This is why Marxists suggest that capitalism today should be described as monopoly capitalism. Despite the monopoly characteristics of capitalism, however, expansion and profit making continue to be the dominant motivations in the economy. Each economic unit tries to maximize its surplus, or profits, to reinvest that surplus somewhere in this country or in another country, and to generate still more profit.

It is precisely this way of organizing the economy that gives rise to some of the most pressing dilemmas and glaring examples of irrationality in capitalist society. If a capitalist enterprise can make profit by producing a given product, that product will be produced and sold. The primary motivation is profit. The extent to which a given product is socially useful, may actually be harmful to people, depletes limited amounts of critical natural resources, is dangerous to the workers' mental or physical health, or absorbs the same human energies and natural resources that might be used to solve some outstanding social problem and to meet some pressing human need—all these considerations influence the decisions made by capitalists about what to produce, only if they are consistent with the profit motive. The reason for this is not found in the absence of social-mindedness of individual capitalists or even in the absence of a socially concerned dimension to business as a whole. The reason lies in the fact that if capitalists fail to maximize their profits, they will go out of business. If enough of them fail to seek maximum growth, the system as a whole will fail. As a result our enormous productive capacity is not directed toward creating socially useful goods and services that will make our lives as rewarding as possible, except insofar as that may happen as a by-product of the profit motive. Rather our productive capacity is directed toward producing whatever will make a profit, and in any way possible.

When capitalism is understood as a system based on these dynamics, a number of economic problems which are difficult to explain from a nonradical position becomes clear. Foremost among these is unemployment. Given that there is much work to be done in the society, that there are many unemployed people who want to work, and that businesses continue to experience a high rate of profit, how can we explain the persistence of percentages of unemployment that reach the high teens for minorities, six or seven percent for the labor force as a whole, and that are unlikely to drop below five percent under the best of conditions, by the admission of leading government economists?

Capitalist factories do not work at full capacity because a capitalist system cannot allow the supply of goods available in the market to exceed the ability of consumers to absorb them. When more goods are produced than can be purchased, the value of those goods is unavailable to capitalists for further investment, since it is tied up on warehouse shelves. Consequently companies limit their productive output. This, in turn, contributes to unemployment. Unemployment is actually created by capitalism and serves a variety of positive functions within capitalism. It is one way that corporations bring pressure to bear against their workers in workers' struggles for higher wages. Workers and capitalists alike know that the unemployed need the jobs of those now working and will take them even at modest wages. Unemployment is not a "maladjustment." It is a systemic by-product of capitalism, and it is functional for the maintenance of capitalism.

The same line of reasoning helps to explain the problem conventionally defined as poverty. When poverty is examined from a liberal or conservative (that is, procapitalist) perspective, it appears as a problem affecting approximately twelve to fifteen percent of the people in the United States.[3] From this point of view, the problem of poverty seems to be a problem affecting a relative minority. It is then analyzed as a consequence of factors such as the personality or cultural characteristics of those called poor, the failure of public assistance programs to provide adequate economic incentives, or weaknesses in job training programs.

However there is another way to look at this issue. The Bureau of Labor Statistics (BLS) estimates budgets for urban families at what the BLS considers a "lower," "intermediate," and "higher" standard of living. In 1975 the lower standard of living requirement for an urban family was $9,588 and an intermediate level was $15,318.[4] Using these figures, 36 percent of families in the United States live on income that allows only a lower standard of living, and 60 percent live within a budget that permits only an "intermediate" standard of living.[5] This includes an even larger number of working people than nonworking people. Looked at in this light, a very large percentage of people in the United States are marginally well-off financially.

For many people who are called poor, the problem of poverty is better understood as the problem of low wages. All workers, those who fall below

---

[3]"Persons Below Poverty Line," *Pocket Data Book, U.S.A., 1976* (Washington, D.C.: U.S. Government Printing Office, 1976), Table 326, p. 226. This figure is based on a poverty level of $5,500 a year for a non-farm family of four persons in 1975.

[4]United States Department of Labor, "Bureau of Labor Statistics Revises Estimates for Urban Family Budgets: Comparative Indices for Selected Urban Areas, Autumn, 1975," *News Release,* May 5, 1976, n.p.

[5]Based on compilations from data in *Pocket Data Book, U.S.A.,* "Family Income Levels in Current and Constant Dollars," Table 319, p. 223.

the so-called poverty line and those who do not, are economically exploited under capitalism inasmuch as they receive less in wages than the value of the goods they produce. The surplus they create is taken from them by the nature of the system itself. This is the essence of the meaning of the concept of economic exploitation, in Marxist terms. Further this is endemic to the system and necessary for its survival. Capitalists inevitably try to pay as little as possible to workers. They cannot return to workers the full value of what workers produce since they must generate a surplus for reinvestment. What we call poverty is more accurately understood as the tail end of a larger pattern of economic exploitation and inequality and is inevitable in a system based on production for profit.

There is an additional and very important criticism to be made of a system based on production for profit. This system also does not work in strictly economic terms. Over time, capitalism is not an economically viable system. It generates dynamics which lead to its own degeneration. It periodically creates recession and depression, which result in unemployment and underuse of its productive capacity such that it cannot maintain itself. The reasons why this is so are rooted deeply in the nature of capitalist economics and are unresolvable within capitalism, as will emerge more fully in the following chapter.

inequality and exploitation

Capitalism is a system that is based on the exploitation of one human being by another. Since the economic basis of capitalism requires competition, a struggle of each against all for survival, and an emphasis on profit and expansion over social well-being, it comes as no surprise that some are winners and some are losers in the competitive struggle. The resulting inequality is a function of the principles on which capitalism operates. This inequality tends to spread from the economic sector to people's overall life opportunities, including their status and subsequent sense of self-valuation.

In addition certain groups have been particularly exploited in capitalist society. Once again socialists are not the only ones who observe the realities facing women, racial minorities, the aged, or gays. What is distinctive about the socialist analysis is that it provides a way to assess the systemic linkages between these particular expressions of exploitation and the basic dynamics of capitalism itself. A socialist analysis questions an ad hoc perspective and develops an analysis that helps to highlight the common rootedness of the specific problems in the workings of capitalism itself.[6]

---

[6]A collection of useful writings on the linkages between sexism and capitalism and racism and capitalism are found in Edwards and others, *The Capitalist System* and Lerner, *The New Socialist Revolution.* A useful discussion from a Marxist perspective of the repression of gays under capitalism is *Toward a Scientific Analysis of the Gay Question,* Los Angeles Research Group, P.O. Box 1362, Cudahy, California 90201, n.d.

There are, of course, particular linkages between racism and capitalism that differ from those between sexism and capitalism. Racism, for example, serves as a mechanism to displace the resentment and frustration of the white working class from capitalism toward minorities. The functional utility of racism for the maintenance of capitalism, through its role in undermining the potential unity of the working class, cannot be underestimated. Racism also provides the basis for paying minority workers less than white workers, and for allowing capitalists to extract even greater surplus from their labor. Similarly sexism, as an ideology, supports capitalism in paying women workers even less than male workers. It also fosters sex role stereotyped behavior which, among other things, has conditioned women to view their well-being as resting on their roles as consumers, manipulated to purchase goods in accord with the latest fads and fashions. Agism conditions the nonaged population to view the aged as an invisible or less than human group of people. Agism, as an ideology, legitimizes the removal of a "surplus" part of the labor force from active contention for scarce jobs and conditions us to view the economic straits in which the aged live, not as an unacceptable problem, but only as a problem.

Each of these problems has a life of its own and would not disappear solely as a consequence of the elimination of capitalism. Sexism and racism have generated their own sustaining ideologies which are now grounded in our values, laws, customs, religious ceremonies, and psychologies.[7] Further, sexism and racism existed in precapitalist societies and are found in some forms in many socialist countries. However these observations are often mistakenly used to discredit the important contribution which socialism can make to the elimination of these difficulties.

It is necessary to analyze the causes and nature of the problems in any society by examining the particular case. While minority populations have been exploited in precapitalist periods, many historians have suggested that the exploitation did not assume the all-pervasive character of modern racism and was not justified by an ideology supporting the idea of the inherent inferiority of the exploited minority.[8] It is analytically and historically unacceptable to make a generalization that equates all forms of racism or that equates, for all situations, the relationship of racism to the maintenance of the basic patterns of a society. Similarly any analysis cannot underestimate the tremendous advances that have occurred in resolving these issues in socialist societies—advances not matched in capitalist societies.

We must also acknowledge that socialist societies have emerged from

---

[7]For example, on the question of the relationship of sexism to capitalism and socialism, see Batya Weinbaum, "Redefining the Question of Revolution," *Review of Radical Political Economics,* 9 (Fall, 1977), 54–78.

[8]For example, see James and Grace Boggs, *Racism and the Class Struggle,* (New York: Monthly Review Press, 1970), especially Chapter 12, "Uprooting Racism and Racists in the United States," pp. 146–60.

feudal and capitalist pasts. Present patterns of exploitation exist, in part, as a legacy of those conditions. However since the full labor power and full social contribution of all people is not only possible but necessary in socialist societies, socialism, unlike capitalism, establishes the necessary, if not the sufficient, conditions for the abolition of these oppressions. When the economic underpinnings of these forms of exploitation are removed, the most significant barrier to their abolition is removed. This is not to say that socialism automatically ushers in the end of all exploitation. It is to say that a society which requires the full participation of all members, which is organized to make use of that participation, and which puts human welfare as a priority in relation to economics, has more likelihood, by virtue of its organizing principles, of dealing with exploitative forms of human relationships.

distortion of human values

Capitalism is an economic system organized on the basis of possessiveness and competition. It fosters a value system and human behaviors which define a meaningful and successful life in the same terms. Capitalism as an economic system is manifested in the personalities and social relationships of the people who live within it. Capitalism distorts the best impulses of human beings.[9]

In part this is a consequence of the artificial creation of scarcity within capitalism. The economy of the United States is sufficiently developed that none of us would need to fear being unable to attend to our basic material needs, were the principles on which available resources distributed more equitable. We could all know that we would always have enough food, clothing, shelter, medical care, education, and other necessities and we would develop mechanisms to cope with problems that might arise if some people chose not to make a reasonable investment of their potential labor power in the society. However because the profit motive and inequality stand between those resources and ourselves, we are all socialized within a culture that promotes the belief that having enough and getting more of it are the primary problems we must solve in our lifetimes. This is not totally incorrect, given the realities of this society. Unless we do work hard, seek every advantage, and compete with everyone else, we will be among those who are the most deprived, and we may well do without the basic necessities.

---

[9]It must also be pointed out that capitalism achieves only a partial success in creating a consistent "capitalist culture." The part in each of us that seeks community, love, and self-expression continues to operate as a force within us at the same time that we are conditioned by the dynamics and necessities of capitalism to operate in a way that denies our humanity. We resist our subjugation to capitalism. It is this resistance which explains, in part, the continuing struggle which people wage against their domination. A useful discussion is James R. O'Conner, "Merging Thought With Feeling," in *The Revival of American Socialism* ed. George Fischer (New York: Oxford University Press, 1971), pp. 22–40.

The consequences of this orientation are staggering. We are suspicious of one another, since we know that each of us must seek advantage over all others. We are isolated from one another, either to protect what we have in relation to others or as part of a process of being denied access to what others have. We are not encouraged to explore the gentle and loving possibilities of life, since we are so heavily involved, and even consumed, by the requirements of meeting survival needs. Life becomes identified with the struggle for physical maintenance at a time in history when we have the potential to assure that survival. In the midst of plenty, although a plentitude is not available to the majority of the people on the earth, we act out the selfishness, fright, and fear, associated with conditions of objective scarcity. Within the logic and workings of capitalism, we are not completely irrational in doing so.

When life is consumed with obtaining things or the physical requirements of survival, more and more we come to see ourselves as things also, although we are not always conscious of the process through which this happens. Consciously or unconsciously we learn to reason as follows. If we ourselves become a certain kind of thing, we will have the job that will produce the income to permit the purchase of a desired style of life. We view ourselves, as in a sense we must within capitalism, as commodities to be sold. If we become better educated commodities, we can obtain a higher price for our labor. If we become "more attractive" women, our purchasing power will buy a more attractive or wealthier husband. In other words, we assess ourselves in terms of our commodity value, and we come to assess one another in the same terms. For many men an important part of meeting another man is assessing his occupational status. For women meeting women, the assessment includes an appraisal of the other woman's power to attract men.

Just as we define our well-being according to the things we own, so we view the people in our lives in terms of ownership. Children "belong" to their parents. Wives and husbands "belong" to each other. Jealousy is rooted, in part, in the idea that the person who is yours is being "taken" by someone else. Further since we view ourselves and each other as commodities, we can wear out; we need to be discarded and traded in on newer models.

The dominant cultural themes of the society are themes that stem from and reinforce the logic of capitalism. The successful person in movies or books is the person who makes it to the "top." For men this usually implies attaining economic or political power. For women it means marrying a man who is rich and powerful. The appeal is to be number one. Alternative ideas, for example, the ideas of community, pleasure, and success through collective action, are rarely, if ever, part of popular culture. The focus is always on the "winner," and while one winner implies many losers, we are encouraged

In other words, capitalism narrowly confines the idea of democracy to the political realm, and even there it operates as much as myth as it does reality. In the very important realm of economic decision making, it does not offer opportunity for democratic input and in fact, justifies the absence of such input on the grounds that capitalism rests on the sanctity of private property. The fact is that in the "most free" country in the world, we have very little control over the people, groups, and forces that shape the circumstances of our lives. We not only have very little control, we have very little voice at all. And this is not a problem that is potentially resolvable within capitalism since economic democracy and capitalism are fundamentally antagonistic ideas. If the increasingly smaller number of people who control increasingly larger shares of the wealth can do as they will with that wealth in the name of further profit making, we will not have a democratic society. This is the essential condition of capitalism.

A Socialist Alternative

We have all been subjected to a great deal of misleading propaganda about the nature of socialism and communism, so much so that for many of us these words conjure up images of terrorism, loss of freedom, and gray bureaucracy. We are not aware of the social, political, and economic conditions of present socialist societies, for instance, the People's Republic of China, Vietnam, Cuba, the Democratic People's Republic of Korea, Yugoslavia, Angola, Mozambique, or Guinea-Bissau.[12] Nor do we have clear ideas about the ultimate potential of socialism in contrast to the inevitably imperfect ways in which the socialist idea has been applied in concrete circumstances.

---

[12]The first socialist society in modern times was the Soviet Union. There is considerable debate in the left today about the extent to which the Soviet Union can be considered to be a socialist society at this time. This is an important debate, though not one that can be addressed here. The discussion about the essential nature of socialism which ensues should help to clarify another point of confusion concerning the Scandanavian countries. They are hazily viewed as socialist by some people. However, the advanced welfare states are just that; they are essentially capitalist countries. The means of production are privately owned, for the most part. Profits, and more importantly, wages, are then heavily taxed to permit an extensive network of social services. As such, these countries do not fit our understanding of what it means to be a socialist society.

To develop a beginning acquaintance with China and Cuba, I would encourage interested readers to pursue Chu Li Tien Chieh-yun, *Inside a People's Commune* (Peking: Foreign Languages Press, 1974); Wilfred Burchett and Rewi Alley, *China: The Quality of Life* (Baltimore: Penguin Press, 1976); David Milton, Nancy Milton and Franz Schurmann, *People's China* (New York: Vintage Books, 1974); Maria Antonietta Macciocchi, *Daily Life in Revolutionary China* (New York: Monthly Review Press, 1972); Ernesto Cardinal, *In Cuba* (New York: New Directions, 1972); Lee Lockwood, *Castro's Cuba, Cuba's Fidel* (New York: Vintage Books, 1969); *The Black Scholar*, Special Issue, "Report From Cuba," 8 (Summer, 1977).

Therefore it seems useful to present some of the rudiments of the socialist alternative to capitalism.

The struggle for socialism, at its most basic level, is a struggle to clear the impediments, of which capitalism is primary, to rationality, humanity, and decency in human affairs. Socialism offers a basis for social organization that can permit this to happen. It is as much method as specific content. The idea that socialists talk about and agitate for socialism because of some larger Machiavellian designs or on behalf of a "foreign power" intent on colonizing the United States for its own aggrandizement needs to be understood as just so much propaganda put forth by those who have a stake in our not thinking about our own lives and about our own possibilities.

Socialism is not a blueprint. It is not a model that I have in my mind or that anyone else has worked out that can be imposed from outside. It is true that socialism, by definition, is based on some guiding principles. However each socialist society in the world differs from each other socialist society in many respects. It reflects both the general idea of socialism and the particular development of the socialist idea in the context of an individual country's history, culture, traditions, and process of transformation.

This will be true for the United States as well. It is useful to learn about other socialist countries and the ways in which they are organized. At the same time, it is not possible to point to another country as a model of the way in which a socialist United States might emerge or be structured. The form in which we create a socialist United States will be unique and will reflect our material level of productivity, our cultural and racial diversity, our traditions of civil liberties, and the way in which the movement for change emerges and proceeds. The outcome cannot be predicted, nor should it be. Nor can it be patterned on another country's experience. What socialism encourages, first and foremost, is that the majority of people take control of their own society in their own best interest as they see that interest.

For many of us political education stopped somewhere in a high school civics class in which we participated in a discussion about "democracy versus communism." Since we all knew that we would rather be "free" than "not free," we relegated the idea of communism or socialism to a corner of our minds clouded with stereotypes and vague prejudices. Subsequently we heard about communism, radicals, or radical organizations in the United States, our response was predetermined. We saw radicalism as a movement or idea that would take something away from us so we regarded it as unpatriotic and generally subversive. In view of this morass of mistaken ideas and obfuscation—a morass and obfuscation that has served the interests of the status quo—it is no surprise that a clear discussion and national debate about the socialist alternative has not yet occurred.

I will present some basic notions about the socialist alternative in three areas. These are social ownership of the means of production, democratic political forms, and a commitment to a satisfying quality of life.

social ownership of the means of production

The essential guiding idea of socialism is the social, public, or collective ownership of the means of production. The means of production are factories, the land, natural resources, and machinery with which we produce the material goods of the society or, put another way, those forms of property which produce income. Under capitalism the means of production are owned and controlled by a few private individuals, that is, by capitalists. In a socialist society the same property is owned by all the people. Since the means of production are commonly, or socially owned, so too are the profits, or surplus, they generate. The wealth created by human labor within the society is wealth which the people of the society control and utilize in accordance with their best thinking about the highest priorities for its use.

Another way to express the idea of public ownership of the means of production is to say that the workers own and control the means of production. In a socialist society there is no capitalist class. The owners and the workers are one and the same group of people. Of course some workers serve as coordinators, planners, and managers. Everyone does not and cannot do everything in a complex society. There is a differentiation of tasks and assigned responsibilities. However the differentiation of tasks is just that. It is a differentiation of tasks and does not imply, as in capitalism, a differential relationship to the surplus that is generated. Profits are not private property as they are under capitalism. Through the political machinery which is developed, a machinery which may assume various forms, collective and democratic decisions can be made about how the surplus generated by the sale of goods will be reinvested in the society.

To say that the means of production, that is the productive capacity and the surplus which is generated, are publicly owned is not to say, as is sometimes thought, that consumer goods which are designed for personal use are publicly owned. To say that the people in general, in a socialist system, own factories, mines, and banks is not to say that individuals and families do not own their own clothing or their homes or that people do not maintain individual bank accounts in which they accumulate savings to spend as they see fit. Socialism is neither centralized nor state ownership of all goods in the society. It is the collective ownership of the society's capacity to produce goods, that is, to produce wealth. The difference between owning a home privately and owning a factory privately, in this sense, is that a home is a consumer item designed for personal use; it does not generate additional wealth, as does a factory. More importantly owning a home does not take from anyone else, or expropriate, a part of the value of that person's labor, in the form of a profit made on the basis of that labor. A home is not an income producing property, unless one is a landlord. Then owning a home and collecting rent from tenants becomes part of capitalist enterprise and is not consistent with the socialist idea.

Notice that this facet of the description of socialism does not address the question of the political and organizational forms which a socialist society might develop to institutionalize public ownership of the means of production. I have indicated that the means of production are publicly owned in socialist societies, but I have not specified the way in which decisions are made, by whom they are made, and on what principles they are made. It is important to recognize that the essential content of the socialist idea is public ownership of the means of production. The form which decision making takes varies a great deal in different socialist societies and will undoubtedly emerge in a still different form in the United States. I will give the question of political organization some attention shortly. For now it is important to recognize that the question of public ownership of the means of production is a different question from that of the way in which the public actually expresses and implements its control.

What can be gained from the social ownership of the means of production? Why do socialists consider this idea so central to socialist theory and so beneficial to people? Social ownership permits us to produce the goods and services that we actually need in order to maximize our well-being. It allows us to make full use of our productive capacity so that people, machines, factories, and tools do not sit idly by while there is important work to be done. And it creates the possibility for us to deal rationally and humanely with the conditions and consequences of work and production, such as pay differentials, work safety, the nature of work itself, and the environmental consequences of production.

To understand the idea of production based on social usefulness, rather than on the profit motive, compare the circumstances which lead to the manufacturing of air conditioners as opposed to the building of adequate housing for low income people, in capitalist and socialist societies. In a capitalist economy a corporation might decide that a new kind of home air conditioner, perhaps one which is more effective in cooling homes, quieter than existing models, and with other special features, might find a market. The company produces those air conditioners and is or is not successful in making a profit from their sale. That same company would be unlikely to consider building housing which might be needed by low income people since low income people could not pay enough in rent or purchasing price to enable the company to make an acceptable profit from its investment.

Now stand back from the question of capitalism and socialism, and look at building air conditioners and building housing as economic processes in general. In a fundamental sense they represent the same process. In both cases raw materials must be converted from their natural state to their form as consumable items. In both cases workers are paid for their productive efforts. Building housing and building air conditioners, in terms of raw materials used, labor expended, money circulated, and the planning involved, are qualitatively the same process.

Under capitalism, however, one of these processes is possible, and one is not. The difference between the two kinds of production does not lie in some essential aspect of one process as opposed to another. It lies in the fact that only one of these production processes creates a product that can be sold for a profit in the market place. The overall social utility and rationality of that choice—the choice to produce air conditioners—is not and cannot be part of the consideration in a capitalist enterprise.

In a socialist United States we could decide to produce housing for low income people, if we decided that it had a high enough priority. We could also decide to create a working system of public transportation, provide universal, adequate health care for all, offer day care and social services as needed, and assure adequate retirement income for everyone. We could also begin to be of more significant assistance to other countries in a world whose exploitation has been the backbone of our own growth for two hundred years.

Can we afford to do all of this? Perhaps not. It is necessary to acknowledge that no society can do everything it wishes to do at this time. We will have to make choices, and we will need to develop mechanisms for making those choices rationally and democratically. Here I am simply making the point that we can turn our resources to the problems that concern us on the basis of rational decision-making processes grounded in social considerations, rather than on the basis of profit-making calculations rooted in capitalist considerations.

At the same time that we will inevitably face choices, we will do so with more resources at our disposal than we have at present. Socialism will allow us to increase our total productive capacity. We will be able to do more than we now do. Capitalist enterprise is increasingly unable to make full use of its own productive capacity. If it did, it would overproduce and eventually drive down profit. Similarly capitalism cannot productively harness the labor power of all of those in the society who are able and willing to work. We underuse our productive capacity significantly at the same time that there is clearly a great deal of productive work that needs to be accomplished. We could guarantee full employment if we undertook to provide adequate recreational, educational, and human services and if we rebuilt the cities and resuscitated the physical environment. We could pay people to do this work by converting the resources utilized for nuclear submarines, private yachts, unemployment compensation, superfluous advertising and forced unemployment, to wages. The only thing that stands in the way of our doing these things is a system in which a few people own and control the resources and activate them only when assured of profits.

Similarly if we were to stop defending capitalist interests around the world, we would be able to transfer the tremendously wasteful and expensive resources consumed by the military to more productive uses, while we continued to maintain whatever military apparatus we realistically needed for self-defense. Resources could be saved and shifted if we eliminated planned obsolescence, based on the need of capitalist enterprise to sell more goods and if we no longer purchased the various consumer luxuries we have been conditioned to believe we need.

Finally social ownership of the means of production would allow us a wide range of options in reorganizing the work process itself. We might decide that some of the present consequences of production are simply not acceptable and choose to alter them even though the cost of doing so would result in decreased production of some other goods. Presently a capitalist enterprise which took serious steps to improve health and safety conditions in a factory might well drive down profit margins and put itself in economic danger. In a socialist society we could decide that safe factories were sufficiently important that we could, in effect, spend the money to buy them—that is, we could invest what was required to make factories safe places in which to work— although that might mean having less of something else for ourselves. We could afford to do it. Again we could not afford to do everything. We could do the things that made the most sense to us, based on social considerations. Similarly we could decide to automate those productive tasks which were most onerous for people to perform, even if doing so did not lead to more production at reduced cost.

Similarly we might deautomate some work, despite increased production costs, because the environmental consequences, when added to the cost-benefit ratios, made production by certain machinery too expensive. These options are possible under socialism. Not all of them would happen. Conflicts of interest would still exist, and trade-offs would need to be made. The point is that socialism, as a system, permits these possibilities whereas capitalism does not.

political organization

The question of how a socialist United States might be organized is, of course, very complex. However I will suggest some operating principles which might provide a useful guide in developing appropriate organizational schemes for ourselves. Each of these principles reflects a single overriding concern, namely, the effort to maximize democratic practice in society.[13] By

---

[13]A helpful discussion is John M. Cammett, "Socialism and Participatory Democracy," in *The Revival of American Socialism*, ed. Fischer, pp. 41-60.

democratic practice I mean, simply, the opportunity for as many people as possible to participate as fully as possible in the decision-making processes that shape the conditions of their lives. Of course not everyone can or wants to participate in all decisions about all matters that affect them. The point is not to force them to do so. Rather the goal is to create the opportunities for such participation and to encourage such participation. Socialism must cut the links that now exist between wealth and decision-making power, and it must open important decisions-making arenas that are now not even considered appropriate for general participation to democratic processes.

For this to happen we will need to develop democratic decision-making bodies where none now exist. We will need to explore the ways in which workers can have more control over their workplaces.[14] Of course, workers will not have absolute control. For example, in the case of human service organizations, we would want to consider the decision-making role that would be played by service recipients and by the community at large. In productive enterprises we would need to consider the key question of social utility in deciding what to produce; we would not depend solely on the desires of the workers in a given factory. The point is not to stress the absolute control of any group in the society over all matters. It is to organize people in appropriate ways so that they can have effective input into decision making. Workers in a given segment of productive enterprise might have quite a lot to say about how their part of production would best be organized. They might, in turn, elect representatives to a larger factory council that would decide questions of production at the factory level. Decisions about what product would actually be produced might be made by a council consisting of representatives from the factory, from the community, and from regional economic coordinating committees.

To maximize democratic participation, to increase the extent to which people identify with the various organizations and political structures of which they are members, it will be desirable to emphasize decentralization of decision making to the greatest extent possible. At present we centralize decision making as much as possible, ostensibly on the grounds of efficiency, but actually because it permits greater minority control over the majority. When we decentralize community decision making and workplace decision making, we encourage greater participation in decision making by those who most directly experience the consequences of those decisions.

We raise, at the same time, the problems of coordination and integration. The solutions lie in creating coordinating bodies consisting of representatives of the various decentralized bodies. For each area of concern we will need to specify the extent to which the coordinating body will have greater authority than will the local body. These are not easy problems to work out,

---

[14]A useful compilation of essays on this theme is Gerry Hunnius, G. David Garson and John Case, eds., *Workers' Control* (New York: Vintage Books, 1973).

but they are not unresolvable.[15] We might devise a system of decision making about production, community services, or regional development in which coordinated plans emerge from a variety of locally constructed plans. The coordinated plans would be sent back to discrete units for review, and be reorganized on the basis of local feedback. In fact this has been the way in which the People's Republic of China, a society with nearly five times as many people as our own, has attempted to reconcile local autonomy and central coordination. Neither that system nor any system we develop will be problem-free. In a socialist society, however, we create the material basis for more democratic and rational problem-solving mechanisms.

Similarly we can find ways to increase direct participation in the larger questions of national interest. One way to do this is through more direct use of referenda—direct voting, after discussion and clarification—on crucial issues affecting us. We will also be able to better ascertain the positions we need to take on national questions when we become more aware of our local priorities. It is difficult to be knowledgeable about these, at present, since we feel so removed from access to decision making, even at local levels. If we make some resources available to all interested people who wish to advance their ideas and if we develop mechanisms for citizen input that actually allow our voices to be heard, we will do much to vitalize political participation at all levels.

At present political participation is a largely symbolic gesture for most people. We do not have real power, and we know it. We respond by disengaging. As these realities change, our responses are likely to change. Political life should relate to the daily questions of our existence. When it actually does concern our immediate experience, we will not need to appeal to one another's civic pride or abstract duty to encourage participation; we will participate. For this to happen we need to open up all areas of decision making to democratic participation, not to confine it to the narrow, symbolic act of voting which is capitalism's idea of democracy. We need to develop a system which in reality allows each of us to be equal members of the society so that when we participate, we do so as real, not symbolic, equals. Socialism is not a cure-all for problems of oligarchy and elitism. It is a base on which we can move closer to the ideal of full democratic decision making in the society.

the quality of life

What we make of a socialist United States will depend on many factors, including the processes by which we achieve socialism, such as the changes in

---

[15]Some potential models have been developed by a variety of social analysts. For example, see Gar Alperowitz, "Socialism as a Pluralist Commonwealth," in *The Capitalist System*, eds., Edwards and others; Arthur Waskow, "Notes From 1999," in *Working Papers for a New Society*, 1(Spring, 1973), 62–74; and, John D. McEwan, "The Cybernetics of Self Organizing Systems," in *The Case for Participatory Democracy* eds. C. George Benello and Dimitrios Roussopoulos, (New York: Grossman, 1971), pp. 179–194.

people's consciousness that accompany and are part of the process of transformation, the willingness to struggle with ongoing problems, and the developments in other countries. A discussion of equality, diversity, and the flowering of human potential serves to indicate how the quality of life might improve in a socialist society.

A socialist society is not a totally "equal" society because each individual will not necessarily have the same resources at his or her disposal. Some may have more than others, particularly in the early stages of socialist development. In part these differences will be a legacy of the patterns of inequality that exist now and may be a matter over which there is ongoing conflict in the society. It is possible that the maintenance of some differentials will continue to be seen as a desirable way to motivate people. In a more advanced stage of development differences may exist on the basis of an assessment of differences in need; for example, workers with larger families might be paid higher wages. Possibly workers with jobs that are viewed as intrinsically less satisfying will be paid higher wages.

Even in its early stages, a socialist society will permit us to develop a far more equal pattern of resource distribution. Significant accumulation of wealth in a capitalist society does not generally occur as a result of wage earning, however well-paid a job may be. Wealth is accumulated through direct ownership and investment. Neither of these accumulating mechanisms is possible in a socialist society. It may be in the best interests of the majority to minimize wage differentials among people. We might structure in some differences, on the bases suggested previously, and make the differences minor. We might feel it to be in our best interests not to allow some people to have a significant financial advantage over others. Our present arrangement, whereby financial inducements are seen as the major motivation for achievement, actually serves very few of us. Most people do not advance significantly. If we consciously plan an egalitarian distribution of resources, we would actually increase the number of people able to achieve more of what they want and need for themselves. These are possibilities under socialism. They are not mandates. Socialism allows us to subject the question of income distribution to rational scrutiny and to democratic decision-making processes.

The problem of inequality can also be seen in the unacceptable differences that exist in the life chances and opportunities of minorities, women, and the aged. Socialism will not automatically eliminate these inequalities. However it will eliminate the underlying economic bases of these problems. In a socialist society we can use and will require the full productive labor of all citizens. What is true even now, and will be clearer then, is that racism hurts us all by depriving us of the potential economic contributions of significant numbers of our citizens.

At the same time that we speak of the possibilities of greater economic and political equality in a socialist society, so too can we speak of the greater diversity that will be possible. Equality is not sameness. Equality, in a socialist sense, suggests that people have equal access to the goods and resources of the society. This kind of access, in a socialist society, opens the door to the flowering of difference.

Capitalism, while presented as a system that encourages freedom of choice, is actually a powerful leveler of cultural, religious, and personality differences. A single overriding drive dominates capitalism, and that is the drive for profits. It reduces all of us to the status of producers and consumers and imbues us all with the ethic of scarcity so that essentially we become similarly controlled by our fears. Our much vaunted emphasis on difference is a cosmetic overlay on a fundamental sameness that thrives on the common oppression we experience.

When our society is organized so that the minimum requirements of survival are assured without bitter competition, and when values other than maximizing production and consumption are allowed to emerge, we can truly contemplate the possibilities of diversity. In such a context it will be far more possible than it is now for religious, racial, and ethnic groups to develop organizations, communities, and life styles to their liking within the general framework of a commitment to the socialist principles of the society. At the individual level people would be far freer to pursue their interests and desires when removed from the constant pressure to survive. As socialism allows for a greater diversity of considerations to enter into decisions about production and economics, by the same logic it allows for a greater diversity of consideration about individual human choices.

Finally socialism opens the door to the possibilities of a fuller flowering of human potential than we have previously known. An economic system built on scarcity, on the brutalities of the market place, on exploitation, and on the single-minded pursuit of growth and profit, regardless of social consequences, will produce responses in people that mirror these dynamics. In order to survive in this system, people have been forced to become self-seeking, competitive, and hardened. When people live under conditions of scarcity, whether the scarcity is manipulated or not, they become protective, guarded, and jealous of what they have. They are less likely to have the sense of security and self-assurance that permits growth and openness.

As we become organized on the basis of other principles, the new reality of the society will inevitably have an impact on the people in the society. Imagine the effect on people's ability to express openness and generosity if we all fully understood that there was no personal gain for any of us in "beating" anyone else at anything and if we all knew that regardless of our race, sex, age or degree of health, we would always have enough of the basic necessities of life. An economic system and a system of social organization that manifested its caring for citizens would be more likely to generate caring citizens.

We would be able to be as creative as our imagination and our social resources allowed in deciding how to use the wealth we had generated for the sake of promoting human potential. For example, at some stage in our development, we might make the decision that minimum, but adequate, housing, food, clothing, and transportation would be made available to every citizen, regardless of that citizen's labor force participation, for one year out of every six. People would not have to work in that year and could depend on a public subsidy that would be adequate for maintenance while they went to school, traveled, developed skills and interests, or did nothing. It is not out of the realm of possibility. We could in fact, institute such a plan right now. We already have sufficient wealth. All that is required is an economic system that allowed us to use our resources in that way, and a collective decision that such an expenditure of our surplus was a high priority.

A socialist society could create a climate of growth in which the very best qualities of human nature would flourish. Again it is not a guarantee of such growth. It is a baseline requisite. An economy based on human need and caring is more likely to support people's genuine humanity. The possibilities of gentleness, love, community, expansiveness, and ultimately true liberation rest on the creation of a material base in a society that mirrors and promotes these values.

3

Processes of Socialist Transformation

On Political Fatalism

Is it actually possible that the basic dynamics of this society could someday be fundamentally changed from their present form? Many people believe not. In fact we have so accepted the notion that a fundamental transformation is impossible that we react against the kind of analysis presented in the previous chapter by claiming that it is futile to pursue reasoning that does not lead to the possibilities for action. We have been conditioned to believe that society, at least our society, cannot change. This belief limits our willingness to explore radical analyses or to investigate the contribution we ourselves could make to basic change processes.

This pessimism is rooted in the political socialization process we receive as children. It is not a result of a reasoned analysis of the possibilities and probabilities of fundamental social change in the United States. Most of us have not made such an analysis for ourselves. In a variety of ways we are conditioned to believe in our own powerlessness, in the irrelevance of our engaging larger social and political issues, and in the inevitability and immutability of the present social order.[1] This is not to suggest that there is no

---

[1]For example, see Paulo Freire, *Pedagogy of the Oppressed* (New York: Herder and Herder, 1971); Herbert Marcuse, *One-Dimensional Man* (Boston: Beacon Press, 1964), and Jonathan Kozd, *The Night is Dark and I am Far From Home* (New York: Bantam, 1975).

truth to the idea that making a revolution is a difficult undertaking. Rather our ingrained and often unexamined fatalism about the possibilities of basic change is not so much a reflection of social reality as it is a reflection of the success of conservative ideas in the society. Those ideas reinforce our beliefs and become a self-fulfilling prophecy. To the extent that we believe that society is immutable, it will be so. Similarly to the extent that we believe that each of us, and especially all of us together, can be key makers and movers of history, we become so.

The Inevitability of Change

contradictions and dialectic analysis

Socialist ideas about the inevitability of social change, and particularly about the inevitability of a transformation from capitalist to socialist stages of development, contain two, somewhat opposing, notions. On the one hand, Marx's analysis of the fundamental dynamics of capitalism posits the inevitability of such change. As Marx analyzed the matter, capitalist societies contain within them opposing, or contradictory, forces which press against one another. These forces and the resolution which comes about through their interaction are the basic dynamic from which socialist transformation emerges. On the other hand, in revolutionary theory much weight is given to the deliberate and conscious creation of revolutionary ideas and revolutionary organizations as a necessary component of the change process. In the absence of such intervention, revolution does not occur. Both aspects of the process need to be considered.

Transformation from capitalism to socialism occurs, according to the Marxist understanding, as a result of the interaction of internally generated conflicts within capitalism while capitalism follows the logical and inevitable path of its own development. This is an important notion in Marxist theory. Socialist revolution is not grafted on to, imported into, or imposed upon an otherwise stable, if suffering, capitalist order. Rather, revolution is the name given to the process whereby a capitalist society is transformed into a socialist society at the point at which capitalism no longer works and no longer contains solutions to the problems it generates. It is most important to understand that capitalism itself has generated the forces which press for and accomplish the transformation to socialism. Socialism emerges out of capitalism as a response to developments within capitalism itself.

In Marxist terminology the process of change generated as a result of internal, systemic conflicts is captured in the concept of *internal contradiction*. This concept is crucial to a Marxist understanding of the process of social change. To make use of it, we need to address three questions: What is meant by internal contradictions; what are the internal contradictions in capitalism;

and why does the existence of these contradictions point to the transformation from capitalism to socialism.

The concept of internal contradictions is an analytic scheme for understanding the general process of systemic change. It suggests that change occurs as a result of the development and interaction of opposing forces that derive from the internal workings of a given system. This interplay of opposites within systems is the key element in the process of development in all systems. It calls attention to the way systems generate their own destabilizing dynamics, to the way internal system dynamics lead to change, as well as to the way the external forces stimulate internal change processes. It helps us see how every system contains elements generating its own change processes. In Marxist terminology the concept of *dialectics* refers to the process whereby internal contradictions lead to systemic change. This analytic scheme conflicts with theories that suggest that change occurs either as a result of the influence of forces external to the system or as a result of the decrease or increase of the quantities of elements within a system.

The opposing forces within systems may be labeled as antagonistic or as nonantagonistic. Being antagonistic suggests opposing forces generated by and within a system which cannot simultaneously be contained within that system as it progresses and develops. Antagonistic forces oppose each other in such a way that their containment within the system, while possible at one stage of development, is not possible at later stages. One set of the opposing forces cannot be eliminated in order to preserve the system, since both sets are necessary to it and help to define it. To do away with one part of the whole is to change the whole. Nor is it possible for the system to maintain an ongoing balance of the opposing forces since the forces compete for domination within the system in an antagonistic, that is a noncompromising, fashion. The forces are irreconcilable at the mature stage of their development.

A nonantagonistic contradiction is of a different order. Nonantagonistic contradictions can be contained and resolved within the existing system. However a weakness of the concepts of antagonistic and nonantagonistic contradictions is that there is no general rule for distinguishing between them. Each particular set of contradictions must be analyzed in the light of the specific circumstances involved in order to determine the extent to which the set is or is not antagonistic within the framework of the system within which it arises. The notion of antagonistic and nonantagonistic contradictions is a classification scheme. It is not a guide to suggest which kinds of forces are which. Rather, it is an encouragement to make a differentiation in analyzing a specific situation.[2]

---

[2]Key theoretical discussions include V. ı. Lenin, "On the Question of Dialectics," *Collected Works* (Russian Edition: Moscow, 1958, Volume 38), and Mao Tsetung, "On Contradiction," *Selected Readings from the Work of Mao Tsetung* (Peking: Foreign Language Press, 1971). A clarifying discussion is found in Michael Albert, *What is to be Undone?* (Boston: Porter Sargent Publishers, 1974), especially Chapter 10, "The Chinese Experience," pp. 206–262.

Marxists utilize this way of looking at the internal processes of systems to understand the nature of capitalism and the nature of the forces within it pointing toward its transformation to socialism. For reasons which will be explored, capitalism generates antagonistic, contradictory forces. As a product of its own logical development, capitalism inevitably gives rise to forces with opposing interests and requirements. These forces compete for domination, but the domination of either force would be incompatible with the continued existence of capitalism. As a result capitalism must give way to another form which permits the resolution of the contradiction. The form this resolution takes has been given the name socialism. The next question that must be addressed, therefore, is the nature of the specific contradictions that Marxists observe within capitalism which lead them to these conclusions.

the primary contradictions in capitalism

As an analyst living in and observing an earlier stage of capitalist development one hundred years ago, Marx saw that the majority of people in a capitalist society generated, but did not control, its wealth. The people who actually did the work of the society which produced its wealth—that is the people who actually turned the natural resources of the earth and the soil into useful things—did so by their labor, but they did not determine how the wealth they created would be used. This is one set of opposing forces, one of the contradictions in capitalism, that plays out as capitalism develops. Acting as a collectivity, although they are not always aware of the interactional, interdependent, or collective nature of their effort, the majority of people produce the real things that are needed by the society, and a few people, the owners or capitalists, control the profits, or surplus. The capitalists do not consult the producers of the surplus about the use to which the fruits of their labor will be put, nor should they, within the logic of capitalism. They reinvest that surplus according to the logic of the system within which they operate. That logic dictates that they reinvest the surplus in a way which will maximize its ability to generate still more surplus. The nature of their personal beliefs and the character of their individual personalities is a secondary factor in their decision-making processes. If they are to succeed as capitalists they must abide by the logic of capitalism. They do what they must do, which tends to become what they believe in doing, as a consequence of the role they play within this particular social order.

The interests of the two major groupings in society, or in Marxist terms, *classes*, are opposing interests. The owners of capital, the capitalists, must maximize profits. Doing so requires minimizing the costs of production, so that the difference between the costs which capitalists incur to produce salable goods or services and the prices which these goods or services command in the market is maximized. This requires, among other things, minimizing the wages paid to workers. The workers, on the other hand, naturally want to maximize their wages. The stage is set for conflict.

In actuality this two class scheme is oversimplified. Society does not consist solely of two classes, each with its own parts, which must be analyzed in relationship to the contradictions within capitalism. For example, of particular interest to social service workers are welfare recipients. On the face of it, they are neither owners nor workers. However, as we delve more deeply, we discover that welfare recipients are a group that is separate from the rest of the working class and yet is also very much a part of the working class. Welfare recipients, to the extent that they receive welfare benefits and do not work, do not fit the model of typical workers. At the same time, many welfare recipients have a cyclical involvement in the labor market. Welfare recipients, therefore, can be understood as a more marginal segment of the labor force who have a wide variety of particulars applicable to their situation. Similarly it is of great interest for the development of radical social work practice to analyze the class location of public employees, among whom we count social service workers. Public employees neither own the means of production nor work directly for capitalists. At the same time, Marxist analysis suggests an intimate relationship between the public sector and the requirements of capitalism, as I will develop in the following chapter. These connections help to clarify the relationship between public sector workers and traditional, private sector workers and to reveal unique qualities of public sector workers, as a product of the more recent history of capitalist development. As this discussion points out, class analysis encourages us to look at groupings of people in terms of their relationship to the means of production.

The basic contradiction in capitalism, however, is rooted in a more fundamental dynamic that underlies the conflict between the classes. The class struggle is the primary manifestation of this underlying contradiction, but it is not the underlying contradiction itself. If we did not extend our analysis more deeply, we would be left with the observation that there are, simply put, two major groups, or classes, in capitalist society; each wants more of the same fixed amount of surplus. At one point, one class may be more successful while at another point, another class may be more successful in winning a larger share of the surplus. This dynamic would suggest that there is perhaps bitter, and even violent, conflict. It is not sufficient evidence for suggesting that a transformation to a fundamentally new system is inevitable.

As we look more deeply, we see a further dynamic underneath this struggle, which gives rise to both the struggle and its inevitably antagonistic and contradictory nature. As capitalists try to reduce wages, among other costs of production, in an effort to increase profits, they reduce the purchasing power of the workers. If they succeed in keeping wages down in a given period, they make it more difficult for workers to purchase back from the capitalists the goods which they, the workers, have produced. If that happens, the profits needed for growth are not generated, since the products are not sold. The economy stagnates. On the other hand, if the workers are more successful in winning wage increases, which leads to an increase in their ability to purchase back the products and services they produce, they reduce the profits the capitalists have available for further investment. If this happens, the economy stagnates from the other direction since capitalists do not have the surplus to make additional investments. Through all this, capitalists want to keep production levels as high as possible in order to generate more profits. Fundamentally then, at the root of this impasse is the problem of overproduction. Goods are produced which do not find buyers.

Several solutions may provide temporary relief. One of these is to expand markets. In fact the capitalist system has attempted to extend its domination and logic throughout the world. It is stopped short of world domination by the reality of socialist and nationalist revolutions, which close off large potential markets to capitalist penetration. Even if this were not so, eventually the same long-term logic of production exceeding consumption would emerge. We see this aleady in the case of the manipulation of domestic purchasing through advertising. Through advertising, consumers are encouraged to buy more than they otherwise would. As consumers we have in fact responded to these efforts. Our willingness and ability to continue to do so is finally limited, both by the extent of our purchasing power and by whatever awareness we develop about the emptiness of consumerism as a way of life.

Another attempt to solve the problem of overproduction is through military spending. The government buys war materials and provides a market for the output of a significant proportion of our productive apparatus. However the money which government uses to buy war materials is tax money, which comes largely from the wages of working people, rather than from corporate profits.[3] So at base, the limits of this solution are also the limits of workers' ability to buy back what they can produce. In addition war production gives rise to inflation which serves to further upset the balance of the economy. Social welfare spending is another effort to solve these problems, since it serves to increase the purchasing power of workers by distributing money to them outside of the usual market mechanisms. The limitations of this attempted solution are analyzed in the following chapter.

Ultimately class antagonisms are rooted in the basic dynamics of a capitalist economy. In order for a capitalist system to grow and survive, it must produce as much as possible, at the same time as it limits wages as much as

---

[3] In 1975, for example, individual income taxes and social insurance taxes were the source of 84 percent of all government receipts. Corporate taxes were the source of only 14.5 percent of government receipts. Corporate taxes as a percentage of government receipts have declined consistently for some time. In 1960 they represented 23.2 percent of all government receipts. These data are from *Pocket Data Book, U.S.A., 1976* (Washington, D.C.: U.S. Government Printing Office, 1976), Table 97, p. 100.

possible. Eventually the reach of capitalism extends as far as the world situation allows, and the logic of overproduction asserts itself. The organization of the material world of production gives rise to insurmountable contradictions. The system must necessarily go through periodic crises, at root the crisis of overproduction, making the life situation of workers exceedingly difficult. Less production is a limited solution within capitalism because any capitalist who produces less reduces profits for a given production unit and runs the risk of demise through absorption by another capitalist. More production is not possible since the surplus available to increase production is limited by sales of the product which in turn are limited by the ability of workers to purchase more.

Put another way, the underlying contradiction is that between the social or collective nature of production (one form of what Marxists call the *forces of production*) and the private or individual control of the means of production (one form of the *relations of production*). The forces of production, in an advanced industrialized society, are collective. That is, they are such that the combined efforts of the majority of people are required to produce the goods and services needed by that society. Because production is advanced and collectively organized, it leads to high output. On the other side of the contradiction, the control of that production and of the surplus that is generated is not distributed among the collectivity that produces it. It is in the hands of a few. The forces and the relations of production, at this point in our historical and material development, are out of phase with each other. It is extremely unlikely that we will return to a more primitive form of production, namely, a form in which each person produces what she or he needs for personal use in a private and individual manner. What we must do is reorganize the relations of production so that they support the most advanced level of productive capacity we can achieve.[4]

As the contradictions between the forces and relations of production mature and escalate, the system makes efforts to preserve itself through various reforms, on the one hand, and through repression, on the other hand. Reform includes welfare state measures, and tax and monetary manipulations. At the present time the system has a fair amount of reform potential still

---

[4]Needless to say, a very complex analytic process and intellectual history has been sketched in this review. Interested readers would be well advised to pursue Marx and his various elaborators and commentators on their own. I have found this aspect of Marx's analysis most accessible in the following. Karl Marx, *Das Kapital*, edited by Friedrich Engels and condensed by Serge L. Levitsky (Chicago: Henry Regnery, 1959.) In addition, an extremely useful work is Paul Baran and Paul Sweezy, *Monopoly Capital* (New York: Monthly Review Press, 1966). Short, direct, and helpful discussions are found in Ernest Mandell, *An Introduction to Marxist Economic Theory* (New York: Pathfinder Press, Inc., 1960) and Gayle Southworth, *An Introduction to Capitalism: Four Lectures on Marxian Economics* (Cambridge, Mass.: Radical America, Box B, North Cambridge, Massachusetts 02140, 1971).

available. It is true that the decade of the 1970s was one of decreased emphasis on reform and increased emphasis on repression. It is also quite likely that we will witness further periods of reform. Quite possibly the limits of reform will be set by the loss of additional markets overseas and by the further loss of resources through war. Also a growing radical ideology may advance the speed at which revolutionary change occurs by creating an awareness of the need for revolution sooner than might be expected if we depended solely on the system to exhaust its ability to reform. The subjective factor is, of course, extremely difficult to gauge and predict.

To the extent that the forces of the status quo do not and cannot attempt to stabilize the system through reform, they do so through repression. In part this repression takes the form of socialization, or soft repression, which attempts to indoctrinate people with the idea that the system works on their behalf, even when it does not. The other form of repression, hard repression, attacks people's efforts to organize for change through punitive legislation, police force, and intimidation. These repressive efforts always carry the potential of backfiring on the capitalist class and the state by revealing to people the underlying coercive nature of the state, and so facilitating progressive organizing. Like the reformist solution to the internal contradictions within capitalism, the repressive solution also has pronounced limits.

the role of the working class

In observing the fundamental contradictions of capitalist societies, Marx was also led to examine the nature and movement of the working class whose material conditions motivated them to fight for basic social change, that is, for the elimination of capitalism and its replacement by a socialist form of organization. That class is the same group of workers who produce the wealth of capitalist society. Why are they assigned such an important role in the change process, according to classical Marxist formulations?

First, they are daily robbed of a full return from their labor. While this fact may not be obvious to all workers, the underlying reality persists none the less. This is the basic meaning of the concept of *exploitation*: The wealth produced by workers is expropriated, stolen from them by capitalists, who control and direct it but who do not produce it. The people who produce the goods and services of the society have a stake in changing things, based on the reality of their daily condition as economic victims of a wage system which pays them less for their work than that work is worth in terms of the value of the things produced.

The working class is assigned a key role in Marxist theory as the agent of societal transformation because workers have a motivation, rooted in the material conditions of their lives, to make such changes. The capitalists and those identified with their viewpoints cannot and will not be the agents of such change. The necessary change rests on the abolition of private ownership of the means of production, and the capitalists will not accede to such change without bitter resistance. Because of its essential logic, capitalism cannot reform itself gradually into a "more socialist" order. Furthermore the psychological commitments of those who benefit most from it are based on processes and values diametrically opposed to those of socialism. Even if some individual capitalists were to become radicalized and attempt to support such change, they would be challenged by other capitalists and by the logic of the very system they represent. Capitalists are welcome to the socialist ranks, and a few may join. Their contribution to revolutionary change will not come through their role as enlightened capitalists, however, but through their role as revolutionaries.

The natural conditions of the working class, then, create the basis on which the working class potentially develops the political ideology capable of supporting socialist transformation. These natural conditions are also the basis of the power which the working class has to actually make these changes. The workers, not the capitalists, constitute the class that is essential to running the society and to making it work. The workers can run the society without the capitalists. They will need to learn new skills and to develop new forms of social organization to avoid replacing present day capitalists with a new breed of worker-capitalists, and they can do so. Capitalists, on the other hand, cannot run the society and produce needed goods and services without the workers because there are not enough of them to do the job. They need the workers; workers do not need them.

Finally the working class is viewed as a key revolutionary agent because the daily conditions of work suggest the collective nature of working-class existence and collective power—although these realities are not readily perceived by workers in nonrevolutionary times. The production of goods and services occurs only because large numbers of working people coordinate their efforts to produce given outcomes. We may not be attuned to the necessity of cooperative, interactional effort among us; none the less the nature of our work within capitalism is collectivist and cooperative in form. We do not expand this logic, normally, to an awareness of our power, inasmuch as we focus more on the subjective experience of being divided by virtue of status differentials, racism, sexism, and so on. However we are already organized in actual fact. Of course the particular organizational forms which will need to be created to advance revolutionary efforts, such as mass organizations, workers' councils, and a revolutionary party, do not exist at present. At a fundamental level, however, the actual conditions created by our efforts to make society work bring us together. For a revolutionary ideology to flourish our awareness needs to come into closer synchronization with reality.

Updating Classical Marxism

Marxism for the 1980s

Up to this point the discussion has generally followed classical lines of Marxist thought. Obviously in the one hundred to one hundred twenty-five years since Marx wrote, in the fifty to sixty years since Lenin wrote, and in the twenty-five to fifty years since Mao Tse-tung wrote, much has changed in the actual conditions of the world and in the ways in which socialists have understood and analyzed the world. In addition any general analysis must be set in the context of particular conditions within a country or sector of world capitalism under study. At least three developments require special attention in an examination of the kind of advanced monopoly capitalist society of which the United States is a primary case. These are the recognition of bases of struggle other than traditional class conflict; racism; and the critical role of government or the state in modern society.

the multiple facets of revolutionary movements

Marxists recognize that there is a basis other than the specific relationship people have to the productive process for the development of radical consciousness. For example, the growth of socialist feminism in the 1970s was rooted only indirectly in the relationship of women to the productive process.[5] The same can be said of the growth of important political movements around ecological issues, against the spread of nuclear power, against utility rate increases, for neighborhood-based organization[6] and so on. Similarly in the 1960s and 1970s campaigns against the reduction of public social services, represented by the work of the National Welfare Rights Organization or the National Tenants Organization, were and are an important part of the political scene. How can we interpret these developments in the light of the previous discussion?

---

[5]Useful discussions of socialist feminism are developed by Barbara Ehrenreich, "What Is Socialist Feminism?" *WIN Magazine*, June 3, 1976, pp. 4–7; *Working Papers on Socialism and Feminism*, New American Movement, 3244 North Clark Street, Chicago, Illinois 60657, n.d. An example of the application of these ideas in one arena of political struggle is presented in Helen I. Marieskind and Barbara Ehrenreich, "Toward Socialist Medicine: The Women's Health Movement," *Social Policy*, 6 (September/October, 1975), 34–42.

[6]Useful discussions of the relationship between urban and class conflict include Manuel Castello, *The Urban Question: A Marxist Approach* (Cambridge, Mass.: MIT Press, 1977); Michael Harloe, ed., *Captive Cities* (New York: John Wiley, 1977); and Stephen Schecter, *The Politics of Urban Liberation* (Montreal: Black Rose Books, 1978). Current reports on these struggles are often found in *Just Economics*, newsletter of the Movement for Economic Justice and Acorn, available at 1735 T Street, N.W., Washington, D.C. 20009.

It is useful to recognize that the problems which give rise to these movements are rooted in capitalism itself. This is not to argue that sexism or ecological destructiveness do not exist in socialist societies. They do. The key question for us is the extent to which, in our situation, these problems are products of capitalism and are capable of solution within the context of capitalism. Each case requires its own analysis. At the same time, I believe that each of these problems is, in fact, not solvable within the context of capitalism.

As would be expected, various movements themselves contain many political currents. Each movement is composed of people holding the view that the particular problem to which the organizing is directed is solvable without fundamental societal transformation of the sort discussed here. There also tends to be a leftist perspective represented within such movements. This cross current of views within the movements reflects the cross current of views within the society as a whole. Ideological struggle takes place within the context of the movements as it takes place in the broader society between advocates and opponents of social change.

To put this in other terms, capitalism, and the destructiveness which it engenders, is at the root of the major social problems we face. Subsequently the consciousness that people develop about that destructiveness may emerge through its impact in various arenas of their lives at a given moment. This is not to be lamented. It simply reflects the fact that the destructiveness of this system affects many parts of the system and can be identified through many of its effects.

What are matters for debate and conflict are the competing analyses of the roots of the problems and the strategies which flow from these analyses. To the extent that a particular problem is understood as being isolated from the basic dynamics of the system itself, the strategies which follow will be reformist rather than revolutionary in nature, and ultimately they will be coopted and will fail. Equally problematic is the question of the potential of political movements to develop the power to affect fundamental change if they are not organized on the basis of people's relationship to the means of production. It is important to organize against racism, sexism, and other forms of human oppression. However, can the women's movement, as the women's movement, or the liberation struggles of minorities, organized as minorities, potentially generate the power to bring about change? Ultimately these movements may make important contributions to a united movement with numerous components.

The multitude of movements around us, only some of which are based on people's relationship to their role as workers, are not inconsistent with a Marxist analysis of the contradictions of capitalist society. They enrich that analysis. They suggest that various contradictions at any moment may provide the basis on which people begin to understand more clearly the nature of our society and their relationship to it. They suggest the omnipresent and the destructive logic of a system oriented toward profit, not toward a decent and fulfilling life for society's members. They suggest that a revolutionary movement may have many contributing streams based on the multitude of ways in which people experience oppression.

racism and class struggle

This discussion provides a context in which to look at a second refinement of classical Marxism, namely, an analysis of racism in the context of the United States. The genesis of racism in the United States is deeply rooted in capitalism itself. Racial oppression, as the basis for generating an unpaid labor force, enabled this country to move from a relatively primitive agricultural state of economic development to a more mature, heavily industrialized stage. It provided a speedy way to accumulate the surplus that industrialization requires. Further, the underlying economic logic of slavery continues to this day. The existence of racism, in economic terms, is another of the ways in which the exploitation of workers is maintained. Racism is a prop for the economic structure of capitalism.

Racism, however, serves important functions within a capitalist system, in addition to these. Racism is also a caste system, supported by a complex and permeating ideological justification. If socialism "dropped on us" out of the sky, an impossibility of course, racism would still be with us. We are left, then, with the following questions: Is the abolition of capitalism necessary, at this point, for the elimination of racism? Would a transition to socialism be a sufficient condition for the elimination of racism? And what is the relationship of Blacks, Chicanos, American Indians and other minorities to the process of socialist transformation?[7]

The abolition of capitalism is a necessary condition for the elimination of racism. The economic roots of racism remain deeply entrenched in capitalism itself in several ways. Capitalism does not permit full employment, for reasons that were developed earlier in this chapter. Racism justifies unemployment and underemployment. The full and equally recompensed employment of minorities would confront the fact that capitalism requires both unemployment and inequality. In addition the continued existence of a caste system serves as a conservative ideological force in the lives of some white working-class members since it provides a scapegoat for the dilemmas of that class (minority group members are "responsible" for crime, for the deterioration of

---

[7] I would recommend James Boggs, *Racism and the Class Struggle* (New York: Monthly Review Press, 1970); William K. Tabb, *The Political Economy of the Black Ghetto* (New York: W. W. Norton and Co., Inc., 1970); Victor Perlo, *The Economics of Racism, USA* (New York: International Publishers, 1975); and Tony Thomas, ed., *Black Liberation and Socialism* (New York: Pathfinder Press, 1974).

city schools, and so on), and it allows the most exploited white working-class members to believe that, however difficult their lives are, they are still better off and better than, another group. At this point in our development, racism is deeply entwined in capitalism and functional for its maintenance, both economically and ideologically. Eliminating racism poses the necessity of challenging the very existence of capitalism itself. It requires abolishing a system that demands economic exploitation of large parts of the population, justifications for massive inequalities, and ready scapegoats as an explanation of the difficulty of life for working people.

Were a revolutionary socialist movement to develop in the absence of the commitment and involvement of minorities, an unlikely circumstance in itself, it would be unlikely to lead to the abolition of racism. Because racism is deeply enmeshed in the workings of all facets of our society, it will need to be confronted and dealt with in the myriad of places and ways it appears. If for no other reason, this reality suggests the necessity of struggling against racism as an integral part of struggling against capitalism. Further, despite the intentions of white radicals, it will and must be revolutionaries from within minority groups who raise the primacy of this issue. To do so may well require the independent organization of minorities capable of bringing racism to the fore of socialist struggles on the basis of minority political power, not on the basis of the intellectual, political, or emotional awareness of the white radical movement, although these are important.

In any case it seems quite unlikely that an effective revolutionary movement can develop in the United States without the involvement of minorities. While I do not believe as some do, that minorities inevitably and necessarily will be the leading sector and major force of such a movement, I do believe that the radical mobilization of minorities is indispensable. There are several reasons for making this assertion. Minorities represent a large and critical part of the working class in the United States. They also represent a numerical majority or a dominant influence in the politics of many cities. Perhaps most important, the mobilization of minorities ultimately is likely to be the major force in challenging racism in the white working class. Racism will be tempered by an awareness of the necessity of cooperative revolutionary work only when minorities are effectively able to challenge racist practices. Parts of the white working class will maintain racist practices and beliefs as long as they are able to do so. Many working-class people have been subjected to years of conditioning in that direction and since they operate within the confines of a capitalist belief system, they assume that their well-being depends on the continued suppression of minorities. Until minorities challenge racism effectively enough that racist practices become less possible, that is, until the white working class develops to the point where collective action seems more desirable than divisive racist action, racism will continue to divert and divide the working-class movement. The liberation of minorities and socialist transformation are not simply two desirable notions which are arbitrarily linked together. They are indispensable allies in the same process.

the role of public employees

Traditional Marxist analysis must also be informed by an awareness of the reality of the enormous growth of government activity in the twentieth century. Approximately one in five workers in the labor force of the United States works for the state.[8] They are not capitalists, and they do not work directly for capitalists. They need to be located in the class structure, and their work must be accounted for. In Chapter 4, I will develop an analytic scheme for assessing the relationship of the state to capitalism. In Chapter 5, I will address the relationship of public sector workers to the traditional, blue collar working class and suggest some influences on the political directions this group has taken and might take in the future. A complete analysis would need to account for other sectors of government activity as well, particularly the military which, together with the social welfare segment, constitutes a significant proportion of government activity and expenditure. Useful analyses directed to this issue are Baran and Sweezy, *Monopoly Capital;* O'Conner, *The Fiscal Crisis of the State;* and Panitch, *The Canadian State: Political Economy and Political Power.*[9]

developing radical ideology

Earlier in this discussion I reviewed some opposing notions within Marxism about the inevitability of change. I suggested that the basis for the argument that fundamental change is inevitable within capitalism is that capitalism gives rise to opposing, mutually contradictory, irreconciliable forces, and that it also produces a group of people, the working class, with the motivation, capacity, and power to make a revolution. The other notion within Marxism is that such change, while inevitable in the long run, is not inevitable in the short run. And the long run might be quite long indeed. Despite the dynamic which Marx uncovered, it is possible that we will not become sufficiently aware of the potential we have to make a humane world for ourselves and so will not act in the ways required to bring such a world into existence. We may not do so because many powerful forces operate to obscure the desirability and block the possibility of such change from us.

---

[8]*Pocket Data Book, U.S.A., 1976*, Table 148, p. 135 and Table 113, p. 111.

[9]Baran and Sweezy, *Monopoly Capital;* James O'Conner, *The Fiscal Crisis of the State* (New York: St. Martin's Press, 1973); and Leo Panitch (ed.); *The Canadian State: Political Economy and Political Power* (Toronto; University of Toronto Press, 1977.)

Let us review these forces. Historically, when members of the working class have attempted to organize, which they have done on a repeated basis, they have met fierce opposition from the capitalist class.[10] In the case of efforts to unionize, for example, workers have been shot and jailed, fired and starved, threatened and even bombed.[11] The impact of such repression is great on those immediately involved and on the many who observe these experiences and conclude that efforts to bring about change are extremely dangerous. In addition capitalist interpretations of these events, publicized through its media, are frequently distorted. These interpretations misrepresent the intentions, methods, and goals of those organizing for change. Those resisting the old order have not developed sufficiently effective and extensive mechanisms to allow them to disseminate an interpretation of their actions to other members of the working class from their own perspective.

In other words capitalists have an arsenal of psychological and attitudinal weapons at their disposal in addition to the actual physical arms they may use to suppress the effort to build radical social movements. The ideological apparatus of the capitalist class, the world view it holds and advances, has dominated social thought, despite the fact that the world view of the capitalist class, that is, the capitalist notion of the good life and means to achieve it, does not serve the best interests of the working class. Similarly the idea that people can better themselves through individual mobility within the structure of the present system, an idea which no longer reflects the realities of our society for most people, operates as a conservatizing force in the society. Our appreciation of our collective strength has also been limited by the racism and sexism which divide us; by our cooptation through a rising standard of living (now much reduced as a conservatizing force by setbacks in capitalist economies throughout the world); by our patriotic commitment to "our country," a commitment which is periodically dangled before us and which unites us in common cause during the repeated wars in which this country engages, and by our deeply ingrained fear of communism, a fear created and manipulated by the capitalist class with the intent of dissuading us from examining alternate possibilities.

For these reasons our subjective experience of our own collective power has been muted, and large numbers of us remain committed to systems of belief, that is, to ideologies, to organizations, and to social processes which

---

[10]Useful discussions include Gene L. Mason, "The Future of Repression," in *1984 Revisited* ed. Robert Paul Wolff (New York: Knopf, 1973) and Center for Research on Criminal Justice, *The Iron Fist and the Velvet Glove: An Analysis of the U.S. Police* (Berkeley, California: 2490 Channing Way, Room 507, Berkeley, California 94704; 1975).

[11]For example, see Richard O'Boyer and Herbert M. Morais, *Labor's Untold Story* (New York: United Electrical, Radio and Machine Workers of America, 1955) and Jeremy Brecher, *Strike!* (San Francisco,: Straight Arrow Books, 1972.)

diminish our lives unnecessarily, which shorten our lives, and which diminish and shorten the lives of persons around the globe. Our subjective awareness of our reality is out of phase with the objective conditions of our lives.

It is this fact which raises question about the inevitability of socialist transformation. It is a doubt which cannot be resolved definitively at this point. It may be possible, though I tend to think not likely, that our analysis as a people will be dominated indefinitely by a world view that serves us poorly. At the same time, it is in this arena, in the arena of our subjective appreciation of our reality and our response to it, that revolutionaries must work. We need to encourage the ideas, the forms of organization, and the initial experiences that point the way to the desirability of radical change and to the possibility of such change. Alternative ways of thinking and of viewing the world and some, even modest experiences of success in creating pieces of that change, are the necessary preconditions for bringing our subjective experience into closer harmony with the realities of our lives. This job is difficult, but possible. We will be assisted by the ongoing, underlying dynamics of capitalism, which continue to generate the objective conditions to make revolution desirable and possible. We will also be assisted by developments in other parts of the world, which increasingly are moving more countries in a socialist direction and which are serving us both by example and by undermining the ability of capitalism, as a world system, to obscure our situation by buying us off with material goods. Finally and crucially, we will move forward as a result of our own conscious efforts to educate and to organize.

The Period of Prerevolutionary Struggle

revolutionary and nonrevolutionary times

As I have explained, socialist analysis of the process of change stems from an analysis of the internal dynamics of capitalist society itself. There is a great deal to say, of course, about tactics, strategy, guidelines, past experience, and the particulars of the ways in which revolutionary efforts have been initiated and sustained. Similarly there is much to concern us about why some movements fail and why some succeed. Note, however, that the analysis of potential agents and processes of change is derived from the underlying social analysis, particularly from the analysis of the economic structure of the society and the social relationships to which the economic structure gives rise.

This is important since it differentiates Marxism from other approaches which conceptualize possible agents and directions for social change. It understands change processes in terms of the fundamental dynamics of the society itself. It does not separate what might be and how we might get there from what is. It is this characteristic of Marxist analysis, its observation of the existing system and its relatively consistent linkages between the dynamics of the old order and the processes and forces pushing toward the new order that has led to its identification as "scientific" socialism. It differs from "utopian" socialism, that is, socialism positing goals which may be quite attractive but lacking notions of "getting from here to there," it can readily be distinguished from liberal reformism which is commited to maintaining capitalism itself.

The Marxist perspective identifies both the confluence of objective conditions (a stage of capitalist development at which the system becomes progressively less able to solve the problems it generates) and the confluence of subjective conditions (recognition by the working class that capitalism has failed and can be overthrown if it is ready to take major risks and to wage major battles. It also suggests that revolution itself is less a single event than it is a process of change, though major social change processes may well have climactic moments. Capitalism has matured from the early stages of competition to the advanced stage of monopolies. In the process it has generated a series of problems for the people of the society, and it has tried to solve these problems. The development of social welfare measures is one effort to solve problems within the context of capitalism. At some time, possibly as a result of wars, economic dislocation, or national liberation efforts elsewhere in the world, further reforms within capitalism could become increasingly difficult to achieve. When this development coincides with the readiness and willingness of the majority of people in the society to make major changes, a revolutionary period might be said to exist.

The coming to fruition of a revolutionary period does not, in itself, assure transformation to a socialist society. Not all elements of the working class will achieve revolutionary consciousness at the same moment, and some elements of that class will continue to adhere to the old world view and will serve the capitalist class in maintaining the old order. Of course they will be among the forces enlisted by the capitalist class to suppress the working-class challenge. As in the past it is most likely that the capitalist class will employ both ideological and violent means to suppress the challenge. It will use the legal system, and it will act in illegal ways. To the extent that the working class has developed its capacity to respond to these efforts at suppression, it will have a greater probability of overcoming the contradictions of capitalism and of moving the society to the higher level of functioning permitted by socialism.

The United States is not presently in such a revolutionary period. This must be clearly acknowledged. None the less pressures do exist for revolutionary change. Although the working class is not conscious of the possibilities of socialism or of its potential for bringing those possibilities about, class conflict continues on a daily basis. Each instance of labor conflict, although not explicitly concerned with a struggle over control of the means of production, reflects the struggle between classes over distribution of the surplus. Each campaign waged by those who depend on welfare state programs is a reflection of class conflict in that it is a contest over the use which will be made of the surplus which the working class has created. Each struggle against sexism and racism, including those which are not explicitly radical, is at base a struggle against the way in which capitalism has divided the working class. These various struggles are interpreted, within a capitalist analytic framework, as conventional interest group competition for scarce resources. To the extent that the conventional interpretation is accepted, these are indeed interest group struggles. However, at the same time, these struggles are rooted in the dynamics of the class system and may presage the emergence of more focused class consciousness.

strategy in a nonrevolutionary time

The key task for radicals, at this stage of revolutionary development, is to identify ways of confronting fundamental contradictions in the material world. They may do this by assisting in the wide variety of particular struggles that emerge, struggles which generally are not seen as radical in the understanding of the participants. Radicals must assist in people's rightful attempts to achieve a better life within the old system, so that by their efforts, the possibility and desirability of altering that system altogether may emerge more clearly in people's minds and then in the organizational forms which are created. Essentially the job of most radicals, particularly to the extent that they work and operate politically within nonradical organizations and among nonradical people, is to find ways to spread radical ideology and to create organizations of people prepared to move forward on radical agendas. Some radicals are and must be engaged in the task of working with other people who are already radical in order to fashion explicitly radical organizations and a radical political party that can provide leadership and coherence to the separate radical elements in the society. For most social service workers who are radical, or who are moving in a more radical direction, participating in building a radical party may be an attractive option. However more characteristically, they will work to bring a leftist perspective to essentially nonradical people and organizations.

The specific reformist struggles which people wage with the old system have very a limited potential to produce desired outcomes. Concessions can be won. Some small part of the surplus can be diverted from existing uses to more socially productive uses. At the same time, the limits of such diversion of resources are firmly set by the nature of capitalism itself. Even the struggles for modest reforms tend to fail, despite their modesty, because they run counter to the necessities of capitalism. None the less, radicals support such struggles and must continue to do so. They represent the ways in which people perceive the issues before them. To ignore these perceptions and the struggles to which they give rise is to ignore the real, immediate dilemmas of daily life for large numbers of people and as such is inhumane. It is also poor political strategy since it isolates radicals from the issues and perceptions of the majority of people.

How can radical consciousness be joined to political organization and nonradical political activities? There is no simple answer to this question. At best there are suggestions about ways to think about the linkages and about the immediate and longer range connections. This is the issue addressed in the following section.

Reform and Revolution

multiple sectors for radical work

In the opinion of most leftists in the United States, the present time does not lend itself to precise judgments about where and with whom it is most fruitful to work for the growth of radical ideology and organization. We cannot clearly say that work within the rank and file of trade unions, among minorities, or with public sector employees, for example, is clearly and singularly where we ought to put our efforts at developing a socialist movement. It may be that a larger number of people in some sector are slightly more advanced in their political thinking than people in other sectors, and that some people are more ready to mobilize in a radical direction. In general, however, there is not a high level of radical political consciousness in the United States. Nor is it clear where the next major surge of such consciousness might appear most powerfully. In the past it has emerged in a variety of sectors, including minority communities, youth, women, and trade unionists. Eventually each of these sectors will need to join together if we are to be successful.

The absence of more widely shared radical consciousness and activity is to be lamented. However the fact that the sector from which the next surge of radical consciousness will emerge is not clearer in itself opens up many possibilities and can encourage us to recognize the varieties of opportunity which exist. Many people are in political motion, though more often in reformist than radical ways. There is an important surge in rank-and-file union activity, a high and growing level of strike activity,[12] a growth in insurgent democratic movements within the large, encrusted unions, and a willingness is many sectors of the trade union movement to engage in militant activity. There is ongoing organization within minority communities, among women,

---

[12]In 1974 there were 6,074 incidents of work stoppage in the United States, compared to 5,353 cases in 1973 and 3,963 cases in 1965. The number of workers involved in these stoppages in 1974 was 2.8 million, up from 1.5 million in 1965. *Pocket Data Book, U.S.A., 1976*, Table 217, p. 168.

around social service issues, among gays, among public employees, on antinuclear and environmental issues and on a variety of utility and housing issues.
All of these offer possibilities for important radical work.

exposing the limits of reformism

Many people who recognize the necessity for political action as a way to
deal with the issues which face them, and who are willing and able to mobilize
collectively to find solutions, continue to believe that solutions are possible
within the overall framework of the present society, that is, within the
framework of capitalist society. In fact capitalism does continue to have the
capacity for further reforms, although its ability to make reforms was limited
by the economic conditions of the 1970s and the pressure on it to do so
slackened as a consequence of the relatively more quiescent state of people's
movements. However, as long as people react to the symbols offered to them
and do not look clearly and specifically at what is actually occurring, they may
continue to be misled about the possibilities for reform.

Therefore one approach for radicals working within reform movements
is to help bring the reality of the limited nature of reform home to larger
numbers of people. Contrary to some naive radical thinking, and to liberal and
conservative stereotyping of radical thought, this does not mean that radicals
ought to oppose the desires of people for "more" or for "better," even when
the "more" or "better" demands are couched in the language and logic of
reformism. They should assist in such struggles. In so doing they should use
their energies and political awareness in such a way that their efforts encourage clearer political thinking and greater feelings of militancy and solidarity
among people. Their goal is not simply to win the given demand being raised.
Hopefully that demand will be won, giving encouragement to people about
the possibility of changing the conditions of their lives through collective
political action. More commonly and increasingly through the period of the
1970s, such demands were not won. In either case the primary objectives of
radicals in these situations is to raise political questions about goals and
strategies so that win or lose, the long-term futility of pursuing nonrevolutionary goals and strategies becomes more apparent to larger numbers of people.
Reform struggles cannot be ends in themselves. They must be seen as stepping stones to a higher level of political consciousness and organization.[13]

---

[13]A useful discussion of this issue, and further suggested readings, are found in the *Basic
Political Education Course,* New American Movement, pp. 40–43, available through the New
American Movement, 3244 North Clark Street, Chicago, Illinois 60657, n.d. See also Ralph
Miliband, *Marxism and Politics* (Oxford: Oxford University Press, 1977), especially Chapter VI,
"Reform and Revolution," pp. 154–90.

The realities of capitalist society serve as an ally in the effort to challenge people's beliefs in the possibility of reform. Even when successfully achieved, reformist gains are often short-lived. Struggles against utility rate increases tend to be defeated eventually by virtue of the fact that resistance movements cannot sustain their energies over as long a period of time as utilities can afford to maintain their pressure for rate increases on the regulatory bodies. Public social services may be expanded when the pressure is sufficiently great and withdrawn when public attention is diverted; employment and educational opportunities for minorities open slightly under pressure and close with the passing of each insurgent wave. Such experiences can help to raise consciousness about the blind alleys into which well-meaning political energies are often channeled. At the same time, repeated failure can lead to a reinforcement of feelings of powerlessness. When the issues are posed in terms of the necessity for developing of a socialist movement, success is not automatically guaranteed. However false belief in the efficacy of short-term struggle is challenged. The long-range view that may emerge can provide a perspective that is more sustaining.

In effect we have a very difficult choice, and we must pose that choice to ourselves and to those with whom we work. On the one hand, reformist efforts often will not achieve even modest gains, and when they do achieve some victories, those victories may quickly disappear. Then again they may be successful, even if partially and temporarily. Reformist efforts are attractive for another reason. The struggle for reform does not require the political risk taking that radical struggle requires, and it does not require that people challenge long held, deeply held, and well-internalized beliefs in the legitimacy of the old system. The hurts and pains can be acknowledged in a reformist struggle, but the falsehood of our present social situation need not be acknowledged. Although reformism leads to frustration in the long run, it can produce a sense of security in the short run.

On the other hand, the socialist approach presses for specific reforms while it recognizes the necessity of revolutionary transformation as a precondition for achieving a decent social order. In so doing it may lead to a greater likelihood of achieving the immediate reform under consideration. Each radical effort however, must formulate a particular campaign as a stepping stone toward radical change—not through the accumulation of piecemeal reforms, which is an impossibility in any case—but through the growth of political awareness and of more unified and radical organizational forms of struggle.

nonreformist reforms

The linkage points of a particular reformist struggle and the larger radical movement that must be built have been suggested by various analysts.[14] A group of activists and writers involved with the Movement for a New Society, formulated three criteria to characterize those political efforts which can be identified as nonreformist reforms. Nonreformist reforms have some potential for partial (not full) realization within the existing social order; they contain the potential of advancing radical political struggle. They are reforms which raise the possibilities and probabilities of building the movement for a transition to a new society.

The characteristics of nonreformist reforms are first, that they involve a "shift in power from established political, economic, and cultural elites and toward oppressed or powerless people."[15] An extension of people's control usually involves an erosion of power from institutions and groups now holding such power in concentrated form; a decentralization of decision-making power to workers and community people; and, an increase in the strength of movement and resistance groups. Second, their objectives are "consistent with long-range goals for a new society, [and] based on a thorough going analysis of present society."[16] In articulating and communicating a new goal for society, revolutionary reforms "grow out of an understanding of the links between oppressive conditions and their causes in social structures, of the consequences of an issue for other parts of the world and for future generations, of viable alternatives that could replace present institutions, and of a strategy for change of which the given revolutionary reform is a part."[17] Finally nonreformist reforms encourage "heightened consciousness among people as to the need for a radically new society."[18] A heightening of consciousness usually involves a more critical view of the present system, greater sympathy for revolutionary perspectives, and approaches on the part of a growing number of people, and a deeper analysis of the social change movement itself, including "an increased ability to communicate with others its analysis, vision, and strategy for social change."[19]

It will be apparent, at this point, that it is not possible to indicate precisely a target of activity for those with radical commitments or a highly

---

[14]The work of André Gorz has been important for many radicals in conceptualizing this issue. See his *Strategy for Labor* (Boston: Beacon Press, 1967) and *Socialism and Revolution* (Garden City, New York: Anchor Books, 1973), especially Chapter 4, "Reform and Revolution," pp. 133–77. Also useful is Rosa Luxemburg, *Reform or Revolution* (New York: Pathfinder Press, 1970, originally published in 1900).

[15]Susan Gowan, George Lakey, William Moyer and Richard Taylor, *Moving Toward a New Society* (Philadelphia, New Society Press, 1976), p. 273.

[16]Ibid., p. 274.

[17]Ibid.

[18]Ibid.

[19]Ibid.

specific way of working with those who are not radical. It is possible to suggest approaches and guidelines. The development of a radical movement and the achievement of radical transformation is possible. To facilitate these ends, we must suit our activities to the particular times in which we live, and they are not revolutionary times. Yet if we are committed to the necessity of revolution and to the possibility of its achievement, we will take the steps that the present time indicates. This is our responsibility, both in terms of increasing the possibility for a more decent life now for more people and in terms of taking steps dictated by our situation to meet our obligations to the revolutionary movements of the future.

more advanced political tasks

If more people were politically radical in their consciousness and if the level of both radical and nonradical struggle were much escalated, other approaches would be possible. For example, under such circumstances we might consider establishing institutions of dual power. In workplaces we could begin to organize workers' councils, and would seek objectives that encouraged workers to give more and more of their allegiance to such councils for increasing amounts of direction in their work. In fact such alternatives can and are being created now in modest ways, and radicals should continue with these efforts. It is unlikely, however, that they can represent a major thrust of political work at a time when most people have not yet abandoned their hopes for the possibility of change through the reform of existing mechanisms. Similarly we could think, in a time of more advanced political development, of alternative, community-controlled governing councils in neighborhoods. Such councils might begin to replace the old mechanisms for meeting community needs and might gain so much loyalty that people would give them control over increasing shares of tax monies. Similarly larger alternative governing bodies might be elected to coordinate workplace and neighborhood councils and exist parallel to the old structures. They might compete with the old structures, for the loyalty and resources of larger numbers of people. At present the alternative institutions and governing forms that exist are only suggestive of the possibilities; they are not a realistically competitive force. Their importance is not to be diminished because of the fact that they are more suggestive than competitive. Again we must recognize the appropriateness of various strategies at various times.

It is also necessary, both at the present time and as we move toward a broader based, more clear-minded level of engagement, to develop a political party that can represent the highest aspirations of people. A "party" does not necessarily imply an organization that would engage in electoral politics. A revolutionary party may or may not pursue that approach, as one strategy among many, to educate people and to challenge existing structures. It will not necessarily do so with a hope of succeeding in revolutionary struggle through electoral means, though such an approach should not automatically be ruled out, as one among many. Such a party can serve to unify diverse struggles by articulating a common politics and by assisting in the creation of organizational forms in which diverse struggles find common ground to plan and to join efforts. At present no such party exists in a form to which large numbers of people can respond.

A revolutionary movement needs to develop mass organizations and a party that contains and articulates explicitly radical ideas. This will give much encouragement and support to the separate and discrete struggles that now take place and that will continue to take place. Because such organizations and such a party do not exist, individual struggles are isolated, both in terms of preople's psychological sense of being alone in battle and in the political sense of each of the separate campaigns proceeding in the absence of the kind of united action that will ultimately be required for success. These realities must be analyzed in a forthright manner so that we can work appropriately from where we are to a level of more advanced and effective struggle.

Toward a Successful Revolution

long term strategy

It seems unlikely that anyone can predict the form that a successful revolutionary movement will take in the United States or that anyone can predict the strategies that ultimately will prove most effective. None the less it is useful to give thought to some possibilities and to some general directions, since too many of us operate with extremely undeveloped conceptions of alternatives to conventional political and social change processes. In addition we need to make some assessments, if tentative ones, about the shape of future movements, in order to develop guidelines for present practice.

First and foremost, revolutionary transformation cannot occur in the absence of a revolutionary movement, and revolutionary movements require the mobilization and political development of large numbers of people. We are not talking about displacing or replacing the individuals who presently control our society. We are not talking about merely changing the distributional principles within the old society. We are talking about changing the operational principles themselves. Doing so will require the participation and alignment of very large numbers of people who begin to see it in their best interests to work toward a transformed society.

A socialist society, involving the active participation of large numbers of people in democratic decision-making processes, involving the alteration of cultural and psychological forms, as well as economic and political forms, will be possible only as large numbers of people change themselves in the process of engaging in widespread involvement with social transformation. This kind of change is impossible unless it is achieved with broad participation. Evidence for this assertion comes from theory, from sheer logic, and from the comparative examples of other countries which have achieved socialism with and without massive cultural transformation in the process. The basis of revolutionary organization lies in the material organization of society. At the same time, the mediating factors are the psychology or consciousness of the people of the society, the organizational forms they create to accomplish political tasks, and the agendas they pursue on a day-to-day basis. It is at these levels that conscious efforts at revolutionary change proceed.

This means we are ultimately talking about the development of radical consciousness and organizational forms that may involve many millions of people. This task is possible. It has been done in other countries. We too can do it. To do so we will need to think now about preliminary forms of political engagement that spread radical political ideas and that involve increasing numbers of people in thinking about and forming a revolutionary movement. At present there are but a few with such ideas to do our work, as defined by our present situation. Our work is to increase involvement. It is the primary task.

We cannot now know the particular forms that revolutionary struggle will assume in more advanced stages. We can say that it will necessarily be broad-based and multifaceted. It will require the united action of a variety of political forces around common agendas. It may develop around several important issues, for example, a growing union movement which develops the will and capacity to disrupt the old system by withdrawing labor power, and reinvesting it under the auspices of worker-controlled governing councils. It may involve, for example, the combination of nonworkplace mass actions on ecology issues with the development of worker and community councils and with electoral politics. We cannot know, and we need not be frustrated by not knowing (except insofar as we might all wish that we lived in such a period and were part of that stage of history). In any case the requirements that any future developments place on us in the present period can be suggested and are the requirements which have been outlined.

civil liberties

We are working to develop a radical movement within the context of a society that gives at least verbal endorsement to people's civil liberties and to their individual rights. These endorsements emerged, in large measure, from capitalism's need to permit the freedom of action that would allow capitalists to make optimal choices for investing surplus and from the need to permit the freedom demanded of workers to move about in accordance with the requirements of production. Despite these dubious origins, many years of struggle on the part of progressive forces have contributed to the achievement of such civil liberties as we have, limited and flawed as they are. None the less to the extent that they are what they are claimed to be, they are a valuable part of our tradition. For moral and political reasons, they must be preserved and strengthened in the revolutionary process. It is not politically realistic to believe that large numbers of people will mobilize themselves for political action if their freedom to speak, to worship, and to form into groups according to cultural affinities will be diminished. Nor should they. By words and deeds, socialists must expose as a political maneuver the antirevolutionary tactic of forces of the status quo, the tactic of suggesting that the socialist alternative implies a loss of civil liberties.

violence

Finally we need to give attention to the issue of violence and, most particularly, to the question of violence and terrorism against people. Unfortunately establishment perspectives have dominated our thinking about the issues sufficiently that any efforts on the part of progressive forces to challenge the existing system run the risk of being identified as violent. In this discussion violence refers to the destruction of property or to the injury or death of people. Terrorism is violence conducted specifically for intimidating effects, and it occurs in the absence of mass support by progressive forces for such action.

The issue of violence is an issue that is most likely to work itself out in the process of revolutionary struggle so that the requirements for success, whatever they may be at a particular time, will be apparent to people at that time. At the present we deal with the question in a vacuum. Revolutionary people and organizations do not have the power to effect change through violence, particularly through violence against people. These are not politically feasible approaches for the most part. Further violence against people is not morally justifiable at this stage of struggle. To engage in violence is to take action hurtful to others when such action is not necessary to move forward in our efforts to liberate ourselves. At present violence is an effort to take a shortcut, but a misleading shortcut since it has conservatizing and counterrevolutionary effects in the present period.

There are at least two implicit assumptions contained in this introductory comment. First, violence against property and violence against people are quite different questions. If violence against property, for example, destruction of a nuclear power plant, could be useful as a strategy for educating and mobilizing, in a fashion consistent with the criteria for work in the present period, then it should be considered. However at this time it does not seem to be the case that large numbers of people could, for the most part, view destruction of property in a way which would contribute to radicalization and mobilization, and for that reason radicals ought to be skeptical about such an approach. In other situations the circumstances might be quite different, for example, in cases where draft board records were mutilated or destroyed during the Vietnam war and where public response was, in some measure, sympathetic.

Violence against people is a more complex question. It is, of course, one basis on which conservative forces stereotype and attempt to isolate radical people from dialogue with others. The characterization of radicals as "violent" needs to be understood as a conservative propaganda tool. It focuses on the isolated actions of a few persons, or on terrorism, a form of political activity which has not been advocated or practiced in this period except by a handful of isolated, nonsocialist radicals. And of course it overlooks the systematic, widespread, commonplace violence of the present order against all of us—a violence which takes its toll in impaired mental and physical health and shortened lives. It also overlooks the very important fact that the violence that has accompanied the effort to produce fundamental change in this country—and there has been a good deal—has been initiated, for the most part, by the establishment in the face of people's movements which could not be controlled and suppressed in other ways. The labor violence of the early 1900s and the 1930s, the violence against the Black Panther Party in the 1960s, Jackson State, the Kent State killings, the murder of the Attica prisoners, and the murder of American Indian Movement activists, illustrate this point.

It is important that we recognize that our information about the relationship of radical struggle to violence comes from media sources dominated by establishment interests. We are told that certain kinds of political activity resulted in violence. It is almost as though several dozen Black Panther Party members were guilty of violent activity by virtue of having been shot to death by various police departments. Most violence that has surrounded political struggle in this country has been initiated by forces of the status quo. Conservative propaganda has obscured and even inverted this reality in many people's understanding.

None the less there might, at some future time, come a period in which revolutionary violence against others would be possible, as a result of the strength and perspective of revolutionary forces. Such violence might be greeted sympathetically by large numbers of people, who would not thereby be alienated from revolutionary struggle.

At such a point, moral considerations will necessarily dictate that a revolutionary movement with a commitment to humanity not engage in violence against people when other viable alternatives are available. I believe that at the point at which such violence is possible, politically and in terms of the actual balance of force, conditions will have changed so that our present judgments and moral considerations will be outdated.[20] None the less since some people will need to consider this question now, I propose the following guideline. Violence against people is justified at the point at which there will be greater physical injury to revolutionary forces if violence is not employed. We are far from that point, if it ever comes. Our job now is to educate and organize, and violence is counterproductive to that end. Of course even as we begin this nonviolent task, violence is done against us. However we are not prepared to defend ourselves from this violence with violence. At such time as we are prepared to defend ourselves, we will have gathered sufficient strength that the entire balance of forces will have changed, and our understanding of the relationship of violence to the change process will likely be quite different. At that point if violence is necessary to protect against greater violence, I believe it will be justified. And I believe, to give this issue a great deal of energy now, other than to counter conservative propaganda, is to focus on a moral and strategic question with little bearing on the practicality of our immediate situation, to our own disservice. Focusing within the movement for radical change on the question of violence against people takes our attention away from the real questions facing us at this point. The question of destruction of property is another matter, to be dealt with now and later on strategic grounds and to be properly divorced, I believe, from the question of violence against people.[21]

[20]A useful discussion on this point is Saul Alinsky's "Of Ends and Means," in *Strategies of Community Organization*, 2nd ed., eds. Fred M. Cox and others (Itasca, Ill.: F. E. Peacock Publishers, Inc., 1974, pp. 198–206. Reprinted from Alinsky, *Rules for Radicals* (New York: Random House, Inc., 1971).

[21]Helpful discussions of this issue are found in Gowan and others, *Moving Toward a New Society*, see Chapter 12, "Why Not Armed Struggle?" pp. 236–51 and Michael P. Lerner, *The New Socialist Revolution* (New York: Dell Pub. Co., Inc., 1973), see Chapter 7, "Violence," pp. 268–283.

4

Social Welfare
in Capitalist Society

Introduction

Thus far I have discussed socialist analysis of capitalist society, and socialist perspectives on the nature and process of social change. At this point I address myself more specifically to those concerned with the contribution they can make to socialism from within the social service sector. The practice of socialists working within the social welfare sector will be more effective if it is based on a sound analysis of the relation of that sector to the institutions, values, and processes of capitalism.

What utility can such an analysis have for the development of radical practice, which is the concern motivating the writing of this book? Is it not sufficient that we can see around us, as social service workers, ongoing reminders of the limitations, inadequacies, and oftentimes brutality of the services in which we are employed? Sensitivity to the immediate realitites of our work situations is crucial. However such sensitivity is not a sufficient basis for developing strategy. If we fail to organize our observations about human services within a comprehensive framework, we face several possible dangers.

One danger, and a widely experienced pitfall for social service workers, is that we may become overwhelmed by the frustrations of social service work, subsequently immobilized, and in short order, "burned out." When we are faced with such a broad array of problems, each so intransigent, a private compromise with the status quo can easily seem the only solution for us.

A unifying analysis does not insure against frustration and burn out. It can be of some help, however, in suggesting the key organizing principles that highlight the common basis of the problems we face. We can understand the linkages between problems, and we can understand the underlying processes and institutions that will need to be altered if we are to effectuate solutions to the specific problems we meet in practice. We cannot approach our work as socialists, however, by neglecting discrete, manifest problems as they arise. Because our analysis has the potential for helping us to see more clearly the linkages between the visible manifestations of the problems and the less visible, but crucial, foundations of the problems, we will have a greater possibility of attacking the foundations of the problems through our work on their specific manifestations.

Another danger of relying on an ad hoc analysis is undertaking projects to achieve reforms that either have no potential for reform or that may achieve a limited reform in one area while simultaneously reinforcing an oppressive process or structure in another area. This is not to suggest that socialists automatically or necessarily quarrel with the struggle for reforms. Just the opposite is true since conditions are difficult, and even small improvements must be fought for and acknowledged when achieved. We cannot passively await the climactic revolutionary moment in which all problems will be solved. Such a strategy would be insensitive to people's pressing daily needs and would be an inadequate mechanism for mobilizing people.

On the other hand, liberal efforts to achieve reform in discrete areas have frequently proven unsuccessful. Despite the modesty of any particular effort, reformers quickly learn that inadequate and oppressive service arrangements are functional for the maintenance of other important social arrangements and institutions and so are most difficult to alter when approached in an isolated fashion. For example, years of effort have gone into the battle for more adequate benefits for public assistance recipients. While these efforts have resulted in some gains, most observers agree that welfare benefit levels are inadequate for maintaining a decent standard of living. Their inadequacy is a function of the fact that adequate welfare benefits would exceed take-home pay for a substantial sector of the labor force not employed at minimum or below minimum wage levels. Given reasonably adequate welfare benefit levels, it would be wise for the working poor to quit their low-paying jobs and receive welfare. Adequate welfare benefits, then, might have the effect of reducing work motivation, as conservatives argue. The example suggests that attention to welfare benefits without attention to the wages of the working class is a limited focus. However giving attention to the question of working-class wages raises very basic questions about capitalist principles of distribution. We are forced then to examine the linkages between welfare benefits and wages in capitalist society. A reformist position ignores these linkages and will be defeated by them in practice; a socialist position recognizes these linkages and connects them, in theory and as a basis for strategy.

Reformist efforts also operate to strengthen the status quo in ways that can be oppressive. For example, when caring social service workers fight for a larger share of money under Title XX of the Social Security Act for services to the aged, a worthy goal in itself, they may well deplete resources available to other populations, for example, the retarded or children in need of protective care. Because the total funds are fixed, successes on behalf of one group are played off against the needs of other groups. Similarly interest groups that are generated as a result of the effort to obtain more resources for the aged, the disabled, or youth compete against one another. Interest group competition, rather than united action, is the consequence.

While socialist analysis is no panacea, it does suggest some alternatives to social welfare reforms (which do not reform but which strengthen the status quo). It points to the commonality of issues. It suggests ways to join in a unified battle and ways to approach derivative problems at a more fundamental level. A socialist analysis potentially provides more than a pretty theoretical formulation divorced from practice. It can be theory with the power to help us reorganize our analysis and develop appropriate strategies.

The socialist analysis of the social welfare sector which I develop here rests on a larger analysis of the role of government, or the state, in a capitalist society. Social welfare activity is overwhelmingly public activity, at this point in our history. It possesses unique qualities which we can explore. Also it is part of the larger context of the public sector which we can subject to analysis. As we become clearer about the role of the state, the particulars of the welfare sector of the state become less confusing and less obscured by the rhetoric applied to that one sector. Therefore I will begin this analysis of the welfare sector by examining the Marxist view of the role of the state.

With an overall framework on the role of the state in hand, it is then possible to analyze the linkages between capitalist institutions and processes and the social welfare sector on several dimensions. In the conclusion of this chapter, I will examine the dialectical nature of these relationships. Dialectic analysis suggests that social welfare is not simply a "tool" of capitalist interests, manipulated by the corporate sector on its own behalf. It also represents the struggles of working people for a more humane society and so contains a potential for liberation as well as a capacity for repression. Both sides of this dialectic must be acknowledged. Clarity about the repressive aspects of social welfare helps us to organize our agendas for change. Clarity about the potential and the people-serving sides of social welfare helps us to recognize the possibility for mobilization.

The Role of the State

There are two major schools of thought about the role of the state in capitalist society. One school, representing the political perspective of conservatives and liberals, who basically accept and defend capitalism, argues that the state serves as a vehicle for mediating the conflicts between interest groups. From this perspective the state is seen as a neutral agent representing groups with competing claims on public resources.

Liberals who hold this position acknowledge that the rich and the corporate sector have greater influence on state policy decisions than do the poor and working people. While they believe in the essential neutrality of the state, they none the less criticize this lopsided influence. However, they see it as an "imbalance" which has distorted the proper, and potentially achievable, role of the state. Conservatives also argue that the state is a mechanism for adjusting competing claims in the society. To the extent that they complain of an imbalance, they protest that the state unduly hinders the free operation of the market and that it panders to some segments of the population through excessive welfare state measures.

Socialists argue, on the other hand, that the fundamental purpose of the state is to serve as a mechanism for the protection and preservation of the capitalist system of private ownership of the means of production. From this perspective the state serves the interests of the capitalist class. Of course the state, as well as every other institution in the society, is a locus of class struggle. The state, therefore, is not simply a captive of the capitalist class. Nevertheless the fundamental nature and purpose of the state is to serve capitalist needs.

I will not spend a great deal of time assessing the conservative/liberal perspective on this question. If I were to criticize this position fully, I would have to explore the following kinds of data and arguments.[1] First, I would have to look, as many have, at the individuals involved in government decision making, as elected officials and key appointees, and I would discover that the leading government figures are very much the same kind of people,

---

[1]A useful discussion is Paul M. Sweezy, "The Primary Function of the Capitalist State," in *The Theory of Capitalist Development* ed. Sweezy (New York: Monthly Review Press, 1942), reprinted in Richard C. Edwards, Michael Reich and Thomas E. Weisskopf, eds. *The Capitalist System* 2nd ed. (Englewood Cliffs, N.J.: Prentice-Hall, Inc., 1978), pp. 133–135. One of the classical Marxist analyses of the role of the state, much of which is devoted to a critique of non-Marxist perspectives, is Vladimir Lenin, *State and Revolution*, reprinted in *Essential Works of Marxism* (New York: Bantam, 1961), pp. 103–198.

and often are the same people, as those who are the major corporate leaders in the society.[2] This would provide some evidence that the points of view and the interests of the corporate sector are the points of view and interests represented by state activity.[3]

Second, I would have to examine the objective outcomes of state policies by challenging the oft-proclaimed ideology of state neutrality and scrutinizing the actual distribution of benefits of direct and indirect state programs and activities. This investigation would uncover the fact that the state, not only fails to equalize the distribution of resources in the society, but actually exacerbates the distributional and decision-making processes which lead to greater inequality in the society.[4] In sum a critical appraisal of the conservative and/or liberal hypothesis discloses the role of the state in preserving and strengthening the capitalist order, rather than in serving all interests dispassionately.

Among socialists there are several schools of thought about the specific ways in which the state serves the capitalist class.[5] These schools are not necessarily contradictory although they tend to stress different aspects of the role of the state. The recent work of James O'Conner has been very helpful in this respect.[6] While the theory he develops is multifaceted, one aspect is particularly useful as a framework for the analysis of the social welfare sector. O'Conner suggests that the state must attempt to solve two major problems in a capitalist society. It must serve two functions. These are *accumulation* and *legitimization*.[7]

---

[2]One of the best known of these is G. William Domhoff, *Who Rules America?* (Englewood Cliffs, N.J.: Prentice-Hall, Inc., 1967). Also key are G. William Domhoff, *The Higher Circles* (New York: Vintage Books, 1970) and Ralph Miliband, *The State in Capitalist Society* (New York: Basic Books, 1969).

[3]Some of the limitations of this line of reasoning, especially its empirical and atheoretical nature, are reviewed in David A. Gold, Clarence Y. H. Lo, and Erik Olin Wright, "Recent Developments in Marxist Theories of the Capitalist State," *Monthly Review*, 27(October, 1975), 29–43 (Part I) and 27(November, 1975), 36–51 (Part II).

[4]For example see James T. Bonnen, "The Effect of Taxes and Government Spending on Inequality," in *The Capitalist System*, eds. Edwards and others pp. 238–43 and Richard Edwards, "Who Fares Well in the Welfare State?" in *The Capitalist System*, eds. Edwards and others, pp. 244–51.

[5]A useful review of these lines of reasoning is Gold, Lo, and Wright, "Recent Developments in Marxist Theories of the Capitalist State."

[6]James O'Conner, *The Fiscal Crisis of the State* (New York: St. Martin's Press, 1973). A useful series of essays, many utilizing O'Conner's formulation, are contained in Leo Panitch, ed., *The Canadian State: Political Economy and Political Power* (Toronto: University of Toronto Press, 1977).

[7]O'Conner, *The Fiscal Crisis of the State*, p. 6.

Essentially accumulation refers to the efforts to "maintain and create the conditions in which profitable accumulation is possible."[8] The state assists capitalist enterprise in amassing the surplus necessary for additional growth and in finding ever extended avenues for the investment and eventual growth of that surplus, or profit.[9] The role of the state in these areas has expanded so considerably over the years, that state involvement in the direct and indirect workings of the economy is now essential to the ongoing functioning of the economy. The role of the state is multifaceted in serving the needs of corporations in these areas. One aspect of state activity is direct involvement in publicly funded production and service provisions, that is, direct state-provided opportunities for profitmaking. We will find a reflection of this role of the state when we explore the social welfare sector. A second aspect of this facet of the state's role is identified as *socializing costs of production*. It is more complex. Because this concept is quite useful in analyzing several major aspects of the role of social welfare, it is important that it be clear.

Any society, capitalist or socialist, with an economy based on increasingly sophisticated technology, requires the coordination and integration of more and more facets of the social order for the maintenance and expansion of productive capacity. Production eventually becomes sufficiently complex that it exceeds the organizing capacity of a single industrial enterprise acting alone and requires a coordinating and facilitating mechanism. Consider the growth of sophisticated production and its systemic requirements in the following examples.

In the 1700s a horse-drawn buggy manufacturer produced relatively simple vehicles. Working alone or with an apprentice, the buggy maker depended on easily and locally available wood, leather, and iron for raw materials. He sold the finished product in a local market to people who came into his shop or, more likely, who ordered buggies on an individual basis. Advertisements, transportation of raw goods, transportation of the finished product, the development of a disciplined and appropriately trained labor force, and what would now be called research and development, were all extremely rudimentary by twentieth-century standards. The buggy maker could and did function relatively autonomously. The requirements of production were few and easily met.

Contrast this scenario with its twentieth-century counterpart. While all modern production is not as complex as that involving automobiles, au-

---

[8]Ibid.

[9]The second of these issues is the concern of an excellent analysis of the dilemmas of monopoly capitalism and the role of the state in relation to monopoly capitalism. See Paul A. Baran and Paul M. Sweezy, *Monopoly Capital* (New York: Monthly Review Press, 1966).

tomobile production is so complicated that a broad spectrum of the social order and many facets of domestic and international society become involved in the process, directly or indirectly. The raw materials required for the modern automobile are drawn from around the globe. To help assure access to these raw materials and to maintain and expand domestic industrial capacity, the United States government has developed a particular pattern of international relations, tariffs, world trade bodies, and military activities. The labor force that manufactures automobiles, researches new technological and stylistic possibilities, and markets the finished product is varied and complex. In some cases it is highly skilled technically; in other cases it is not highly skilled but is highly socialized to encourage acceptance of difficult work conditions. Government facilitates the task of appropriately training and socializing this labor force. Modern production depends on a high probability of sales for a given quantity of the finished product, and markets must be assured before the product is manufactured to avoid economy-wide disruptions. As a consequence consumers must be well prepared, psychologically and financially, to buy a new car periodically. In short the successful manufacture and distribution of automobiles is a process that reaches out into international relations, educational processes, the psychological attitudes of consumers, as well as into transportation, basic research, and labor relations.

Clearly no single enterprise could manage to manipulate all of these societal variables for the sake of a smooth production-sales process. Nor could it afford the large investments in education, roads, and armies that are required. The state comes into play to meet these complex requirements. The state can organize the society-wide requirements of production through its capacity to tax, conscript, build, and regulate. This is what is meant by the concept "socializing the costs of production." Certain costs of production, for example those associated with transporting products on public highways, are made into social costs. They are met, wholly or partially, by public dollars, that is, by our tax dollars. This is a process that operates, in different forms, in both capitalist and socialist societies.

The contradictory aspect of this process as it occurs in capitalist societies arises from the fact that while many of the costs of production are borne by government, which actually means by the tax dollars of the people of the society, the profits are not socialized. They remain in private hands and are reassigned by capitalists.[10] Capitalists withdraw some of the surplus that is generated from production for their own personal use. Most of it is reinvested according to the primary criterion by which surplus is invested in capitalist society—namely, its ability to generate additional surplus for its owners. Through taxation, all of us help to generate surplus since we finance

---

[10]A useful discussion of this dynamic is found in Rick Deaton, "The Fiscal Crisis of the State," *Our Generation*, 8 (October, 1972), 11-51.

governmental mechanisms that support production. However just a few people dispose of the surplus, and they do so without considering the benefits of reinvestment for the majority.

The second overall function of the state suggested by O'Conner is legitimization. Legitimization involves the process of justifying the existing social order, obscuring the class divisions in the society, and helping to control social disorder as it arises. The social welfare sector represents one facet of state activity in the process of legitimization. It makes a contribution to capitalism's requirements for internal social tranquility in ways that will be explored.

On the one hand, the state assists the process of capitalist expansion by providing opportunities for direct profit making and by socializing costs of production. On the other hand, it obfuscates its own role and the nature of capitalism itself by controlling and managing the unrest that emerges in the society. Now our task is to explore the utility of this analysis of the state to clarify the role of the social welfare sector, in which we have the greatest interest.

Socializing Costs of Production: The Social Welfare Sector

At various times during the process of developing an increasingly sophisticated industrial capacity, the corporate sector realized the necessity of extending state activity into the social welfare arena in order to meet the newly emerging needs of the industrial sector. Although this process occurred over a long period of time, the takeoff point in the United States was the New Deal period.[11] Social welfare activity, which takes place almost completely within the public sector, represented a further extension of the already expanded role of the state in helping to socialize costs of production. In the case of social welfare, the costs of production did not involve creating access to raw materials or building roads to facilitate distribution of goods. Rather these costs were and still are related to (1) directly preparing and maintaining the labor force; (2) subsidizing low and/or irregular wages; and (3) stimulating consumer purchasing power by an influx of cash benefits during periods of high unemployment and/or recession.

preparing and maintaining the labor force

Several important areas of social welfare can be analyzed in terms of their role in helping to prepare workers for labor force participation or in maintaining workers in a sufficiently healthy condition to work or to return to work if they become disabled. Key among these is education. Social policy

---

[11]A useful discussion is Robert Heilbronner, "Phase II of the Capitalist ystem," *New York Times Magazine* (November 28, 1971), pp. 30, 76–90.

analysts do not generally consider education a social welfare measure in the United States although it is included in several official indices of annual social welfare expenditures. It does serve as a useful illustration of social welfare functions.[12] To analyze the ways in which education serves the requirements of production, it is not necessary to deny or negate the beneficial, people-serving component of public education. We must make a rounded assessment, however, of the multiple functions served by any given measure, and we must judge the extent to which it serves various interests.

Education is related to the requirements of production through its heavy emphasis on technical training, especially for those students tracked into the blue collar and service sectors of the work force, and through its socialization techniques that make students adopt conforming modes of behavior.[13] Public education does help some students to develop a broader world view and an ability to analyze social reality. At the same time, it attempts to diffuse critical thought, to promulgate conservative attitudes, and to encourage acceptance of in-school tracking that prefigures postschool class differentials. In these ways its primary emphasis is on creating attitudes and skills consistent with the requirements of a stratified labor force.

Health and mental health services, as well as various rehabilitation services, can be understood in the same light. For most such services the standard of "successful" treatment is the ability of a worker to return to regular employment. If the patient is female, a viable and "healthy" alternative may be to return to homemaking and mothering.

Each of these cases illustrates the first way in which social welfare programs socialize a cost of production. These social welfare measures help to maintain a domestic labor force that requires training and upkeep to function effectively. The emerging programs do help to educate and rehabilitate. However the standard by which education and rehabilitation are judged successful tends to be the extent to which they facilitate employability. Government programs in these areas serve activity in the private sector, at public expense.

subsidy of low wages

The second way in which social welfare programs help to socialize costs of production is by subsidizing wages which are too low to allow a minimally self-sufficient standard of living or by subsidizing work which is seasonal or in

---

[12]A readily available quantitative measure of educational expenditure levels and other social welfare expenditures is the annual summary of social welfare expenditures and trends over time in such expenditures published in the *Social Security Bulletin*, usually in the January issue.

[13]A useful compilation of essays on this issue is found in *Schooling in Corporate Society: The Political Economy of Education in America and the Alternatives Before Us*, ed. Martin Carney (New York: D. McKay Company, 1972).

other ways episodic. Unemployment Insurance, Social Security benefits, public welfare, and day care are among the programs which belong in this category.

The extent to which we invest in day care, for example, is closely related to the extent to which women are required in the labor force.[14] Because of the low wages women receive for their work and because primary child care responsibility falls ọn their shoulders, women often cannot afford to work unless they are supported in that effort by publicly funded child care. When women's labor is not required in the labor market, the importance of women as full-time mothers and homemakers is stressed. When women's labor force participation is necessary, for example, during wartime, the value of day care socialization experience for children is emphasized. The ideology surrounding optimal child care arrangements varies widely and is significantly influenced by labor market requirements. In the same way the availability of public monies for day care increases or decreases as a function of labor market needs.

This framework is similarly instructive in examining the role of welfare. Contrary to popular stereotypes, welfare recipients are active participants in the labor force since they tend to work before, during, and after their involvement with public welfare.[15] However they frequently work at seasonal labor, performing migrant agricultural work, low paid jobs with frequent layoffs, such as nonunionized piecework in the garment industry, or tenuous service work, as domestics.[16] Each of these jobs produces some goods or

---

[14]Katherine Ellis and Rosalind Petchesky, "The Politics of Day Care," *Social Policy*, 3 (November-December, 1972-January-February, 1973 combined issue), pp. 14-22; and Alicia Frohmann, "Day Care and the Regulation of Women's Workforce Participation." *Catalyst: A Socialist Journal of the Social Services* 2(1978), 5-17.

[15]See Martin Rein, "Barriers to the Employment of the Disadvantaged," in *Social Policy*, ed. Rein (New York: Random House, 1970), pp. 374-414; and Mildred Rein and Barbara Wishman, "Patterns of Work and Welfare in AFDC," *Welfare in Review*, 9 (November-December, 1971), 7-12. These observations are also supported by the growing documentation of the fact that those in the United States who fall under the so-called poverty line are not permanently in this status. Both individuals and families become "poor" and "not poor" in repeated cycles, some of which is attributable to their variable labor market experience. One such study, conducted by James N. Morgan and associates of the University of Michigan was reported in "Poverty Is Found Less Persistent But Wider Spread Than Thought," *New York Times* July 7, 1977), p. 1.

[16]A useful analysis of the relationship of this superexploited strata of the labor force to welfare roles and to the unemployed has been made by the National Labor Federation, an organization devoted to organizing this population. Their paper, "Sociology and the Unrecognized Worker," is available from the National Labor Federation, 200 West 20th Street, New York, New York 10011, mimeographed, n.d. While this analysis is helpful, readers should be aware that the overall politics of the National Labor Frederation are viewed with considerable suspicion by some segments of the left. A critical discussion of the National Labor Federation is found in Harvey Kahn, "NCLC/U.S. Labor Party: Political Chamelion to Right Wing Spy," *The Public Eye*, 1 (Fall, 1977), 5-37. This journal is published by the Repression Information Project and is available from them at P.O. Box 3278, Washington, D.C. 20010.

services which segments of the society want or need. However these are also jobs for which the economy is reluctant to pay a living wage. Welfare benefits permit some workers to take the jobs, even though they are paid a wage which cannot sustain a decent standard of living. Welfare benefits, paid through public taxation, subsidize low wages in selected areas of the labor market and help to socialize the costs of production. The United States, with its enormous wealth, its enormous rates of profit in the private sector, and its enormous Gross National Product, does not pay large numbers of its workers enough to allow them to live a decent life. Welfare programs by no means fully compensate for this. However they do make the difference between starvation and low levels of maintenance for many people. All of us subsidize a cost of production—paying a living wage to workers—through the taxes we pay. While some of those tax dollars benefit welfare recipients, to a larger extent they benefit the corporate interests which thereby maintain an exploitative relationship with workers.

stimulating purchasing power

Finally welfare programs help to socialize costs of production by helping to maintain a cash flow in the economy during periods of high unemployment and/or recession. This factor was one of the prime motivations for the introduction of many welfare measures, including the first major public employment programs and the retirement benefits of the Social Security Act during the New Deal period. It was clear to government planners and economists during the Depression that government expenditure, rather than budget reduction, was required to stimulate the economy. The programs that emerged then are the basis of much of the current social welfare structure. They continue to be rationalized by arguments that they operate as a counter-cyclical influence, by pumping money into the economy at times when people are unemployed and underemployed. Social welfare measures have become part of the larger strategy of attempting to control the more gross manifestations of periodic depressions and recessions.

Social Control

the safety valve function

It is possible to identify a number of ways in which social welfare programs serve to maintain the existing social order as mechanisms of social control. The first of these derives from the observation that the major spurts in social welfare programming in the United States have occurred during significant periods of social unrest, namely, the Progressive Era (roughly 1900 to 1920), the New Deal period (approximately 1933 to 1940), and during the 1960s. Each of these periods was characterized by an upsurge of vocal and visible resistance to the particular economic and social conditions of those times. In each period corporate and government planners concluded that social welfare reform could be used to respond to some of the demands for improved living conditions while they continued to preserve and even strengthen capitalism. Social welfare measures have developed in reaction to popular unrest and pressure and have provided some minimum, yet important, benefits for selected populations. However the forces for change have not been sufficiently strong and sustained during these periods to achieve the structural changes required to meet demands fully.

One of the most thorough studies of the safety valve function of social welfare, elaborated for the case of public welfare, is *Regulating the Poor* by Frances Fox Piven and Richard Cloward.[17] Their argument is that public welfare rolls expand and contract in relation to the extent of social unrest in the society. This process is in turn related to the degree of unemployment and to market requirements for additional labor. When there is more unemployment and consequently more social unrest, relief rolls expand, and eligibility standards are relaxed. As the need for labor increases, recipients are pushed off the welfare rolls back into the work force. Relief serves, in this way, as a safety valve for some of the pressures that periodically build up in a society that is unable to assure full employment at a living wage for significant numbers of its citizens.

Similarly the spurt of social programming in the early 1960s, notably the War on Poverty, the Great Society programs, and the creation of mental health centers, is partly attributable to the social change efforts of the civil rights movement, the New Left, and the black liberation movement. Once again social welfare provided a safe and relatively inexpensive response to people's movements that had potentially profound implications for social change.

While the costs of social welfare measures are decried in some circles, in reality social welfare does not comprise an overwhelmingly large proportion of government expenditure or of the GNP, particularly if we remove that part of social welfare expenditure financed by the special Social Security tax. In the absence of this large program, government social welfare expenditures for health, education, and welfare, constituted 35.2 percent of all government expenditures in 1975. This is a fairly modest increase from the 30.8 percent that such expenditures represented as a percentage of all gov-

---

[17]Frances Fox Piven and Richard A. Cloward, *Regulating the Poor* (New York: Vintage Books, 1971).

ernment expenditures in 1950.[18] Recognizing that social welfare strengthens, rather than weakens, capitalism, an expansion of social welfare programming as a response to mass unrest seems a small price to pay. In fact it has been a small price to pay.

electoral politics

Social welfare as a mechanism of social control has also been used to tie various interest groups more firmly into the web of conventional electoral politics. As Piven has suggested, the Great Society programs, many of which were targeted at urban minority populations, can be partially understood as a mechanism to secure the wavering loyalty of those populations to the Democratic Party.[19] Nixon's political strategy, designed to develop southern electoral strength, led him in part to endorse a revised income, maintenance program, the Family Assistance Plan, which would have provided disproportionately large benefits to the southern states and minimal benefits to the northern states. This use of social welfare is not surprising. It is simply another way in which the particular political party in power rewards segments of the electorate loyal to it through the selective dispersal of government largess.

divisiveness

A related mechanism is the way in which social welfare programs divide individuals and groups of people from one another, for example, through the principle of individual entitlement to benefits. The common

---

[18]These figures are derived from Alfred M. Skolnick and Sophie R. Dales, "Social Welfare Expenditures, 1950-75," *Social Security Bulletin,* 39 (January, 1976), Table 5, p. 13. It was important for political elites to argue, during and immediately after the period of the Vietnam war, with its attendant economic dislocations, that these dislocations were not attributable to military expenditures, since military expenditures had actually decreased as a percentage of all government expenditures and represented, at some point in the late 1960s, less than half of all government expenditures. This calculation relies on manipulations of the data in the Unified Budget. If Social Security benefits are included in the total package of health, education, and welfare expenditures, then social welfare expenditures can be shown to represent 58.4 percent of all government expenditures for the year 1975. This reduces the proportion of all government spending represented by military expenditures. If Social Security is removed from these calculations, military expenditures climb significantly as a percentage of all government expenditures.

[19]Frances Fox Piven, "The Urban Crisis: Who Got What, and Why," in *1984 Revisited,* ed. Robert Paul Wolff (New York: Knopf, 1973), pp. 165-201. See also Richard A. Cloward and Frances Fox Piven, "The Urban Crisis and the Consolidation of National Power," "Urban Riots, Violence and Social Change," *Proceedings of the Academy of Political Science,* 29 (July, 1968), 160-168 and Frances Fox Piven, "The Great Society as Political Strategy," *Columbia Forum,* 1970 (Summer), pp. 17-22.

bond of being similarly dependent on one or another government subsidy is thereby obscured. In the most oppressed communities, it is not uncommon for neighbors to report each other to welfare authorities for activities which might affect eligibility, for example, receiving gifts from a man, in the case of Aid to Families of Dependent Children (AFDC) mothers.

A more widespread source of divisiveness derives from the fact that social welfare funds are often distributed on the basis of competition among elegible groups for limited pools of social welfare dollars. In the absence of objective mechanisms for setting priorities, the planning processes for distributing resources established a set of rules which encourage interest group competition. Money goes to those groups best able to compete in the political arena. Various groups of low-income people, as well as the professionals and interest groups which identify with their service demands, compete and have competed over limited funds in the War on Poverty, Model Cities, and more recently, Title XX programs. While the policy makers may not have intended to exacerbate these divisions, in effect they have managed to promote competition and hostility between groups that have more to gain from unified action than from competition.

legitimizing exclusion from the labor force

Social welfare programs maintain social control and social stability through their role in isolating and minimally maintaining people labelled as "useless" in the society. Typically usefulness is defined by an individual's employability and desirability in the labor market. If the United States had a full employment economy, we could creatively employ many persons now identified as developmentally disabled who are isolated in institutions or other nonproductive niches. We do not seem to need the productive efforts of all citizens; in fact we face the opposite problem of legitimizing the exclusion of large numbers of people from the labor market. The United States has a large population which has been diagnosed and defined as "surplus," which is not now productive, and which might become disruptive, either through its own actions or in concert with others sympathetic to its plight if some charity mechanisms did not exist. These mechanisms are not very satisfactory for the people involved. However they create an impression of caring. The same argument about social welfare as a mechanism for the disposal of useless persons can be made for addicts, the aged, physically disabled persons, and others.

maintaining an image of concern

Social welfare measures create the impression that government is concerned about the well-being of the people of this country. Since there is so much available evidence that other government programs and policies primarily benefit corporate interests, it is important that government preserve its image as the disinterested servant of all groups in society. The relationship between social welfare and the needs and interests of the corporate sector can be readily explicated. However this relationship is not widely understood. In fact many people view social welfare measures as contrary to the logic and requirements of capitalism. Social welfare is politically confusing. This confusion helps to maintain the status quo since social welfare measures can be and are touted as one indication of government's benign concern for all. To the extent that government is viewed as committed to the quality of life for all citizens, its true role is obscured, and the need for a fundamental challenge to the state is deflected into reformist directions.

day-to-day control

In some cases social welfare measures exercise direct, day-to-day control over people's lives. In some programs, for example, those directed toward juvenile and adult offenders, the control function is explicit.[20] In other programs it is less explicit, though no less controlling, for example, in public welfare where a wide variety of rules and regulations govern the work habits, sexual behavior, purchasing patterns, and family relationships of welfare recipients. In still other cases social control mechanisms are integrated into the regulations governing eligibility for benefits. For example, strikers are often denied welfare benefits; welfare mothers are granted lower benefits for their fourth child than they received for their third child; and the unemployed are required to maintain weekly contact with unemployment insurance offices to receive benefits, even in areas of massive unemployment. Every social welfare program has explicit or implicit standards of behavior as a condition of its receipt. On inspection the standards of behavior reinforce system-conserving, that is conservative, patterns of activity on the part of recipients, and so help solidify the institutions and values of the status quo.

individual socialization

Another dimension of the control function is the effort at individual socialization that occurs in specific programs. In many programs, for example, an explicit or implicit measure of success is that men go to work on a regular basis. The standard for women is more complex since success may

---

[20]The case for the juvenile justice system has been well made by Alexander Liazos in "Class Oppression: The Functions of Juvenile Justice," *Insurgent Sociologist*, 1 (Fall, 1974), 2–24. The model developed in that analysis offers a useful set of analytic categories for exploring the control functions of other social welfare measures.

mean a return to work or it may mean a return to "appropriate" domesticity, a form of unpaid labor. If publicly funded mental health centers were to take seriously the mission of helping people to become mentally healthy, they might well encourage a revolutionary spirit among service users. After all a healthy response to a distorted social order is to struggle to change that order. Clearly this is not the way in which mental health centers view their mission. They are much more concerned with helping so-called disruptive youth to return to school, alcoholic workers to control their drinking sufficiently to permit steady work patterns, or depressed mothers to resume full-time housemaking and parenting more willingly. The values inherent in these services on which the outcome of a service is assessed, are values deeply ingrained in the capitalist understanding of the successful individual and the good life.[21]

stigma

Finally it is important to recognize the control functions of social welfare in relation to persons who are not recipients of social welfare benefits but whose situation is such that they might at some future time require such services. Receiving many social welfare services is a stigmatizing process, not because of some stigma inevitably arising from receiving services, but because of oppressive policies making social welfare programs unattractive and even degrading. As a result people tend to view turning to public welfare programs as a last resort. In this way the inadequacy and demeaning nature of the social welfare system discourage people from using it. It pressures people who are presently working to keep working, even when they perform dangerous and distasteful work at low pay.

Direct Profit

Historically social welfare has not been a sector where corporate interests have developed extensive opportunities for the direct investment of surplus and for subsequent profit making. The linkage between public social services and the corporate sector has been less direct. However in the 1940s, with the advent of a national public housing program, escalating in the 1960s with the introduction of more extensive publicly funded health programs, particularly Medicare and Medicaid, and in the 1970s with the expansion in a number of directions of purchasing service provisions, the private sector is

---

[21]A useful discussion of this dynamic for the case of child care institutions is David Gil's "Institutions for Children," in Gil, *The Challenge of Social Equality* (Cambridge, Mass. Schenkman, 1976), pp. 79–103.

coming to play an increasingly significant role in the provision of public social services. Apart from these developments, the private sector has had a modest history of independent service provision in areas that overlap with or are identical to service areas also encompassed by government programs, for example, education, day care, and nursing homes. Health care, of course, has been an exception in that it has long been an area of significant profit making for private interests. However, these arrangements are of less concern for this analysis than are those in which government assumes primary financial responsibility for service provision and arranges for provision of service through commercial, entrepreneurial interests.

It is useful to examine the relationship between the social welfare sector and the private sector as the private sector becomes more directly involved in public programs. In programs like Medicare and Medicaid, the role of government is primarily to finance services. The services are provided by corporate or private interests. For example, it is only partially accurate to identify public housing as public housing. To the limited extent that public housing exists, it is better described as publicly financed housing built by and enriching private developers. Whatever the benefits of public housing to its tenants—and there are benefits—there are extremely lucrative returns to the builders of public housing who are guaranteed generous profits on their sometimes surprisingly small investments.[22] Similarly Medicare and Medicaid, for the most part, have been limited to serving as mechanisms for public financing of privately provided medical care, hospital care, and drugs. The well-documented outcome has been enormous benefits for the health industry, significant tax increases for the general public, and marginal health care gains for the intended consumers.[23]

Increasingly the public sector is relying on the private sector for a broader range of service provision.[24] In part this is grounded in the general

---

[22]A still useful discussion that highlights this pattern for the period when a more significant initiative was made in housing is Charles Abrams; *The City Is The Frontier* (New York: Harper and Row, 1965).

[23]For example, in one Cook County, Illinois study, 100 of 1700 doctors were listed as available to Medicaid patients. They earned an average of $21,000 each in one year from this program. Similarly, in 1970 it was estimated that 10,000 U.S. doctors received an average of $25,000 in Medicare and Medicaid payments. These studies are reviewed in Thomas Walz and Gary Askerooth, *The Upside Down Welfare State* (Minneapolis: Elwood Printing, Commissioned by Advocate Services Inc., Minneapolis, 1973), p. 35. A useful analysis of the health establishment is Barbara and John Ehrenreich's *The American Health Empire: Power, Profits and Politics* (New York: Vintage Books, 1971).

[24]The growing involvement of corporate interests, for the case of day care, is reviewed in *Corporations and Child Care: Profit Making Day Care, Workplace Day Care, and a Look at the Alternatives*, Cookie Arvin, Georgia Sassen and the Corporations and Child Care Research Project, a Publication of Women's Research Action Project, Box 119, Porter Square Station,

reform does not threaten, but actually can serve, corporate interests. Social welfare programming has subsequently come to be seen as a relatively harmless "lesser evil," benign in comparison with the more fundamental, anticapitalist agendas that are often implicit in powerful social movements. The dynamic unfolds as follows: protest activity and political organization develop periodically, partially as a response to the difficulty of economic and social life under capitalism; protest gives rise to demands for social change; government and corporate planners, thus far successfully, respond to and channel this protest into system-maintaining avenues. One of these avenues has been social welfare programming. However even as demands are coopted, the resulting programs generally contain some element of the initial demands that were raised.

Social welfare, then, can be seen as the outcome of class conflict, although the outcome has clearly favored the corporate class. It is, in effect, a temporary compromise that is reached between conservative and progressive forces. It represents both the struggle of progressive forces for a more decent world and the continuing ability of conservative forces to channel and contain progressive forces within the logic of capitalism. It is this interaction of forces with basically opposing interests that helps to explain the conflicting tendencies within social selfare. On the one hand, it is undeniable that some people would be worse off without the social welfare programs of which they are beneficiaries. (At the same time, some people would be better off without welfare programs in their lives.) Social welfare programs are of some immediate utility to people, and social welfare workers who believe that they are useful to the people they serve are not "dupes" or willing "agents of capitalism." On the other hand, social welfare programs are inadequate and often repressive and misdirected. Further they help to support and strengthen the very social order that creates the misery with which they deal. This is the way in which social welfare programs are contradictory.

In considering the class interests served by welfare legislation, we should recognize that the alignment of social welfare in service of capitalist interests is not total. Because the rationality and foresight of capitalist planners is limited, because much of social welfare is an ad hoc response to particular circumstances, because social welfare measures partially reflect the political power of the working class, and because the capitalist response to working class needs and political demands is imperfect, the struggle continues. If, in fact, capitalist planners were as rational and farsighted as we sometimes hypothesize, we would not be able to explain the emergence of significant political turmoil in the social welfare arena. Despite the best efforts of the planners, and they are sometimes quite strenuous efforts, these programs do not maintain social stability for long periods of time. In fact by the very mechanisms through which they attempt to assure stability, they simultaneously lay the groundwork for new political initiatives. For example, a public welfare program, designed to quiet labor unrest, gives rise to a newly created political group with a stake in collective action and political struggle.

Summary

I have reviewed the ways in which social welfare is integrated into the overall logic of capitalist society by utilizing three analytic categories; socializing costs of production, maintaining social control, and offering opportunities for direct investment and profit making by the private sector. I have also stressed, however, that these forms of integration describe only the "response" side of the play of conflicting class interests. It is also necessary to be aware that the initiation of change has tended to come from the working class and from progressive political leadership. Welfare state programs are not simply a device for cooptation and repression. They also provide needed assistance to people, as we would expect them to do, since one branch of their lineage is the political demands of working people in this country.

An awareness of the dialectical nature of social welfare is of more than theoretical interest. It provides one basis on which we can assess the past successes and failures of efforts toward progressive change. We can avoid repeating earlier mistakes if we examine the cooptation and repression that social welfare represents. We can avoid a sense of impotence if we examine the efforts which brought about even modest reforms.

The repressive aspects of social welfare serve, in part, to mobilize people to struggle against their oppression. The progressive aspects hold out promises, as yet unfulfilled, and visions of a better world. Both aspects of this reality, the frustration and the hope, must be accounted for in our efforts to organize. To deny the repressive aspects of social welfare is to succumb to liberal naiveté. To deny the progressive aspects is to overlook the history and successes of our own political efforts and to ignore the real dependence of many people on social welfare as an important element in their struggle to survive. Also we would run the risk of failing to develop allies for collective political effort. By exploring both the failure and the promise of social welfare, we can paint a more complete picture of the potential for change, the junctures at which people can be mobilized, and the issues that can be exploited. This is the subject matter to which the following chapter is addressed.

5

Linkages Between the Social Service Sector and Socialist Transformation

Assessing the Political Context

locating social service workers politically

The actual and potential political power of social service workers is unlike that of truck drivers, coal miners, or steelworkers. When coal miners strike, the country experiences profound dislocation and even crisis in short order. If coal miners were to develop sophisticated radical consciousness and begin to form workers' councils with the avowed aim of collectively managing the coal mining industry and taking control of the surplus generated by that industry, the shock waves would be felt around the country. On the other hand, when social service workers strike, relatively little pressure is generated. In fact, periodic strikes of social service workers and other public employees tend to ease the financial burdens of the state and result in savings for public institutions.

An assessment of the potential contribution of social service workers to revolutionary struggle based solely on their short-run ability to disrupt essential system-maintaining processes would lead to the conclusion that the concept of radical social work, or its potential contribution to revolutionary transformation from within the social service sector, is unrealistic. However the process of broad scale social transformation is multifaceted. Many forces contribute to the preparatory phase of revolution and to the revolutionary phase itself. Some of the contributions are direct, and some are indirect. As I will suggest in this chapter, the contributions that can be made by the public sector in general, and the social service sector in particular, are potentially as significant as are the contributions that can be made by other sectors. In the future other sectors of the working class may play a more important role in advancing revolutionary ideas and movements. At such a time, the relative role of the social service sector may be reduced although revolutionary activity in any sector of the population is never insignificant in making some contribution to the larger processes that are occurring.

At this point such discussion must be speculative. What we can do now is examine the current political situation and assess on that basis the contributions that can be made from within the social service sector. To do so it will be helpful to identify the distinguishing characteristics of the political landscape that have particular relevance to the formulation of strategy for radical social work.

the level of revolutionary development

From a socialist perspective the distinguishing characteristic of the current political environment is the absence of significant revolutionary movement in the United States. Few people explicitly and openly identify themselves as socialists. Only a few avowedly socialist organizations are viable, and they are not well known. Furthermore they are relatively isolated from nonradical mass organizations, for example, from trade unions and liberal reform groups, and they tend to war among themselves as vigorously as they war with the capitalist system.[1] The majority of people in the society do not have the background and experience to allow them to discuss the nature of capitalism and socialism objectively and critically. Many people espouse an uncritical and unexamined commitment to "the free enterprise system" and to the "American Way." These realities must be acknowledged. We need not and must not confuse our desire to foster a revolutionary momentum with a falsely optimistic assessment of the present condition of radical political development. The United States is not in a revolutionary period, and no one can predict confidently when such a period will emerge.

---

[1]There are many reasons why the existing leftist groups wage political struggle against one another. The future of that struggle is by no means clear. That the struggle has been destructive for the development of a more powerful left in the United States is conceded by many on the left. The kinds of political disagreements and perspectives that inform this infighting can be reviewed in *2,3 Many Parties of a New Type?*, the Proletarian Unity League (New York: United Labor Press, 1977). Also see Jim O'Brien, "American Leninism in the 1970s," *Radical America*, 12 (November, 1977-February, 1978), 27–63.

However we would assess the current political situation incompletely, and therefore inaccurately, if we did not attend to other features of the political landscape. Central among these is the fact that the capitalist system is working less and less well for more and more people. Since the mid-to late 1960s, the destructive nature of capitalism has become intuitively more obvious to many more people. Various indicators of well-being suggest that people find it increasingly difficult to live their lives with dignity and pleasure. It is significant that this is also true in the economic arena where capitalism has traditionally been best able to compensate for its social irrationality. U.S. capitalism has not been able to provide a rising standard of living for increasing numbers of people, as in the past, and these people are finding that they actually have less and less real purchasing power at their disposal.[2]

The manifestations of capitalism's growing irrationality are varied. Some are obvious. The cost of essential goods and services, such as medical care and housing, is rising rapidly. Other forms of the breakdown are somewhat more subtle and less obvious to everyone. For example, industrial injuries, always quite high in the United States, continue to be a tremendously important factor in the lives of many workers.[3] In any case the point here is not to reemphasize the destructiveness of capitalism, but to indicate that more and more people are recognizing that the capitalist system is not working very well for them in important areas of their lives.

This does not mean that most people are prepared to make an explicitly radical analysis of their situations. They are not. Many people will acknowledge that some or many of the major institutions of the society do not seem to be working on their behalf, especially if their assessment of these institutions is solicited in ways that do not trigger off programmed anticommunist and "proAmerican" responses. For example, if people are asked if they believe that most politicians look out for the interests of the average citizen, many will say that they do not think so. On the other hand, if people are asked if they think that government is an instrument of the ruling class, they

---

[2]For example, in 1972–73, spendable weekly earnings for workers in the non-agricultural sector of the economy (excluding public employees) were 1.1 percent lower than they were in 1967, once the effect of inflation was taken into account. In 1973–74 they were 4.9 percent lower than in 1967, and in 1974–75 they were 0.4 percent lower than in 1967. In other words, the average person is not "getting ahead." The source of these data is *Pocket Data Book, U.S.A., 1976* (Washington, D.C.: U.S. Government Printing Office, 1977), Table 209, p. 165. A useful discussion of these dynamics is *Why Do We Spend so Much?* 3rd ed. Popular Economics Press, Box 221, Somerville, Massachusetts 02143, 1977.

[3]The magnitude of this problem is revealed by these data. Each year, approximately 14,000 people are killed in on-the-job accidents, and more than two million people are injured. While fatalities from job-related illnesses are difficult to assess, reasonable estimates place the figure at about 200,000 additional fatalities a year. Les Boden and David Wegman, "Increasing OSHA's Clout: Sixty Million New Inspectors," *Working Papers for a New Society*, 6 (May/June, 1978), 43.

will respond with the stereotyped responses to leftist thought that their political socialization has induced. When people speak on the basis of their own direct experience, they are often radical. When they respond to abstract conceptualizations, they tend to be more conservative.

The destructiveness of the society and the radicalism which that destructiveness encourages are important aspects of the political scene. They suggest, among other things, that radicals need not concern themselves with "making things worse" in order to stimulate revolutionary sentiment. Conditions are bad enough, and they continue to deteriorate on their own. Rather one of the important tasks facing radicals is to help people understand that our previous interpretations of the nature of our dilemmas and our past solutions to these problems no longer serve us well. The interpretations do not explain our situation. Conventional solutions, based as they are on these interpretations, do not succeed.

We must also reckon with the fact that many people experience a profound sense of cynicism, helplessness, and frustration when they address themselves to political questions. They are unable to analyze situations clearly or to conceptualize alternatives to conventional politics and conventional outcomes. We must facilitate people's efforts to find ways, even if they are preliminary to full scale revolutionary commitments, to express themselves politically. This is necessary so that people can gain experience with the process of political engagement, so that they can enjoy some success in influencing social conditions. At present, even nonradical progressive organizations have some contribution to make to the larger process of radicalization since they encourage collective work and political involvement. Through collectivity they help people with a lack of knowledge about how to organize for social change and with defeatist psychological predispositions to overcome their limitations so that they can engage more fully in radical work.

Another facet of the current political situation is the continuing hold that the existing political parties have on the loyalties of many people. This accounts for absence of a united revolutionary political party or organization to which people can turn for leadership. Of course the level of voter registration in elections is low, which may reflect people's sense that such participation does not matter much as a means of influencing major policies in the society. None the less most people do not seem ready to think in terms of an alternative party, especially one which would clearly be radical in its orientation.

We must acknowledge that the further development of radicalism among larger numbers of people is much inhibited by the absence of visible, and particularly organizational, expressions of radicalism. This suggests that radicals should be quite conscious about building radical organizations and should do so with a dual focus on local organizations, which can speak to the immediate needs and interests of people in their local situations, and on national organizations, which are the only basis for organizing that ultimately can create the leverage required to make the necessary changes.

fiscal dilemmas of the state

The economic pressures on the state since the late 1960s have stimulated some significant political developments. This has particular relevance for those of us who work in the public sector and who deal with people in the society whose well-being is dependent on the state's financial resources. In fact it is possible that the critical economic pressures and demands now facing the state may become quite significant in providing the basis for developing further radical consciousness and organization in the society.

As discussed in the previous chapter, the state sector has become essential to the maintenance of the existing social order. The role it plays is critical to social and economic stability—although as we shall see it also makes a significant contribution to instability. State services are not an appendage to an otherwise smoothly functioning society. The capitalist system is so organized that it requires the state to provide an ever expanding array of services and goods. In fact the demands on the state are escalating at the same time that the ability of the state to meet these demands is becoming more limited.

The potential of the state to respond to fiscal pressures by reducing services is limited by the fact that state-provided services are essential to maintaining the status quo. Of course the state can reduce the cost of government by limiting services to particularly vulnerable segments of the population. Benefits for welfare recipients are a notable example. However the effort to save government dollars by these measures is largely symbolic and diversionary, since the money spent for public welfare or for some of the other human services that are favorite targets for budget cutters is small, relative to the military budget, special corporate tax privileges, or the total level of state expenditure.[4] In the short run such efforts can divert attention from the underlying dilemma. In the long run they cannot resolve that dilemma.

What exactly is the dilemma? Basically, it is that the state must spend more money than it can raise through taxation.[5] It is called on to spend

---

[4]In 1974, public assistance programs, which then included Old Age Assistance, Aid to Dependent Children, Medical Assistance, and General Assistance, cost $20.7 billion. The Federal share of this amount was $10.2 billion out of a total Federal expenditure in that year of $254 billion. Data are from *Pocket Data Book, U.S.A., 1976*, Table 298, p. 211 and Table 74, p. 98.

[5]Between 1960 and 1976 there were only two years in which federal government receipts exceeded outlays (1960 and 1969). In every other year the federal government operated with

money for reasons that were reviewed in the previous chapter. Private corporations depend on extensive state involvement to maintain their economic stability and growth potential. This is the state's role in accumulation. Also the social and the economic problems created by capitalism require patch-up efforts by the state in order to avoid outright social chaos and the development of revolutionary alternatives. This is the state's legitimization function. The state must engage in these activities in order to maintain social order.

Socialist societies as well as capitalist societies face mounting internal pressures for increased spending. These pressures can and do result in domestic conflict over the allocation of resources. The underlying dynamic in the two kinds of society, however, differ in a fundamental way. Socialist societies are able to draw directly on the resources of the productive sector in order to finance public services. Socialist societies do not face the structural dilemmas experienced by capitalist societies in raising monies for public spending. To understand why this is so, we need to understand the choices the capitalist state faces as it deals with the problem of raising money for public services.

In the face of growing pressures for more spending, the state naturally attempts to tax more heavily. To raise the funds necessary for public services, a capitalist state turns to two primary sources of tax revenues— corporate tax and individual income tax. If a capitalist state attempts to increase state revenue by taxing corporations more heavily, it will reduce the surplus the corporations have at their disposal, which in turn will reduce their levels and rates of growth. This leads to decreased levels of production and to increased unemployment. Higher corporate taxes entail the risk of stimulating recession. During difficult economic periods when more people need government support, government does not provide more services unless there is also serious political agitation. One reason it does not is that it is in these very times that taxable income is reduced, and government is less able to raise additional tax revenues. During such times government actually tends to reduce corporate taxes in order to stimulate additional corporate investment. The ability of government to raise additional taxes by taxing capitalist enterprise is limited structurally, not so much by the powerful antitax lobbies of corporations, as by the necessity within capitalism to allow

---

deficit spending. In 1975 the deficit was almost $44 billion. In 1976 it was $76 billion. From 1960 to 1976 the aggregate deficit (not including interest) was $241 billion. Data are from *Pocket Data Book, U.S.A., 1976*, Table 95, p. 99. Similarly, state governments experienced collectively a $65 billion debt as of 1974. *Pocket Data Book, U.S.A., 1976*, Table 110, p. 109. City governments experienced collectively a debt of $61 billion as of 1974, up from $23 billion in 1960, data also from *Pocket Data Book, U.S.A., 1976*, Table 112, p. 110. Two useful discussions are Hugh Mosley, "Is There a Fiscal Crisis of the State?" *Monthly Review*, 30 (May, 1978), 34–46 and the editor's, "Debt and the Business Cycle, *Monthly Review*, 30 (June, 1978) 1–11.

and even to encourage the accumulation of large surpluses in private hands in order to maintain the economy.

The other option open to the state is to increase taxes paid by workers, and this the state attempts to do. However it is limited by several factors. One of these is that people fight back. They wage political struggles over tax increases, and to some extent, they are successful in their fight. When they win these battles, however, they also suffer, for example, when the effort to hold down or reduce property taxes results in school closings and other cut backs in vital services. Increasing taxes on working people has another serious consequence which tends to limit its effectiveness as a solution to the fiscal dilemmas of the state. To the extent that taxes increase, the lives of working people become more difficult, and they turn more and more to public services for survival. They thereby exacerbate the original problem by demanding still more public services.

In short it is difficult for government to raise the revenues required to respond to the needs it is asked to satisfy. The consequences of this impasse are obvious. Many social problems seem insoluable in the absence of extensive government involvement. At the same time, existing services are barely surviving the financial assault to which they are being subjected. The fiscal crisis of the state has become one of the critical political realities of our times. The problems we face require solutions on the national level, but government is not able to raise the funds or the political will to solve them.

What we see is that the state itself has become an important arena in which the crises of capitalism are played out. This has serious implications for social service workers who are themselves public employees and whose work involves the distribution of public benefits to social service recipients who also depend heavily on the availability of public dollars.

unions and the new working class

One of the developments in the United States and other advanced industrialized countries that is significant in shaping our particular political environment is the growth of what has been identified as the new working class (NWC) sector of the labor force. This sector did not exist at the time Marx analyzed the class structure of capitalism and so was not incorporated into his analysis of potential revolutionary elements in capitalist society. We must now account for and consider the meaning and role of this large group of workers.

The NWC is that part of the labor force which consists of white collar workers, both professional and nonprofessional, technicians, and managers. They are identified as the *new* working class in order to distinguish them from the traditional working class, the blue-collar workers. In 1975 there were 42 million white-collar workers in the labor force whereas in 1960 there were fewer than 29 million white-collar workers.[6] In contrast to this growth, blue-collar workers, the traditional proletariat, or working class, as it existed in Marx's time, increased from 24 million people in 1960 to only 28 million people in 1975.[7] The sector of the labor force whose numbers declined, as would be expected, was farmers and farmworkers.[8]

In analyzing the NWC it is important to note that, not only are the number of persons in this segment of the working class growing, but also that the percentage of the total labor force this group represents is growing. In 1960 white-collar workers comprised 13 percent of a labor force of 66 million workers. In 1975 they made up 50 percent of a labor force of 85 million workers.[9] They are increasing both in absolute numbers and as a percentage of the total labor force, and this trend promises to continue. When we speak of the working class in the United States, we are speaking, not only of traditional blue-collar workers but increasingly of secretaries, data processors, teachers, and social workers.

These figures are provocative. For such a large proportion of workers in the labor force not to be manual workers in the traditional sense is quite a new development historically. Since the turn of the century, the white-collar segment of the labor force has been growing. We are accustomed to their presence, and therefore we may overlook them and ignore their impact on the labor force. Writing at a time they simply did not exist, Marx could not assess them in his analysis of the potential role of the working class in waging revolution. Twentieth-century Marxists have had the task of analyzing the actual and potential political role of this new segment of the labor force.

One of the important facts about the NWC is that many of its members are public employees. In fact much of the growth in the white-collar sector of the labor force is accounted for by growth in public employment. In 1960 public employees constituted 13 percent of the total labor force; (they constituted 17 percent of the labor force if the military establishment is included). By 1974 they comprised 17 percent of the labor force (and 20 percent if the military is included.[10] Public employment now accounts for the jobs of one in five workers in the United States. Again this is quite a significant change

---

[6]*Pocket Data Book, U.S.A., 1976*, Table 206, p. 164.

[7]Ibid.

[8]The number of farmworkers decreased from 5.2 million to 2.9 million between 1960 and 1975. The other major occupational group is service workers whose numbers increased from 8.0 million to 11.7 million in that same period. *Pocket Data Book, U.S.A., 1976*, Table 206, p. 164.

[9]Ibid.

[10]*Pocket Data Book, U.S.A., 1976*, Tables 148, p. 135 and 113, p. 111.

from the period in which Marx analyzed the composition and political potential of various segments of the labor force.

There is an additional piece of information that will be important to an analysis of the political potential of this population. That concerns the change in patterns of unionization among the working class. In recent years the increase in unionization has not kept pace with the growth in the labor force as a whole. In the traditional blue-collar unions, the absolute number of unionized workers has actually decreased in recent years. Total union membership increased from 15 million people in 1950 to 21.6 million people in 1974. However between 1970 and 1974, the growth was slight, rising from 20.8 million to only 21.6 million people.[11] In 1976 and again in 1977 union membership actually decreased in absolute numbers. Union membership is now hovering at around 20 percent of the total labor force.

In contrast with these figures white-collar workers are experiencing more rapid unionization. Although the percentage of white-collar workers who are unionized is lower than the percentage of all workers who are unionized, the white-collar unions, particularly public employee unions, are growing rapidly.[12] While we cannot predict their future, several factors are likely to make this sector ripe for expanding unionization. These include the fact that unionization drives on a massive scale in the public sector are relatively new. We are only beginning to see the potential of such drives since both tradition and law had inhibited white-collar unionization efforts for many decades after the period when blue-collar unions got their start. Equally important the growing fiscal crisis of the state may propel increasing numbers of public employees toward unionization in an effort to fight layoffs and pay cuts (although it is also possible that a tightening labor market can inhibit further unionization drives).

There is disagreement among leftists about the political future of the NWC. There is a good argument to be made on behalf of the potential of the NWC to develop a more radical consciousness and to play an important role in future radical struggles. It is true that NWC members have not traditionally been prone to think of themselves as part of the working class. White-collar workers and other members of the NWC have generally held

---

[11]*Pocket Data Book, U.S.A., 1976,* Table 215, p. 168.

[12]Between 1970 and 1974 the number of government workers who were union members increased from 2.3 million to 2.9 million people in *Statistical Abstracts of the United States* (Washington, D.C.: U.S. Government Printing Office, 1977), Table 680, p. 419. Between 1964 and 1974, membership in the American Federation of State, County and Municipal Employees (AFSCME) increased from 235,000 to 648,000. Membership in the Service Employees International Union increased from 320,000 to 550,000. Membership in the American Federation of Teachers increased from 100,000 to 444,000, and membership in the American Federation of Government Employees increased from 139,000 to 300,000. This data is also from *Statistical Abstracts of the United States,* Table 682, p. 400.

themselves aloof, attitudinally and organizationally, from blue-collar workers. They have tended to receive higher wages than blue-collar workers and to perform work which carries higher status and more autonomy than that performed by blue-collar workers. However this is changing. Conditions of work for the NWC increasingly are replicating those for blue-collar workers.[13] Members of the NWC may want to maintain special status as professionals or be otherwise distinguished from blue-collar workers. However the conditions of work for white-collar workers are increasingly becoming factorylike. In the term used by NWC theorists, the NWC is becoming "proletarianized." The traditional advantages of white-collar work, such as relatively higher degrees of discretion on the job, are giving way to more routine, bureaucratized, and closely supervised conditions of work. Even the more elite sectors of the NWC, those considered professionals, are increasingly likely to work as functionaries in large bureaucracies, rather than as solo entrepreneurs. They receive salaries, operate within bureaucratic guidelines, and are closely supervised. More and more they are likely to be union members and to depend on their union, rather than on individual efforts, for protection of basic job rights and career development.

In addition to changes in the workplace itself that may contribute to a radicalization of the NWC, the high level of personal expectations and the technical and analytic competence of the NWC may have an impact on its political outlook. A higher proportion of the NWC than of the old working class is college educated. Potentially a college education leads to raised expectations about the opportunities for creativity and satisfaction that work will entail. When work does not encourage or allow growth and self-expression, frustration can result. NWC members have been socialized to view themselves as relatively advantaged, and many react with surprise and then anger to the realities of the work situation. Further, by nature of their advanced education, many are reasonably well-equipped to analyze and comprehend the basic nature of the dilemmas they face. They may also be in a position to project the possibility of alternative ways to structure their work in a fashion that enhances the role of workers, since their training tends to encourage mastery of more of the job situation.

On the other hand, there are good reasons to question the extent to which workers in this sector will become more radical, or at least become radicalized more rapidly than workers in the blue-collar sector. The doubt rests partly on the fact that people in the NWC, despite increasing proletarianization, continue to be privileged in relation to the traditional working class. As a result they may not develop the political outlook that would lead them in the direction of an alliance with blue-collar workers. Their

---

[13]Bill Patry, "Taylorism Comes to the Social Services," *Monthly Review*, 30 (October, 1978) 29–37.

commitment to the status quo may be firmer than proponents of NWC theory argue.[14]

No one can predict, of course, the exact political direction this group will take. There is growing unionization and militancy in that unionization among white-collar workers and public employees. There is also a self-conscious left in some segments of the NWC as represented, for example, by the development of a radical presence in the social services. At the same time, we can readily uncover evidence documenting conservative attitudes and behaviors among NWC members.

While we cannot predict this group's political future, it is useful to recognize that members of the NWC are indeed workers. We ought not to dismiss their political relevance to socialist transformation out of hand, on the grounds that they are not the traditional blue-collar workers of whom Marx spoke. The assessment of their political future must remain open. For the present I believe this is an important segment of the working class for radicals to look toward and work among. It follows that inasmuch as social service workers are members of the NWC, an assessment of the political potential of social service workers will be much influenced by an assessment of the political potential of the NWC as a whole.

stability and instability

An additional aspect of the current political scene that is particularly worthy of mention revolves around the question of whether the quietude that seems to dominate the current political landscape represents a fundamental inertia or whether other forces are operating beneath the surface that can give us hope for more vibrant politics in the near future. This question cannot be answered with certainty. It is not possible to say if and when a more radical politics will emerge as a significant force in the United States. However it is important to identify some of the factors that would lead us to challenge, or at least to question, the picture of complacency and disinterest in radical politics that is painted by representatives of the status quo.

One thing does seem certain. Beneath the relative passivity of large numbers of people is a great deal of anger, rooted in the experience, whether or not consciously understood, of exploitation. The direction that anger might take is unclear. That there is anger is undeniable. What seems at first

---

[14]For example, see the case developed by Barbara and John Ehrenreich in *Radical America* (March-April, 1977 and May-June, 1977) and by Stanley Aronowitz, "Does the United States Have a New Working Class?" in *The Revival of American Socialism* ed. George Fischer (New York: Oxford University Press, 1971), pp. 188–216. "The Professional-Managerial Class," *Radical America*, (March/April), 1977, pp. 3–21 and "The New Left and the Professional-Managerial Class" *Radical America*, 11 (May/June, 1977), 5–24.

glance to be a pervasive quietude appears on closer inspection to be frustration and explosive rage. If radical ideas and organizations emerge in the near future, what will need to be explained is not only why they emerged at that point in history, but also why they did not emerge until that point in history, given the many reasons why one would expect a socialist movement to develop.

Of course there are many ways in which people demonstrate their willingness and ability to fight back against the society that oppresses them, even in these quiet times. We can be encouraged by the high level of strike activity, expecially unauthorized wildcat strike activity among blue-collar workers; by the continued vitality of some segments of the women's movement; by the growth of community organizing in many cities, with a focus on neighborhood issues and issues of economic injustice; by the strength of the gay liberation movement; by the growth of interest in Marxism among increasing numbers of NWC members; and by the ecology movement, particularly, the antinuclear power movement. These movements and others are not well reported in the conventional press. We will not know about them unless we seek out newsletters, magazines, and organizations on the left. That these movements are not well reported in the conventional media is partly a reflection of their relatively small size and largely a reflection of the unwillingness of the conventional media, representing as it does the established forces of the society, to give exposure to people's movements. It also reflects a bias against grass-roots movements, whatever their strength, in conventional news coverage. Grass-roots movements are seen as insignificant to national politics, on the grounds that politics are what the elite do and not what the masses of people do. In any case it is important that those of us committed to revolutionary change keep informed and keep each other informed of developments in various sectors, if for no other reason than to dispel the illusion created by conventional media that no one is in political motion. When we are so informed, we will better understand that the political landscape, while not enormously promising from a radical perspective, is not as bleak as is conventionally pictured.

The Social Welfare Sector: Points of Linkage

developing a sense of political direction

Thus far in this chapter I have reviewed some aspects of the current political environment. It is now necessary to elaborate more specifically the ways in which social service workers can utilize this understanding to identify their relationship to a revolutionary process as it could emerge in the United States. This section examines those structural links between the social welfare sector and the contradictions of capitalist society that offer promise for furthering revolutionary ideas and revolutionary movements and which subsequently can provide the basis for suggesting more specific strategic approaches. I will consider points of linkage in three areas: the fiscal crisis of the state; NWC theory; and the social services themselves.

social services and the fiscal crisis of the state

Analysis of the fiscal crisis of the state provides some guidance in exploring one facet of the relationship between the social service sector and broader social change processes. The dollars which fund social services and social service workers are primarily public monies. To the extent that a more adequate system of social services and more adequate wages for social service workers become issues for political struggle, we can press against the inherent inability of the capitalist state to meet the fiscal demands made of it.[15] In pressing for more adequate services and higher wages, we do two things. We raise demands which speak to the immediate and legitimate needs which people have—people who are service recipients and people who are service providers—and we exacerbate a fundamental contradiction in capitalism, represented in part by the fiscal crisis.

There are two ways in which social service workers can escalate pressures on the state for increased social spending. The first is through their own wage demands. This is happening as more and more social service workers become unionized and as they gain strength in their unionization efforts through higher degrees of solidarity among themselves and with other public service workers. This should not suggest that unionization easily or automatically leads to higher wages. However there is a noticable relationship between increased unionization and higher wages in the labor force, when other variables are controlled.

The second way in which social service workers can push against the fiscal crisis of the state is by organizing for more adequate social service provision. This occurs both through our own independent efforts to represent the valid needs of service users and through our efforts to work with organized groups of social service users who press similar demands. Once again we bring pressure to bear on a dynamic in capitalist society that is already strained. We do so though a vehicle which has the long-term potential to upset the fragile stability of the present arrangements and which speaks to immediate and legitimate needs of the moment.

---

[15]The important role which public service unions have played in aggravating the economic dilemmas of the cities has been analyzed by Frances Fox Piven, "The Urban Crisis: Who Got What, and Why?" in *1984 Revisited* ed. Robert Paul Wolff (New York: Knopf, 1973), pp. 165–201.

The political developments that accompany the fiscal crisis of the state are of considerable strategic importance. In itself, a deepening fiscal crisis will not automatically lead to the emergence of radical politics. We already have before us many examples of the inability of the state to meet social needs. This inability is likely to grow. However the state will respond to the resulting pressures in a variety of ways, all designed to defuse and coopt the radical political potential represented by those pressures.

For example, the state will deny social services selectively, choosing politically vulnerable groups to attack, isolating them when possible,[16] and maintaining the fiction of responsiveness to the majority as long as possible. Similarly it is commonplace for the state to respond to the wage demands of public service workers by appealing to the populace at large to help the state resist. The basis of the appeal is that higher wages for state workers necessitates higher taxes. In this way the state attempts to pit workers in the private sector against workers in the public sector, and it has been somewhat successful in doing so.

In the face of growing demands for more adequate services for one segment of the population, the state will typically divert funds from some other, less well organized, segment. For example, in some states the aged were successful through the mid-1970s in eliminating the means test requirement for social services to the aged under Title XX. Representatives of the aged argued that such a high proportion of the aged are poor that it does not make sense to administer an expensive and offensive means test to sort out the small percentage of them who seek hot meals or social services and whose income is above the eligibility levels set by Title XX. To the extent that such campaigns have been successful, they bring about a welcome reform. However we ought to be clear about the overall impact of such reforms. Each state has had a predetermined amount of funding for Title XX programs, and that funding had to be distributed among programs for all

---

[16]Richard Cloward and Frances Fox Piven discuss the way in which the Social Security Act, while providing some real benefits to working people, weakened the momentum of the more radical Townsend Movement which had been organizing and pressing for pensions of $200 per month. It did so by providing pensions at a much lower level than the Townsendites had been demanding and by doing so, not for those already aged, but for the future aged. This effectively cut off support of the majority of those active in the work force from those already retired who supported the Townsend plan. See Richard Cloward and Frances Fox Piven, *Poor People's Movements* (New York: Pantheon, 1977), p. 31. Similarly, in the 1960s, the National Welfare Rights Organization found that it could organize and agitate around provisions for special benefits for winter clothing contained in welfare regulations. In response to the growing pressures created by the Welfare Rights Organization through its utilization of these procedures, states responded with flat grant allotments for special needs. On the one hand, this change made it easier for larger numbers of people to receive such allotments. On the other hand, the grant was small and, more important from an organizing point of view, it weakened the Welfare Rights Organization's ability to utilize this provision of welfare policy as a vehicle to mobilize pressure on the welfare system. These examples could be multiplied many times over.

categories of persons utilizing public social services. To the extent that an increased number of the aged became eligible for Title XX programs, less funding was available for other populations whose need is different, but equally pressing.

There are no simple solutions. The complex and necessary strategic approaches to avoid these pitfalls involve building larger coalitions of service users and providers who are alert to the trade-offs that are made this year, to the advantage or disadvantage of one group, and next year with the priorities reversed.

Another response on the part of the state, in the face of growing needs and growing demand, is doing nothing, and to a large extent that is what the state does. Of course doing nothing tends to be accompanied by a barrage of propaganda. Such propaganda may stress a variety of themes, depending on the political party in power or the climate of the times. At one point we may be told that we need a period of benign neglect or of lowered expectations. This may accompany the theme that the American people cannot expect government to do everything, nor should it do everything since that weakens our moral fiber and weakens the traditional problems-solving mechanisms that have made our country strong. At other times we will be told that the government is responding immediately and directly to the problems people face, even when the government is doing nothing. At still other times the legitimacy of the need itself will be questioned. These all have been, and will undoubtedly continue to be, responses on the part of the state to demands for more adequate public services.[17]

Our efforts to secure legitimate social services are met with equally determined efforts to avoid the fiscal crunch that such demands produce. We must understand that there are no automatic successes and no sure-fire strategies in political life. For several reasons, however, we are on sound political footing in following this path. One of these is that the demands raised are themselves legitimate and fundamentally reasonable. When people are unemployed, despite their best efforts to find employment, their demand for unemployment benefits of sufficient amount and duration to meet legitimate needs is understandable and reasonable. Second, we must recognize that unmet needs, whatever the accompanying propaganda, increase people's anger and thereby provide another possibility for organizing. The state can attempt to obscure its role and deny the legitimacy of people's needs. Those needs persist, none the less. When the state does not respond, it weakens its claim to moral legitimacy. This is happening already. It is becoming clearer to more people that the state is either unable or unwilling to meet legitimate needs. Increasingly people are less willing to believe that

---

[17]A useful discussion is S. M. Miller, "The Recapitalization of Capitalism," *Social Policy*, 9 (November/December, 1978), 5–13.

the state represents their best interests. As we help to raise demands for adequate social services, and as the state is unable to respond, we weaken the state's claim to legitimacy, and we undermine its ability to manipulate social services for the purpose of social control. Again this does not happen automatically. It happens to the extent that we are able to link the growing fiscal crisis with vigorous organizing efforts that help people to understand the nature of the crisis they are facing, to develop effective vehicles for challenging the state, and to formulate analyses that prevent the state from turning people against one another in a search for easy scapegoats.

These then are some of the potentials, as well as the pitfalls, represented by the fiscal crisis of the state. The fact that the state is called on to meet pressing needs and must do so to help maintain the society in its present form while the demands on the state outstrip its ability to meet those needs creates a situation with much potential for social change. As social service workers we are not immediately indispensable to the maintenance of the economic order. By virtue of the relationships described previously, we are related to less direct, but critical, economic dynamics in the society. Our task is to organize around the crises that are developing in a way that furthers the building of revolutionary ideas and a revolutionary movement.

social service workers and the new working class

An understanding of NWC theory provides an additional way to assess the relationship of social service workers to revolutionary efforts in the society. Perhaps the most crucial implication NWC theory for social service workers is its suggestion that we take ourselves seriously in politics; that is, that we view ourselves as worthy of our own political attention. According to some traditional leftist analyses, analyses which are unpersuaded by the political potential of the NWC, working with and among social service workers with an eye toward their contribution to radical politics is a wasted effort. It is argued that this population is unlikely to become radical in its outlook and is powerless to make a significant contribution to radical politics, even if it were to move leftward.

From a liberal perspective work with and among social service workers also has a different meaning than it does to proponents of NWC theory. Progressive change is understood to derive from sources of power other than from the working class organized as a class. An example of this contrast is progressive change through the elite lobbying efforts of social service leaders, rather than through the collective action of the rank and file. To the extent that a liberal perspective endorses organizing among workers, it tends to restrict the focus of that organizing to the achievement of more limited "professional" objectives; it ignores or denies the potential for larger change. Social service workers are encouraged to organize as professionals with their own special turf to protect, rather than as workers with a commitment to their common interests with other workers. NWC theory supports a progressive perspective on the question of organizing among social service workers.

Increasingly social service workers are organizing as workers, regardless of their point of view about their larger political role and regardless of anyone else's point of view about their actual or potential role. They are doing so as part of a trend among public service workers and white collar workers and in response to the pressing problems of their work situations which require their collective action. None the less the majority of social service workers are not yet unionized, and relatively few of those who are, view it in political terms that go beyond the bread-and-butter issues of trade union protection and individual advancement. They are not to be condemned for viewing unionism in terms of its impact on their own immediate circumstances. From a radical perspective the issue is to find ways to encourage the unionization of larger numbers of social service workers and to help advance their understanding of unionism into the context of a broader framework of radical politics.

One implication of the political direction provided by NWC theory is that social service workers should unionize. There are risks involved, as will be discussed in a subsequent chapter. The unionization of social service workers is no guarantee of more secure jobs, higher wages, or revolutionary politics. None the less if we are to encourage radicalism in this sector of the NWC, we are likely to be more successful by stimulating collective efforts than by encouraging the isolated development of individual service workers. Unionization is by no means the end point of our efforts. It may be a useful starting point.

social service workers and the welfare state

Earlier I discussed ways in which welfare state services help to integrate people more closely into the values and structures of capitalist society. I suggested that the social services are one vehicle at the state's disposal for what has been identified as the state's legitimization function. This function has become increasingly important in the last decade as conditions of life have become more difficult for increasing numbers of people. In the first part of this chapter I discussed the growing malaise of ever larger numbers of people. In this context it becomes more apparent that the role of social services is to encourage people to feel that the society will care for them, if their individual efforts to sustain themselves fail. In reality our present arrangements of income supports and social services will not do that. They none the less continue to preserve some illusion that we live in a caring society committed to its citizens which makes it more difficult for people to sort out the political realities around them. The social services are one of the props in an illusory balancing act. By virtue of that fact they are also potentially useful tools for political ends quite different from those they now serve.

I will develop some of the strategic approaches suggested by this analysis more specifically in Chapter 7. Here I am highlighting another of the larger political dynamics that can inform radical social service practice. To the extent that we social service workers organize against the repressive nature of social services, we can help to demystify the nature of those services. To the extent that we are able to facilitate the organization of social service users through our work, rather than to divide people, albeit unwittingly, we can lend encouragement to an additional constituency for radical change. To the extent that we become clearer about the way in which conservative values appear, in our practice, we can experiment with ways to deliver services that clarify and promote radical perspectives.

Social services play a more important role in maintaining political quietude during a difficult period than they do in a calm period. Clearly this is a difficult period. Social service workers have not always understood the political role they have played. If they have understood, they have not always known how to act in a way that challenges that role. Radical social service workers can work to educate their coworkers and to organize for radical change with the knowledge that they bring the struggle for revolutionary change into one additional area of the society, an area which is of some importance in maintaining the status quo. Once again the social services are not a direct link in the structure of capitalism. They are an important indirect link and by virtue of that fact, offer possibilities for contributing to radical change.

APPLYING THEORY
TO PRACTICE

6

An Orientation
to Radical Practice

Appropriate Expectations of a Model for Radical Practice

Having reviewed some of the theoretical perspectives that underlie radical practice, in this part of the book I turn to practice guidelines, that is, to the application of principles of radical change within social work. The following chapters bring a socialist perspective on change to the specific circumstances of social workers.

Radical social workers are attempting to integrate their politics with their social work practice more completely. It is helpful to acknowledge that we are not able to do so fully, given the limitations of theory and the modest level of radical activity in society. However as we make the attempt we gain more clarity about the problems involved in developing radical practice. That clarity sharpens the issues, creates the possibility for further conceptual and theoretical development, and reinforces the next round of practice efforts. As the level of revolutionary struggle advances, new practice possibilities emerge that were not anticipated at an earlier stage since conditions did not exist for their expression. Then further theoretical advances become possible.

That our efforts are circumscribed by the level of radical struggle in the larger society does not suggest that is it futile to work on developing radical practice and theory. In fact those with radical political commitments have no alternative but to advance things from their present point to the next point. As we make radical practice in social work more concrete, we will develop the insights and perspectives that make it more sophisticated. Our progress will not be smooth and evolutionary. As the world changes and as our knowledge of it changes, we will uncover successive contradictions. At times we will be quite clear about ways to advance class struggle, and at times we will be stymied.

We are not likely to have at our disposal, now or in the immediate future, a blueprint for radical practice or a set of "how to do it" guidelines applicable to each situation. If we expect them, we will be frustrated and discouraged. On the other hand, we can acknowledge the part of our life experiences and analysis that has pushed us in a radical direction and the fact that we have chosen social work as an occupation. Our task is then to find, over time, increasingly satisfying ways to integrate these facets of our lives. [1]

Primitive Rebellion and Radical Social Work

From one perspective what radical social workers are attempting to develop is quite new. From another perspective, developing a theoretical model and a radical practice in the society builds on a great deal of existing sentiment and experience. The idea of radical practice strikes a responsive chord in many people since it is practice that relates to the critical analysis of the society and its social services which many social service workers have already made. That critical analysis may not be couched in socialist terms and may not be well articulated in any terms. None the less a radical analysis of the social services frequently strikes social service workers as just what they had been searching for, even when they were not aware they had been searching for it.

Social service workers often practice primitive political rebellion. Many resist existing policies and the more oppressive aspects of the work they are expected to do. This resistance is a social service version of indus-

---

[1]For whatever consolation it provides, those people and groups working to develop greater clarity about the theoretical basis and conceptual foundations of conventional social work; that is, social work that operates within a procapitalist, liberal to conservative stance, do not have a clear alternative to offer to the radical model. Further, they have been at the job considerably longer and have more resources at their disposal. In the estimation of most radicals, they cannot be successful since their efforts will necessarily be confounded by their unwillingness to think in radical terms when that is so clearly required. The debates and limitations of these efforts are reviewed in a special issue on conceptual frameworks in *Social Work*, the Journal of the National Association of Social Workers, 22 (September, 1977).

trial sabotage; it corresponds to the action of an assembly line worker who purposely does not complete a task according to specifications, or who destroys a machine. For social service workers acts of resistance on behalf of those they serve involve breaking rules and regulations, lying, falsifying records, and refusing to engage with people for whom involvement with a social service agency might be destructive.[2] Analyzed in political terms, these kinds of actions can be viewed as a precursor of more organized, systematic, and politically informed efforts to change the social order. They are still primitive, however, because they are individualistic; they are not viewed or executed as part of a collective movement-building strategy, and in fact, they are not generally couched in political terms at all. Nevertheless they stem from the same impulses that can lead to a self-consciously radical practice if directed in different channels. They are rebellious acts of saying "no" to established procedures. They are based on anger and frustration, and they recognize that there is a serious schism between what people need and what social policy allows for and provides.

While we are in the initial stages of conceptualizing about and practicing radical social work and need to be cautious about having unrealistic expectations for theory and practice, we are not working completely against a prevailing tide, and we are not introducing ideas and suggestions into an arena where they will seem unrelated to people's daily experiences. Just the opposite is true. These ideas will help many people to make sense of the frustration they have experienced; that is, to make sense of their experience in terms of the contradictions of capitalist society. The ideas will prove exciting and energizing by offering people a more systematic way to analyze and to act.

When social service workers analyze their practice in terms of a radical political perspective, they enhance the possibility of their acting in resistance to established mandates in a more guilt-free way. A common experience for primitive rebels within the social services, and to some extent for all rebels, regardless of their arena of practice or their degree of sophistication, is the feeling that they are acting improperly. This feeling is a reflection of the political ambivalence that is part of all of our lives and that will be discussed more fully later in this chapter. To the extent that we have internalized norms that stress doing what we have been told to do and being "good boys and girls," we will feel that we are doing something "wrong" when we practice in a radical way.

---

[2]For an elaboration of this point see Geoffrey Pearson, "Making Social Workers: Bad Promises and Good Omens," in *Radical Social Work* eds. Roy Bailey and Mike Brake (New York: Pantheon 1975) especially pp. 24–43. Anyone who has worked as a social service worker in a large, public social welfare bureaucracy will not need to read the article to be convinced of the prevalence of this type of behavior among social service workers.

On the other hand, to the extent that we operate within a principled framework that expresses our humanity and our caring for others, we will have a powerful weapon with which to combat our concern about being deviant. A radical analysis can be very helpful in influencing whatever part of us feels illegitimate by letting us see ourselves more fully as protagonists in class struggle and as people who are operating on the basis of principled political convictions.

To put this another way, a Marxist perspective encourages us to explore the materialist base of our feelings. Our sense of right and wrong is indeed our sense of right and wrong. However our sense, feelings, and internalized morality are rooted in the concrete realities of society. In a society, ideologically dominated by the propertied or capitalist class, it is inevitable that our feelings will largely mirror a conception of the world that legitimizes capitalist domination. A Marxist analysis helps us in sorting out the extent to which the ideas, feelings, and morality emanating from and sustaining a capitalist economic system actually serve us. As we better understand the ways in which the whole system fails to serve us maximally, we will be better able to evaluate the ways in which the parts of the system which we have internalized, such as our sense of right and wrong, serve us.

Radical social work practice builds on a view of the purpose and nature of practice that differs significantly from the conventional view. The radical model does not offer a new bag of tricks, a unique methodology, or a comfortable practice setting in a "radical agency" with radical colleagues and radical agendas. However a radical model can support the sentiments that people often have already and can offer some sense of direction for acting on those sentiments. A practice model, resting on radical assumptions about people, the social order and social change processes, can profoundly influence the ways in which we perceive ourselves and others. While we will still experience confusion and doubt about continuing the struggle from within social service agencies, and we will have less than perfect clarity in political direction, the changed analysis and consciousness we bring to our work can set the stage for significant growth in our ability to bring our politics and our daily work into closer alignment.

With this in mind I turn to a discussion of principles that can guide radical social service practice. The material in the following chapter elaborates, in more operational terms, ways in which radical theory can inform social service work in a variety of arenas.

Meeting Immediate Needs and Building a Revolutionary Movement

A troublesome question for many people considering radical social work practice is whether or not it fosters inattention to the immediate needs of social service users by pursuing larger political ends. The question is a reflection, within the social welfare sector, of a central concern of revolutionary theory, that of the relationship of reform to revolution.

Beginning in the late 1800s influential segments of the capitalist class came to a new understanding about the relationship of reform to the maintenance of capitalism. Until that time capitalists and their managers and planners had resisted even relatively minor reforms. They thought that reforms, ameliorative measures within the structures of capitalism, were unnecessary concessions to the working class and would threaten capitalist power and profits. As the working class became more organized in its resistance to the capitalist class, however, the level of struggle escalated. Then capitalist resistance to all reforms seemed less efficient, and selective concessions were made to maintain the system. From that point on, the capitalist class, primarily through the organs of the state, conceded reforms when the pressure was sufficiently great. While capitalists moved toward begrudging acceptance of the necessity and desirability of reform, their interests were maintained by virtue of the fact that the reforms they granted cooled unrest, created the illusion of a caring ruling class and a unified society, and lessened the probability of more profound and disruptive changes.

It would be inhumane and politically destructive for radicals to oppose reforms despite the limitations of reforms and the way they solidify oppressive mechanisms in the society. At the same time, if the efforts of radicals are entirely absorbed in reform movements, we will be diverted in our efforts to challenge a system which makes life so difficult for people and which will not be significantly changed, however hard and long we work for reforms.[3]

Our work within the social services reflects this dilemma. Social services are one type of reform that has been won by the working class. Social services matter to people. They can be helpful in meeting some immediate needs, and they would not exist at all—even in their present bare-bones fashion—if working class people had not fought for them. At the same time, social services are organized in such a way that they provide very limited help to a minority of those needing help. Frequently they hurt people rather than help them. Furthermore social welfare services help to solidify and stabilize capitalist institutions. The critical issue, therefore, is to discover how to work in such a way that we support the legitimacy of social services in their people-serving aspects while we simultaneously use social services to help build a revolutionary movement.

We must work toward a theory and practice that address both immediate needs and revolutionary agendas at the same time. Although our practice will necessarily be imperfect, our goal must be to integrate our short

---

[3]A fuller discussion of the Catch-22 of reformism is found in Jeffry Galper, *The Politics of Social Services* (Englewood Cliffs, N.J.: Prentice-Hall, Inc., 1975), see Chapter 5, "Social Reform: The Liberal Response," pp. 73–87.

and long-term concerns. It is not possible to achieve such integration perfectly. However, advancing such integration as an expectation and a standard
against which to measure radical practice is useful. We do ourselves and
others a disservice to pose the choice in an either-or fashion.

If we are lax in striving to build a revolutionary movement, we can
rightly be accused of failing to take seriously our own analysis of the need for
fundamental change. If we are not committed to challenging the destructive
operating principles of the system, we will be supporting the status quo and
the irrationality and inhumanity that it represents by the nature of our work.
On the other hand, if our efforts to build such a movement cause us to ignore
the short-term, helpful things we can do, we will deserve to be politically
isolated since we will have demonstrated the irrelevance of radicalism to the
immediate needs of people.

Cloward and Piven, in their introduction to a British publication on
radical social work, discuss this issue in a way that poses movement building
and social service provision as antagonistic concerns. They fully understand
the destructive nature of social services. However they do not relate the
anticapitalist analysis on which their critique rests to a socialist perspective
on change. They argue as follows:

> If we manage to get people who are hungry a bit of bread, or to protect the
> weak against the assaults of the courts or the mental hospitals, then we will
> have gone a short way toward redressing the wrongs of a harsh society. Which
> of us is so arrogantly unfeeling, or so confident of the prospects for revo-
> lutionary transformation as to think these small gains are not important?
> In the longer run, if we fight for the interests of the people we claim are our
> clients, then we will also be waging a struggle against the institutions of the
> capitalist state. There is a kind of tautological trick inherent in some Marxist
> arguments, to the effect that any actual effort to deal with the contradictions
> created by capitalism will produce reforms that paper over the contradictions.
> The trick is a professionally convenient one, for it enables us to say that no
> action short of the final cataclysmic one ought to be taken. But revolutions are
> not made all at once.[4]

This line of reasoning does a disservice to those attempting to formulate and practice radical social work. It equates aggressive individual
casework services with anticapitalist work. It argues that meeting the needs
of individuals through case advocacy represents a challenge to the logic and
structures of capitalism. While this kind of work can produce useful outcomes, it does not challenge capitalism in and of itself. Capitalism can ac-
commodate these kinds of individual challenges. In fact if the challenges are
not challenges to the operating principles of capitalism itself, they may well

---

[4]Richard A. Cloward and Frances Fox Piven, "Notes Toward a Radical Social Work," in
Radical Social Work, eds. Roy Bailey and Mike Brake (New York: Pantheon, 1975), p. xlvii.

be coopted into existing institutions which can then function more smoothly while maintaining their larger oppressive functions. There is little evidence, either in current political life or historically, to support the notion that the accumulated efforts of individual workers to provide adequate service within the structures of existing institutions influence the basic processes of those institutions.

Cloward and Piven anticipate such a response from critics. In the statement quoted, they reply to that criticism of their position by arguing that some Marxists believe that nothing should be done until the final, cataclysmic revolutionary moment. If revolutionaries were to argue such a position, they would deserve to be condemned by Cloward and Piven and by many others, at the least for holding such a naive view of the process of revolutionary transformation. However, by posing the issue as either working in a militant, but traditional, fashion or taking no action, they overlook the more creative approaches that lie in between and that form the heart of revolutionary work in a nonrevolutionary time. Cloward and Piven present a simplified conception of revolutionary struggle. Here they have not helped us to develop a more integrated and organic perspective on the linkages between daily work in social service settings and movement building. Movement building, like revolutionary transformation, is a process, and it is hard work. The question that is most useful to ask, and which Cloward and Piven do not ask, concerns the ways in which the daily struggle on behalf of service users can also make a contribution to movement building and to structural changes.[5]

In fact there may be occasions on which we will have to choose between these two concerns or in which they will be incompatible. However, we can maximize the compatibility of meeting immediate needs and building a revolutionary movement if we keep the following three notions in mind.

First, working within the framework of a socialist analysis is often the very best way of meeting people's individual needs. We are frequently quite limited in what we are able to do on behalf of social service users, even when we raise issues that are not system-challenging. In order for us to be effective on behalf of a particular problem, it may be essential that we help individuals to organize with others to raise wider challenges through collective political action. Organizing or facilitating the organization of service users in a way that attempts to raise the question of their rights to adequate services and

---

[5]It is possible that Cloward and Piven do not ask this question because they have relatively little faith in the effectiveness of conscious organizing efforts by radicals and nonradicals alike to generate political motion. In fact, they have argued that efforts at movement building are destructive to the achievement of short-run gains which are most easily achievable when large numbers of people press their demands without the fetters or energy diversions involved in building formal organizations. They have developed this position most fully in *Poor People's Movements* (New York: Pantheon, 1977).

that fosters their sense of collective empowerment may be the most reasonable way of trying to meet the immediate and pressing needs of individuals. It may represent the logical expression of our full commitments to helping others as social service workers. A socialist framework is not incompatible with social work practice. Rather, it takes the commitment to social work practice seriously. The real deviance is not in radicalism; it is in traditional practice that is based on a profound ambivalence toward social work's stated commitment to social welfare.

Second, we ought to recognize that at best we meet only a small portion of the need that exists for whatever kind of service we offer. Therefore, we are always in the position of making choices about whom to serve and which needs to service. Often we are not conscious of making such choices because they are dictated by the logic of agency policy or are determined by so-called professional criteria which orient us toward some problems and away from others. Greater clarity about the need to integrate immediate service provision and movement building can provide a framework in which we can be more creative in making choices about whom to serve and what needs to address. We always make such choices. What would it mean if each of us consciously added our commitment to building a radical movement to our criteria for making choices? This question may need to be answered in different fashions by workers in different settings. Despite the fact that the question has no single answer, it is a productive one to ask.

Finally in responding to the challenge of Cloward and Piven's remarks, and in outlining a response to the dilemma of integrating service with movement building, it is helpful to recognize that we always have choices in the way we respond to an individual's social service problem. To what extent do we link that individual with other individuals who have the same problem? To what extent do we encourage people to examine the more fundamental roots of the problem? To what extent do we take one person's problem somewhat further by questioning the policies and issues that create the problem? In raising these questions, some of the choices we face emerge. To ask questions is not to provide a blueprint for radical practice nor is it to limit ourselves to questions which only radicals would ask. To ask questions is to illustrate the thesis that each problem can be addressed in many ways. From a radical perspective we will attempt to respond to particular problems in a way that builds organization and that expands radical consciousness, through the process of working for structural changes.

To summarize we do ourselves a disservice if we pose immediate need-meeting efforts and revolutionary work as antagonistic concerns. There may be situations in which we will have to make choices between the two. However, there is a significant difference between seeing the two concerns as fundamentally contradictory and seeing them as parts of the same process. A radical analysis offers a way of viewing our commitments to others in the light of an anticapitalist and prosocialist perspective. As such it speaks to the daily issues and events of life. When it fails to do that, our task is to develop ways to make it do so and not to retreat from facing the real challenge by posing radicalism as a luxury that we cannot afford when people are hurting.

Education, Movement Building, and Structural Reforms

introduction

As I have suggested, it is hard to make a strong case for the argument that the essentially orthodox social services will make a long range contribution to the radical transformation of society, even when those services are provided aggressively. This assessment is not based on some vague theoretical considerations or on esoteric evaluations of historical Marxist documents. Rather it comes from what seems to be a straightforward observation that without a revolutionary movement, we will not generate sufficient power to bring about changes in the system so that human services can serve humans. Therefore the central question before us, as we go about our daily work, is how we can best spread radical ideas and build a revolutionary movement.

educational work

Peter Leonard, a radical British social worker and social work educator, has suggested that "the key task of radical practice is an educational one. This role aims at contributing to the development in people . . . of a critical consciousness of their oppression and of their potential, with others, of combating this oppression."[6] He suggests that facilitating the linkage of people with larger systems of people and building counter-systems, in other words, movement building, are additional aims of radical practice. There is no mystery about the criteria that must guide our practice. To the extent that we help to spread radical ideas more widely and deeply among those with whom we come into contact and facilitate the building of organizations that express those ideas, we will be helping to build a revolutionary movement.

In working to integrate political education with daily service efforts, we must be conscious of the requirements for any effective educational effort. In particular we must start within people's experience. There is little to be gained in presenting a complex theoretical analysis of the fiscal crisis of the state to a person whose overriding concern is to obtain a specific benefit. On the other hand, since recipients of social services, like anyone else, tend to

---

[6]Peter Leonard, "A Paradigm for Radical Pracitce," in *Radical Social Work*, eds. Roy Bailey and Mike Brake, p. 57.

view their situations by mixing conservative and radical perspectives, we have some common ground for pursuing the more radical side of their analyses. For example, some welfare recipients have internalized beliefs about the stigma of welfare and feel that receiving welfare represents a personal failure. Simultaneously they may be aware that they are oppressed by a system that does not provide adequate opportunities to work for all those who would like to do so. A radical worker would support these ideas as they came up or raise them when the opportunity presented itself. It might even be desirable to extend the discussion into such issues as the cooling out and coopting role of public welfare and its relationship to the maintenance of a reserve labor force. Such education starts with individual consciousness and individual experiences. This does not mean that the radical will not challenge ideas or introduce new ideas. It does mean that the worker supports the individual in questioning traditional assumptions about a given situation. Radical educational efforts of this sort do not impose an analysis onto the situation from the outside. Rather they help clarify a radical analysis based on an individual's own thinking.

Working in this fashion with social service users represents only one possible way of using our work as a tool for consciousness raising. As an example, we can dispel uninformed notions such as that doing radical educational work means pounding a foreign doctrine into unwilling ears. All of our interactions as social service workers have an educational aspect, whether intended or not. If we are not conscious of facilitating a particular interpretation of someone's situation, we may, perhaps unwittingly, be lending support to conventional conservative interpretations of the problem. Each interaction, each helping situation, each discrete aspect of our work, offers the opportunity for us to become clearer about a socialist analysis of that particular experience. Each such moment offers the opportunity to extend that understanding more broadly.

Introducing a radical perspective to others is not only a matter of clarifying the systemic roots of a particular problem. It also involves helping people to reexamine the widely shared assumption that we are unable to create change. People would be more ready to examine a radical analysis if they were not blocked by the sense that such analysis will not serve them as a basis for action. The anticipation of having no way to act on the basis of a radical analysis limits the possibility of becoming more radical. Developing a more integrated socialist outlook involves more than a radical analysis of capitalist society. A socialist perspective also involves understanding that the development of a revolutionary movement is both possible and likely and that we each can contribute to that movement. A socialist perspective is not a static analysis of what is. It is an analysis of what is and what is in the process of becoming. We are all limited in developing that analysis insofar as we feel and are powerless to intervene in the events of the world.

The sense of isolation we experience is a powerful conservatizing force. It undermines our developing a radical consciousness by limiting our awareness of the sense of the power we could have if we acted together. It encourages each of us to see ourselves, not only as having particular problems, but as being the exclusive cause and source of our burdens. Isolation leads to an individualistic, privatized, and self-critical analysis. Engagement with others is a potent mechanism for reevaluating that conservative analysis.

To the extent that we see ourselves as powerless, our perception becomes a self-fulfilling prophecy. A key part of radical practice is understanding that people's movements are created by people just like ourselves. The creation of such movements is difficult and long term but possible. We can participate in the creation of such movements, and we can develop the necessary skills of analysis and organization, just as we have learned other modes of analysis and action in our lives. In short radical social work is distinguished by its commitment to consciousness raising, political education, and collective action that can change social conditions.[7] Political education occurs when people learn the techniques of coming together for politcal action and when they experience the excitement and power of making a difference in social and political events.

movement building

We will not always have the opportunity to contribute to the building and strengthening of organizations that can promote radical change. However, we will often have such opportunities if we are alert to them. At various points we may be able to facilitate organization among service users, among coworkers, and among citywide and nationwide organizations. Many situations offer the possibility, if we are creative, for building collectivity, for challenging existing distributions of power, for struggling to shift power to the level of workers, service users, and community residents, and for devising alternative structures that can challenge organizations of the status quo. This may occur at a modest level, for example, through developing a radical caucus within a union. On the other hand, it may involve building a citywide organization of radical social service users, with a variety of possible agendas and directions, and with the potential of forming alliances with other political organizations, including those of social service users. The point that needs to be emphasized is that we must think in terms of building organizations based on a radical analysis with the goal of contributing to the development of a larger revolutionary movement. We may not always be willing or able to

---

[7]This dual focus is nicely formulated by John F. Longres, a paper and annotated bibliography entitled "Radical Social Work," presented at the Council on Social Work Education, Annual Program Meeting, March, 1977, Phoenix, Arizona, mimeographed.

make a full-time commitment, and we may not know how to make the perfect contribution in every situation. However, each of us can always make some contributions to the movement-building process that are consistent with our abilities, interests, and particular situations.

structural reforms

Structural reforms, or nonreformist reforms, represent those kinds of intermediate goals toward which we can strive, in a nonrevolutionary period. These reforms challenge basic structures and processes of capitalism, but they do not represent the achievement of socialist outcomes. For example, in the chapters which follow I will explore the possibilities for developing a socialist approach to direct service work, to change efforts within social agencies, to trade unionism among social service workers, and so on. In each case I do not suggest that a given strategy will "achieve socialism." However it will help to encourage the possibility of radical transformation by shifting more power into the hands of the working class as part of the process of achieving intermediate gains.

Not all issues contain similar potential to contribute to building radical momentum in the society. Wherever possible, it will be useful to focus on issues that highlight critical dilemmas of the social services and that reveal contradictions in the society as a whole. For example, organizing social service workers and helping them move in a collective and progressive direction draws attention to the larger analysis of the NWC and the fiscal crisis of the state. Enabling more social service users to challenge the social control functions of social services helps to expose the repressive political tendency of social services. On the other hand, bureaucratic infighting, even when it leads to more adequate delivery of service, does not necessarily organize and politicize the people we need to reach.

However, general guidelines are no substitute for the detailed and difficult work of making particular analyses of specific agencies, policy arenas and local power structures. In relation to a particular agency, we need to become as clear as possible about the functions it serves in the larger social and/or political arena. Similarly it is useful to analyze an agency's connections with other institutions and people to uncover and specify the role it plays, the political interests it serves, and its points of vulnerability. Where is the agency culpable? Who, in addition to service users, benefits financially, politically, or in other ways from agency policy? In what ways does the agency serve as a mechanism of control? In what ways does it fail to serve the best interests of service users? In what ways are workers exploited?

When we have addressed some of these questions, even if only in a preliminary way, we can begin to explore issues that raise the potential to organize. Then we will need to make choices. We will do so on the basis of several criteria, including the relevance of our particular choice to the larger social and political dynamics involved in radical change. We will also select issues on the basis of their viability as organizing foci.

Issue viability refers to the potential of a particular issue to stimulate people to take political action and to do so in a way that opens the possibility of deepening their analysis of social and political realities. Similarly the extent to which a given issue offers the potential to move from a more discrete concern to broader concerns is critical. Issues may arise that reflect gross injustices and irrationalities in the society. However, they may not be issues around which people can be mobilized, for any of a variety of reasons—for example, the constituency involved may be scattered or internally divided. Alternatively people may be mobilized around issues in a conservative direction that is not immediately amenable to influence. There is not a single guideline for the question of choosing issues. However, we will have a more clear-minded basis for selecting issues if we think about issue selection with these multiple criteria in mind.

Issues frequently emerge on the basis of a conflict that arises in a given situation, rather than on the basis of a conscious decision that a given issue makes sense as an organizing tool. A strike will occur among agency workers; a citizen's group will mobilize in response to a particularly atrocious policy; a budget cut-back will galvanize the formation of a service user's group. It is important to stay attuned to these developments and to the opportunities they present for mobilizing larger numbers of people into political action. Life will not always present us with choices about the political issues that are lively. We need to be prepared to engage issues as they arise as well as to stimulate motion during a more quiet period.

Paying Attention to Ourselves

personal readiness and commitment

Earlier I suggested that the pursuit of long-term radical political goals and the immediate requirements of direct service delivery must not be conceptualized as mutually exclusive or antagonistic concerns. By the same line of reasoning, our commitments to larger radical agendas and our perfectly reasonable need to nurture ourselves in the short run are best understood as complementary processes. In order to integrate our political work with our personal needs and desires, we must legitimate caring for ourselves as we commit ourselves to radical politics, and we must develop approaches to our political lives that facilitate both kinds of concerns.

If we are to be responsible in undertaking any sort of action in the world, we must inevitably consider our own preparedness, abilities, needs, commitment, and levels of energy as we make the decision to act. This is as it should be. We will not be successful, and we will be limited in our ability to sustain our efforts if we feel consistently overextended, if we act without the internal and external supports we need, or if we simply do not have the personal skill to do the job. For a number of reasons this common sense observation is frequently overlooked as people consider moving in a more committed, radical direction. They too often stop assessing themselves as an important variable, and for a period of time they hold out the single standard of total, full-time commitment to radical organizational work. For some this means that they can never begin to be more engaged, since so much seems to be required. Others engage and quickly disengage as the demands prove too heavy. Either response limits the growth of the individual and the strength of the movement.

It is useful to ask a series of questions of ourselves as well as of the external political environment. These include, What feels right to me? What represents a next step for me? How can I extend my commitment and energy beyond where I am now, and yet not so far that I am quickly forced to retreat? What kinds of engagements will facilitate my growth? What political work will be consistent with my interests and abilities? Not everyone is willing or able to make the investments of energy and to take the risks that would accompany a full-time commitment to radical politics. An accurate assessment of ourselves is a legitimate and necessary component of our political analysis.

ambivalence

Many people are unclear about their political views and about their willingness and ability to commit themselves to political activism. To some extent we are all murky about our politics, and we are not helped to become more clear-minded by the incomplete and confused political education we usually receive. Therefore a useful starting point in assessing our own willingness and ability to become radical political people is acknowledging that we are not always completely clear about what a radical commitment implies, in terms of a larger analytic stance toward the world or in terms of the implications of such a commitment in our daily lives. To acknowledge that confusion means to accept it as our present condition. We should not disqualify ourselves as political people because we are not completely clear about the implications which follow from our radical inclinations. At the same time, we cannot be complacent about our shortcomings in analyzing social life and our relation to it more clearly. We can allow ourselves to participate on the basis of our present level of sophistication about radical politics and simultaneously strive to be active in our efforts to become more clear and purposeful.

It is helpful to acknowledge that all of us, without exception, are somewhat ambivalent about our commitment to radical politics. We are all a mixture of radical and conservative impulses and ideas. In fact it is inevitable that we should experience this mixture and confusion. We all have a conservative side as a consequence of having matured in a society which encourages noncritical thinking, which promises substantial rewards for conventional behavior, and which does not accept the validity of a critical or socialist perspective. We all have been raised within the value system and ideology of capitalist society. In all of us there is a part that clings to the belief that what we have been told about the meaning of our lives and about the legitimacy of our society is true, and that wants fame and fortune. No one wants to assume a deviant role or to view life in terms of struggle. None of us has completely overcome our sense of powerlessness, naivete, and fear of difference. Though we may have moved in a radical direction, we can never completely eradicate that part of our analysis and consciousness that is conditioned by conventional social views.

At the same time, we all have a radical side to our personalities and to our social analysis. Though the most vehement anticommunist among us might become enraged at explicitly radical ideas, it is entirely possible that the same person would support them if they were presented in a way which does not tap into the stereotypes created by leftist jargon. At the same time that we are socialized in the conventional modes, we are living in a society that does little to nurture our hope, joy, and sense of self-fulfillment. Frequently society makes our lives more difficult. Whatever the rhetoric about the role of government, for example, and however much we accept that rhetoric, the common experience of our lives is that public services neither do serve us in the way we would like nor act in our interests. Our experience tells us the truth about the society, and that truth encourages our radicalism. The fact that our analytic scheme does not support our experience gives rise to the ambivalence and confusion we feel about radical ideas and radical politics.

What attitude and stance should we take toward this ambivalence? Unfortunately the attitude that some people take (also the attitude assumed by many people active in the left) is often not helpful. It disqualifies others as contributors to socialist transformation. We must find ways to accept more people investigating a more radical stance even though they may be unsure about their level of commitment and understanding. Similarly the position of some leftists that people are either "with us or against us" guarantees that most people will be against us. People on the left have too often assumed a "lefter than thou" posture which does not facilitate openness, questioning, or an honest exploration of political ambivalence. We must find ways to question and challenge without condemnation that part of ourselves and others that is not radical. And we cannot afford to overlook or dismiss that part of ourselves and others that is open to radicalism and to political growth.

We can meet ambivalence by recognizing that all of us are a mixture of radical and conservative ideas and impulses. The most conservative person is not totally conservative, and the most radical person is not totally radical. It cannot be otherwise. The differences between us are differences in the balance of the two perspectives. This does not mean that we can or should be indifferent to our conservative sides and that we need not struggle against that side in ourselves and others. We should. However we need to do so in a way that supports efforts to grow and to engage and that does not disqualify actual or potential allies in progressive change efforts. This stance allow us to participate in the process of exploration and activism at whatever point on the political spectrum we find ourselves and to move forward from there. We will not change ourselves or the world if we wait for a time when we are free of ambivalence or a time when we have found the moment, project, or people that perfectly fit our images of what it means to us to "be radical." Being more radical in our lives, that is, becoming more consistent with a socialist analysis, is not an event. It is a process.

changing ourselves

There are a number of concrete steps we can take to help ourselves move toward a clearer stance that allows us to express our political concerns less ambivalently. We are not compelled to wait passively for "things to change," and we cannot afford to do so.

I have already suggested that we accept our own confusion and ambivalence. Part of this process involves looking critically at the aspects of our lives that actually satisfy us and provide us with the greatest value. It is best done in conjunction with others, but it can be initiated alone. Our society has told us a very lengthy story about ourselves. The story is based on assumptions which are either false or only partially true. They are assumptions about life which capitalism generates and perpetrates to encourage us to commit ourselves to the capitalist system. They do not fit the realities of our lives as we find out when we examine our lives on the basis of our own direct experience.

We need to tell the truth about ourselves to ourselves. This is not an easy process since we have been told lies about ourselves and we have internalized those lies. We need to cut through self-destructive beliefs about ourselves. For example, we may have come to believe that we work and struggle in order to make more money and in order to "get ahead" and that this is both necessary for our survival (which it is) and also the fullest expression of our basic human impulses (which it is not). We must reconnect with that part of us which wants to serve others, to be socially useful, to experience love and community, and to be creative in our work and our lives.

Similarly we need to confront our unwillingness to become involved in social and political life. Very few people are "born organizers." Few of us spontaneously thrive on organizational life, as we now know it. Most of have vaguely frightening or explicitly alienating visions of what it means to involve ourselves in radical organizations. These ideas will not dissolve without conscious efforts on our part. We can simultaneously be true to and respect our ambivalence, and we can push ourselves to investigate ways to become more involved in organized expressions of our radical commitments. As we do so, we can ease the process by recognizing that, as with any new endeavor, we will at first feel unsure of ourselves and somewhat uncomfortable. Many people are uncomfortable in the role of novice, especially when they have achieved competence in some other areas of their lives. And just as surely we will change over time as we participate. We will become more confident and we will find radical work a more natural expression of our interests and commitments. It will not happen magically, and it will happen only if we persist.

The importance of contact with others who have like-minded ideas or who are wrestling with the same issues cannot be overestimated. In the process of internalizing conservative ideas and values, we have borne the weight of most of the significant people and significant institutions that touch our lives. To develop a counterideology on our own is to face a very powerful and subtle opponent without collective support. Even our preliminary efforts to work with others on political issues has the value of reducing our sense of isolation and uneasiness about the radical ideas we hold. The official organs of society offer very little validation for the legitimacy of a radical perspective, and we cannot expect them to do so, given the class interests which they represent. Working with other radical or even ambivalently radical people, reading literature that analyzes events from a socialist perspective, and engaging in a left political culture may seem unfamiliar initially. However these are extremely useful and necessary steps in our efforts to deal with our own confusion about political directions.

Finally as we consider the question of becoming part of a larger political process, we must face the reality that movement groups and movement work have too frequently *asked of* participants, and not often enough *given to* participants. In saying this we need to be careful not to blame some group of people, whom we locate as existing "out there" in the political universe at a distance from ourselves. "We" and "they" are the same people. All of us who have been involved in organized political work have been shortsighted in failing to attend to our own needs to make organizational work pleasurable, growth producing, and personally satisfying, as well as on-target in its larger political goals. In fact not only has the left too frequently failed to attend to the personal and group needs of left activists, in some cases it has argued that to attend to personal and interpersonal issues distracts from the most important work to be done, and reflects traditional kinds of individualism or excessive self-preoccupation.

One result has been the high burn-out rate among political activists. However creative a political project might be, it will not sustain personal energies and will not nurture activists unless it offers opportunities for supportive interpersonal contact, individual growth, and for personal political development, and unless it is fun, at least part of the time. The legacy of left political work as grim, humorless, cold, and self-denying haunts us too much. The women's movement, by focusing on the lives of women inside and outside the movement, has helped to legitimate the idea that the personal is political and that political work and personal growth need to be, and are, integrated concerns. This thinking needs to be extended more broadly.

As we engage in left political work, we will often find that such work is not supportive and pleasurable. We must face this reality squarely. Part of our commitment to building a viable movement should include efforts to influence these aspects of political work. We must think of our personal needs and the needs of those we involve. We must help to move organized political work in the direction of providing a supportive culture for individuals. At present we often seek personal support and growth outside of the context of the political work we do. The left has been antipsychological and too often not supportive of opportunities for personal growth. On the other hand, the multitudes of therapies and personal growth opportunities that abound in the society are limited by their lack of understanding or by their inability or unwillingness to address the social and political issues that have such enormous impact on people. Our job is to learn from such activities so that we are better able to integrate their power with the political and social concerns and visions of the left.

For example, in organized political work, we need to become involved with other leftist people on a personal level. We need to make time in political meetings for personal feedback, for criticism and self-criticism, and for recreation. We must attend to the maintenance needs of the groups we form as well as to the externally directed tasks of the group. In general we ought to take care of ourselves. And in fact we have the opportunity and potential to do so in a way that can prove richer and more fulfilling than the conventional version of satisfaction and of growth. The left is based on collectivist notions which are, at least theoretically, supportive of community. The left encourages the notion of struggling against repression, both within society and within the individual. The left has a way of looking at the impact of the broader society on our individual sense of well-being or lack of well-being. On the basis of that analytic perspective, the left has the opportunity to fashion organizations and approaches to issues that serve us fully in a personal sense. To struggle within political organizations to make political work an enriching personal experience is not to graft a foreign body onto political work. Rather it is to struggle to hole our political involvements true to their promise of representing a better way to approach and live life. Our political work can immediately pay off for us in personal terms if we all attend to the personal issues in a caring and collective fashion.

7

Direct Service

Technique versus Direction

This chapter focuses on ways to bring a radical political commitment to bear on the dynamics of direct service to people who use the social agencies in which we work. Most workers will express their socialist commitments in this arena of social work practice simply because they spend a good deal of the time and energy on direct service delivery and on the problems of service users. We must stay attuned to the possibilities of expressing our politics in a variety of ways beyond the immediate circumstances of service provision. At the same time, if we can find ways to integrate our politics with the daily occurrences of work, as I believe we can, we will have tapped a good deal of potential for reaching a significant number of people and for creatively directing our political energies toward the most substantial part of our practice.

The ways in which any worker or group of workers bring their socialist commitments to their practice will vary a good deal. The nature of the setting and the characteristics and interests of those who use the service will be critical factors in shaping the possibilities for radical work. The issues that arise, the readiness of service users to explore alternative perspectives and actions, and the risk involved will differ in a counselling situation in a mental health center, a youth program in a community center or settlement house, a welfare office, a day program for senior adults, an institutional setting for delinquent youth, or a social service unit in a hospital, to name just a few of the many and diverse settings in which social workers find themselves.

Because there is such variety in social service settings, and because conditions vary so widely even within ostensibly similar settings, it is not possible to make simple generalizations about strategy in direct service situations. However it is possible to suggest some unifying themes since radical practice focuses on the central concerns of movement building and revolutionary change, as well as on meeting immediate needs.

It is important to emphasize the necessity of developing our practice within a larger political framework. We will not accurately understand or deal with the parts unless we can grasp the totality. Another way to make the same point is to say that radical practice requires radical theory. Even with only a brief introduction to socialist theory and commitments, social service workers can find ways to act on their views and will, in the process, develop a more specific set of practice guidelines.

I emphasize the critical importance of working within an overall political analysis for a specific and practical reason. There is a logic to social service agencies as there is a logic to capitalist society as a whole. It is not a logic that serves us maximally, and yet it is a logic that provides a way of looking at each situation by offering a plausible rationale for conventional practice. If we act on the basis of conventional wisdom, or make what seems to be the most immediately expedient choice in a given situation, we will most likely operate within the logic of the existing system and so will make our small contribution to re-creating that system. Socialist theory suggests an alternative logic, and it is that logic which must direct us in our practice. Since a socialist perspective is not contained in the daily messages we receive from conventional sources, we will need to be as clear as possible about guiding principles as we proceed with daily work. Otherwise in the face of the rationalizations presented on behalf of the status quo, we can lose sight of our political direction.

For example, in the conventional views about our society which are reinforced through most books, newspapers, and television, there is very little analysis of people's ability or willingness to examine the world from a radical perspective. Of course the conventional analysis of capitalist society does not focus on its inherent contradictions and does characterize radicalism, when it examines it as deviant, rather than as a logical response to an unhealthy society. If we focus our own attention on the surface of social life instead of on the underlying reality, we too may conclude that a radical response to the society is idiosyncratic. On the other hand a socialist analysis directs us more toward the repression that keeps radical impulses from spontaneously expressing themselves. These alternative views influence the way we practice, for example, by influencing our willingness to put our energies into facilitating radical activity among service users.

The fundamental assumptions and commitments of radical practice and conventional practice differ and oppose each other in significant ways, so they can easily be distinguished. In saying this it is useful to acknowledge that it is not always possible to act in a completely consistent way in every situation. In these cases we will need to look to facets of our work other than direct contact with service users to express ourselves politically. At the same time, the experience of radical social workers is that there are always some arenas of work in which radical politics can inform their practice.[1]

Radicals do not express their commitments through particular techniques. In fact the techniques radicals employ, even when they are most self-conscious in developing a radical practice, are not inconsistent with humanitarian liberal techniques. For example, when liberals formulate practice principles in a caring way, they are likely to emphasize equalitarianism in the helping relationship, their responsibility for facilitating service users' sense of competence and empowerment, and their commitment to helping people sort out real world oppressive situations from internal distortions. Radicals have no monopoly on openness or personal sharing in the helping relationship. They are not the only ones to shift a helping situation from a one-to-one encounter to an organizing effort on behalf of a group of service users facing a similar problem.[2] Nor is it necessary to approach an agency situation from a radical perspective to know that agencies often operate on the basis of destructive policies and that social work practice may involve efforts to organize workers within an agency to challenge agency practices. Certain techniques are common to any organizing effort. For example, first approach a few coworkers, then a larger number of coworkers, identify issues

---

[1]The number of studies of the actual practice of radical workers in social service settings is limited. The analysis and reporting of efforts to develop radical approaches to direct service delivery is one of the needs of radical social workers and is one thrust for a contribution to the development of radical social work practice.

In addition to the experiences which I have directly observed, been part of, or which have been reported to me by participants, I have had the benefit of the following documents. Paul Neustadt, "Radicals in Clinical Social Work: How Their Radicalism Is Expressed In Their Practice," A paper presented to the Graduate School of Social Work and Social Research, Bryn Mawr College, May, 1977; Carolyn Kott Washburne, "Social Work After the Revolution," Paper Presented to the School of Social Work, University of Pennsylvania, 1971; and Philip Lichtenberg, "Therapy Within a Radical Political Context," School of Social Work and Social Research, Bryn Mawr College, 1977, mimeographed.

[2]For example, see Ruth R. Middleman and Gale Goldberg, *Social Service Delivery: A Structural Approach* (New York: Columbia University Press, 1974) for a presentation of moving from individual to collective solutions, written from a political vantage point that does not rest on an explicitly radical analysis.

on which people can be mobilized, hold an organizing meeting that engages people and stimulates them to act, and formulate strategies that are designed to produce the desired results. The best practice techniques from a liberal or humanitarian perspective will provide radical practice with a methodology of intervention at the level of technique. The use to which technique is put, rather than technique itself, distinguishes radical from conventional practice.

Political Organizing as Social Work Practice

introduction

In order to emphasize the linkages between direct practice and a commitment to revolutionary change, I am introducing the discussion of direct practice by focusing on linkages between the immediate interaction of worker and service user, and on the possibilities for moving to more organized expressions of political activity. The sections which immediately follow explore three possibilities for facilitating the organization of service users; uniting service users involved with a direct service setting; linking service users with outside, existing political organizations of service users; and supporting those organizations in other ways. I will then consider ways to bring a socialist perspective to bear on the casework dynamic in situations where no immediate organizing possibilities exist. That situation presents greater problems of political consistency and must be explored. Finally I will suggest some approaches to a socialist perspective on the community-organizing task within social work. Since, from a socialist perspective, the practice of casework must move toward organizing, the explicit discussion of community organization will be relevant for other arenas of practice as well.

organizing service users in a clinical setting

The caseworker who is intent on facilitating political organization among service users must necessarily see the opportunities present in any situation for bringing service users together to address political issues that have a progressive impact. In these times it is unlikely that an explicitly socialist agenda will be in the forefront of such organizations. That is simply not where most people are at this time (though it may be possible in some cases, and we should not make the mistake of lagging politically behind those we hope to mobilize). However if we can organize a constituency, encourage the development of heightened political consciousness and power, and facilitate struggles for self-determination in the face of system-maintaining bureaucracies, we will have made some contribution.

Settings vary, of course, as does the political climate that is so influential in shaping any particular organizing effort. However even the most quiet times and unlikely settings may offer some possibilities if we are alert to them. Residential settings, such as mental hospitals or youth detention centers, by virtue of the total control they maintain over residents, present obvious problems for organizing. At the same time, structures that offer some opportunity for more advanced organizing work may already exist in such settings for example, resident advisory boards. While these patient or client committees tend to be relatively insignificant in their impact on critical institutional issues, they may provide a base for more serious political work over time. They are an obvious assignment for progressive workers. Creating a bill of rights for service users is another organizing focus for such settings, as are campaigns for greater self-management and self-governance. Institutional settings also lend themselves to creating linkages with outside groups who have a stake in the institution, whether they be groups of ex-offenders, mental patients, or friends and relatives. In the last decade organizers have created important political momentum even in the most repressive institutions, for example, prisons. While the circumstances differ in each setting, the existence of progressive movements even in these residential settings suggests that there are ways to make a difference wherever we are.

The National Welfare Rights Organization, established in the mid-1960s, is a notable example of the kind of impact that progressive social workers can have in facilitating the organization of service users. There were many strands in the development of the organization, including a decade of political activism on civil rights issues that established a supportive climate for further political struggle. That climate influenced large numbers of welfare recipients, who were increasingly prepared to view themselves as having legal and moral rights to welfare, and it also influenced a generation of social service providers, many of whom were imbued with the sense of political activism that characterized the 1960s. Social service workers employed by War on Poverty agencies were a significant force in helping to establish the first Mothers for Welfare groups that were a prototype for the more sophisticated National Welfare Rights Organization. Organizers hired by the antipoverty agencies helped bring together potential activists while caseworkers identified particular problems in welfare policy, referred potential recruits to the organization, and carried on a bureaucratic dog-fights with welfare offices over the specific injustices done to the people with whom they were working.[3]

---

[3]A useful discussion is Frances Fox Piven and Richard A. Cloward, "The Welfare Rights Movement," *Poor People's Movements,* eds. Frances Fox Piven and Richard A. Cloward (New York: Pantheon, 1977), pp. 264–361.

To illustrate more fully the idea of moving from direct service to organizing, I offer an extended example from the child welfare sector, with special emphasis on the issue of foster home placement.[4] Foster home placement agencies are frequently private agencies, though they generally work closely with public welfare agencies which provide referrals and which ultimately are the source of much agency funding. Social workers in such settings have a hard time doing their jobs. When they remove children from their natural parents, they must deal with very angry parents who, whatever problems they have in raising their children, frequently do not want to lose their children. In dealing with foster parents social workers face a situation in which the foster parents develop an investment in raising their foster children and fear that they will lose them, given their secondary legal status. Workers are asked to make very difficult choices which require weighing the rights of natural parents, foster parents, and of course, the children themselves, in a situation marked by a lack of resources or misdirected resources. They must deal with the paradoxical and cruel policy that allocates monies to foster parents, not to natural parents. Similarly more money is available to a foster parent than is available to a natural parent through public assistance payments. In any case the total amounts of financial support available to sustain families, whether foster or natural, is very limited and additional resources, for example, trained home aides who might intervene in the natural family to help tide a family over a crisis, are simply not available on the scale required. An additional tension is introduced when, as is frequently the case, white social workers are called upon to deal with a disproportionate number of minority cases.

Faced with this difficult situation, many social workers do their utmost to work out decent compromises among valid and competing claims and pressures. The worker burn-out rate is high, as would be expected. The task is frustrating. It is difficult to achieve solutions that satisfy all parties. The solutions that are worked out are often successful for only a short time, and the value questions involved in these decisions are complex and contradictory in their implications.

What are the possibilities within this setting for organizing service users in a way that has both immediate service implications and long-term political potential? One way to approach this question is to analyze the political ramifications of the service as it presently functions.

Several political realities stand out. The state intervenes in the family life of large numbers of minority people in this country. While foster agencies may nominally be located in the private sector, both the funding sources and the policy mandates within which they operate make them functional

---

[4]This example emerged from conversations with Linda Barth, a friend and social worker in a child welfare agency.

extensions of the public sector. The state extends it reach, as it has increasingly done throughout this century, into the innermost fabric of our personal experiences. In the case of child welfare issues, the state mandates when a child will be removed from its natural family, where it will be placed, if and when it will be returned to the natural family, and how acceptable its family's life style is. Even if the standards by which the state assessed suitable family life were completely acceptable to those whose lives are directly affected (which they are not) those affected would still feel helpless because of the way in which the state uses the power it has.

In some situations, the best interests of the child would be sacrificed if the child remained with the natural family. In such cases changes should be made in children's living arrangements. Further, child welfare agencies often do make particular situations more tolerable and even more life-supporting than they were prior to intervention. However, these benefits do not alter the fact that the same service also helps to establish the omnipresence of the state in the lives of working people, especially the lives of those who have low incomes and who are minorities.

A second strand of the analysis highlights the fact that the process of foster care creates considerable antagonism between natural and foster parents. They come to see each other as competing groups since the child is taken from the natural parents, given to the foster parents (with visitations and so on worked out as possible) and then, in some cases, removed from the foster parents and returned to the natural parents. This approach to the problem assures enmity, or at least mutual suspiciousness.

Standing back, we can see that foster and natural parents often have a good deal in common. Both kinds of families tend to be working class and disproportionately from minority groups. The differences that do exist are real and need to be acknowledged in any service situation. However from a larger political perspective, we cannot overlook the fact that child welfare services have the effect of introducing a competitive, divisive dynamic into the life of minority communities.

Finally foster agencies tend to operate on the basis of a white, Anglo-Saxon, heterosexual emphasis on the nuclear family as the primary appropriate environment for child raising and tend to overlook the power and potential of the often quite viable extended family and extended network that operate within minority communities. Child welfare services undermine the sustaining psychological power and political potential of the extended network.

How might social workers attempt to bring service users with a stake in foster care together in a way that speaks to their immediate concerns and to long-range political development? One issue that can mobilize both foster and natural parents is their sense of powerlessness over their personal affairs in relation to the agency and, with varying levels of awareness, to the state. A possible organizing focus, then, is the issue of self-determination in decision making on child welfare cases.[5]

Child welfare agencies often create advisory boards of various sorts and just as frequently the agencies are frustrated by parents who do not exhibit a great deal of interest in participating on them. However, the role of such boards tends to be quite limited; their impact on critical issues is minimal. So it is hardly surprising that members invest little time or energy in an advisory role.

Perhaps, then, a social worker might take on the following tasks in this setting. Organize the parents and foster parents who show some ability to make a more systematic analysis of their situation. This organizing work might be an extension of the work of an existing advisory board or it might take place outside of a preexisting structure through contacts with individual cases. Devise a possible agenda for this group based on the idea that parents and foster parents can press for a central role in deciding about contested cases or can serve as an appeal panel for parents, foster parents, or children who feel unfairly treated by the agency. Such a group might challenge the agency's definition of a suitable setting for children and might develop new understandings of the possibilities for child care, for example, by pressing for the acceptance of an extended family or a network as a suitable arrangement for children. The group might also formulate political strategies that would link them with like-minded people who seek to challenge those larger policies that do not support families in the society, for example in economic ways. They might advocate total control of family services by local communities and supportive state grants with no strings attached.

Why pursue this possibility? What is to be gained? How can a concerned worker endorse the transfer of such powers to a service users' group when the worker makes the argument, as many can well do, that professional judgment is an important and helpful tool in many child welfare cases?

This strategy brings people together around issues that are of both immediate concern and of longer range political potential. In the short run a service users' group with the suggested focus and with some organized power would undoubtedly influence an agency's policies in a proservice user way, even though it would be unlikely to achieve its ultimate goals. In the short run the sense of empowerment that service users felt as a result of this

---

[5]It is true that the level of personal pathology in some people is so great that they cannot function effectively in the larger political arena. Regardless of the root causes of that pathology, we cannot expect all persons with whom we work in a service context to be capable of or open to political involvement. However, too often social service workers err in the other direction. They make blanket assumptions about the organizational and political disinterest or incompetence of the entire category of people with whom they work. It is this latter assumption, I believe, which poses the greater danger to human welfare.

political involvement would surely have a positive effect on their ability to deal productively with their immediate child care situations.

In the longer run the issues that such a group could raise would point in the direction of community empowerment, of challenge to the state, of confrontation with unsatisfactory aspects of social policy, and of attempts to reverse and even to capitalize on the divisive influence of much social policy. Such a group could help to make explicit the implicit, conservative, political nature of child welfare services. It could help make child welfare services another arena in which the controlling and often racist role of the state is exposed and confronted. In the process it would provide a living laboratory for both political education and for education in organizing and developing strategies.

Such a group might not be successful in achieving a victory in peer review and decision making procedures for placements by child welfare agencies at least in the short run. Such a shift would violate too many professional canons and would also confront too directly the state's desire and need to maintain control. If the efforts of the group were joined with the efforts of many such groups, however, and if this were to take place in a more vitalized climate—which is not unreasonable to anticipate—some movement in this direction might very well be possible. It would be unlikely to be fully successful in the absence of a powerful revolutionary movement since even these relatively simple agendas challenge a great deal in the present pattern of social services. However, even partial success would be potentially meaningful when we assess success using the criteria of its impact on long-term political development and on immediate improvements in the service situation.

In view of the personal investment many individuals have made in the outcome of these decisions and what child welfare workers see as high degrees of personal disorganization in the lives of many of those with whom they work, this assessment must address the issue which caring social workers will rightly raise about the appropriateness of user-controlled service. Whatever the shortcomings and the larger political implications of current modes of decision making, at the least, argue concerned workers, their best, disinterested judgments can prevail with the hope of introducing some increased sanity and humanness into a given situation.

In the short run this may be true. It may be that some decisions would be made that would not serve the best short-term interest of individuals as well as would a conventional approach. On the other hand, we must not underestimate people's ability and willingness to be creative and to serve others when they have won the power to do so through their own political efforts. Nor can we overlook the fact that the mistaken or unhelpful judgments such a group might make must be weighed against the unhelpful or mistaken judgements that paid workers now make.

Equally significant, we must assess our approach against a larger political perspective. The long-term empowerment of people is the critical variable in revolutionary change. It is also the critical variable in challenging oppressive agency policies and in creating a society in which adequate resources can be devoted to problems, such as those addressed by child welfare agencies. In the absence of larger radical change, child welfare workers will always be forced to make choices between painfully and marginally acceptable alternatives, and they will never have the resources they need to be helpful to families in the way that concerned workers would like to be. The directions for organizing and empowering service users suggested here create new problems, but they also point to a way of linking short-term service issues with longer-term political development. To the extent that social service workers are committed to adequate child welfare and family provision, they will need to shift from a short-term perspective on their role, in which they attempt to mediate an essentially unworkable situation, to a longer term view in which they recognize that participating in radical organization makes a powerful contribution to meeting the needs of children and families.

facilitating political engagement: linking service users with existing political organizations

Thus far in exploring ways workers can facilitate political organization among service users, I have focused on developing new political groupings. Workers may also find a variety of ways to encourage people to engage in collective political activity through existing political organizations.

Many social service workers are not fully aware of such organizations or the work they do partly because radical or progressive organizations are not now sufficiently powerful to establish a well understood public presence. Our knowledge of such groups and their work is also limited by the fact that what we do know about them comes to us largely through public information sources dominated by a class which has a stake in minimizing the impact of such organizations and in distorting their analyses and work.

Social service workers operating from a conventional political outlook make it their business to learn about resources in the community that can be useful to those with whom they work. They learn the ins and outs of applying for welfare, of negotiating with job placement services, and so on, as well they should. By the same token, as we develop a radical approach to social service work, we must set ourselves the task of investigating appropriate political resources in the community and determining their relevance to the particular issues faced by those with whom we work.

There are a number of steps we can take to learn more about what is happening in our communities in the arena of radical politics. Many people find that more information about the existence and the work of radical groups comes their way as they themselves become more open to a radical perspective. Information about radical groups is, in fact, more available in society than we believe. When such groups are more visible in society people tend to screen out the information they present. One step we can take to learn more about the important political work they do is simply to be open to learning about that work. As we become more open, we will discover that information is available.

There are other steps we can take to learn more about what is happening in the radical movement. As we participate in political work, we will necessarily put ourselves into a network in which news of other political work will be part of our own political environment. We can also subscribe to the newsletters of various organizations as well as to the alternative presses that carry notices of political events and reports of left political organizations. If and when we commit ourselves to this level of political education, there is no doubt that over time we can considerably enrich our awareness of the political resources of our communities.

Each city and state will vary in the political organizations it has to offer in support of those we serve and as a vehicle for political involvement. Larger urban areas will be likely to have more resources than smaller communities, though even smaller communities may have several relevant organizations. In larger cities there is scarcely an area of concern to social service practice in which some progressive political group is not at work. For example, in many cities there are active women's organizations concerned with abortion, women's health care, rape, and wife abuse. Given the disproportionate number of social service users who are women and the extent to which the problems they bring to social agencies have deep roots in the prevailing sexism of the society, it seems natural that radical social service workers would inform themselves about these groups, the kinds of work they do, and the kinds of people whom they attract. Radical social workers should make efforts to facilitate the connections between women's groups and at least some of the people with whom they work.[6]

Similarly in many cities there are organizations specifically concerned with the political rights as well as the personal and cultural issues of gay people. Here, too, a radical social worker might well benefit many social

---

[6]This suggestion illustrates an earlier point about technique as opposed to political direction. In effect, I am suggesting here an extension or version of a classical piece of social work practice, namely, referral. The techniques will not necessarily differ from any well done referral. This may require that the worker learn first hand what the political group is about so that the chances of the connection being an appropriate one are increased. The worker may alert people in that group to the possibility that a new member or potential member may be on the way. The worker may follow up with the person referred to help interpret what that person found when encountering a group of new people, possibly a specialized political jargon, and so on.

service users by becoming familiar with some of these organizations and their work, and by legitimating and facilitating the involvement of gay service users with such groups. The range of organizations devoted to this one issue is wide and includes in many cities, a gay bookstore, a gay community center, a gay counselling center, and various political groupings concerned with legislative and policy issues of particular concern to gays. Similarly in many cities there are a variety of community based groups which organize on a neighborhood basis around local, city, and statewide issues.

We will often discover a variety of organizations structured on the basis of interests that parallel those of the social agencies themselves. In many cities, for example, political groupings of mental patients and ex-mental patients operate on the basis of a fairly sophisticated analysis of the political nature of the mental health establishment, its repressive characteristics, and its linkages with capitalism. They engage in educational work, research, and direct organizing and action in an effort to stimulate political action through the mobilization of mental patients themselves. Groups of addicts and ex–addicts, in similar fashion, base their challenge to current practices on a radical analysis of the nature of services to and for addicts. They also work to mobilize and organize those most directly influenced by such services.

Areas in which there are relatively long histories of organizing are housing and welfare. Some tenants' groups have developed a quite sophisticated political analysis.[7] They may assist tenants with individual housing problems, help to organize rent strikes or other collective action, and work to bring people who become involved with them through these efforts into coordinated action, focused on a tenants' bill of rights, cooperative home ownership, and so on. To the extent that those with whom we work have housing problems, facilitating their involvement with such organizations can make a good deal of sense both in working to solve an immediate problem and in encouraging them to develop a political self-concept through the linkage that can be made between their particular problem and the larger issues. Similarly the Welfare Rights Organization, though not at the height of its political powers, continues to provide both case assistance and a vehicle for political action for welfare recipients in some cities.

A characteristic shared by many of the service-related organizations is that each, in its own way, challenges the social welfare establishment's definition of the given problem. That can be of particular importance to those with whom we work. The underlying analysis that informs the way in which a particular problem is defined is as much an arena for political struggle as is

---

[7]Some examples are the National Tenant Organization (348 W. 121 Street, New York, New York 10027); the Cambridge Tenant Organizing Committee, publishers of the Somerville Free Press (38 Union Square, Somerville, Massachusetts 02143); and, Shelter Force (380 Main Street, East Orange, New Jersey 07018).

the response to the problem once it is defined. For example, when social service agencies or social service workers define homosexuality as deviance even the most caring individual response will be based on a distorted understanding of the actual reality of the service user. Gay liberation organizations operate on the basis of fundamentally different assumptions about homosexuality. By their very existence and by the specific issues they address, they challenge understandings of homosexuality that are derived from deviancy theory. For example, they assert the right of gay couples to adopt children and to be supported in their efforts to do so by social agencies. The Welfare Rights Organization has helped to shift the self-definition of some welfare recipients from beneficiaries of charity to entitled recipients of legally mandated services. Organizations of mental patients have helped to challenge the apolitical definition of mental illness by raising questions about the political purposes served by various kinds of diagnoses and by the treatments which then follow. In each of these cases, the specific therapeutic impact on those involved can be significant in a way that no amount of counselling in a traditional agency could match. Equally important, the changed consciousness that results has an appropriate vehicle for expression at the next level of political engagement on the problem.

supporting existing organizations of service recipients

There are a number of ways in which radical service providers have facilitated the work of existing political groups of social service users, in addition to referring new members. These possibilities represent another way to encourage the political activism of service users.

Sympathetic workers can alert organized groups of service users to internal agency policy developments around which they might mobilize.[8] For example, in one case, workers in a state mental hospital and an organized group of ex-mental patients developed a useful linkage to fight against abuses of mental patients in hospitals and to challenge the control functions of the mental health establishment. This linkage enabled the outside group to publicize the abuse of patients in the hospital and led to a major investigation of the hospital which resulted in progressive changes. At the same time, it provided the group with a useful organizing focus that enabled it to build strength and to reach new people with a political analysis of the functions of mental health agencies. In another case a progressive administrator in a large mental hospital used his position to encourage his hospital to sponsor a conference for a wide range of advocacy groups concerned with

---

[8]Useful case material and suggestions are found in Robert Knickmeyer, "A Radical Critique of Political Activism in Health, Education and Social Service Institutions," State University College at Oswego, New York, June, 1975, mimeographed.

mental health and mental retardation issues. The conference was a useful means for the groups to learn more about each other and to develop a more coordinated approach to service issues.

If we engage in any undercover work, naturally we will experience anxiety both about moral wrongdoing and about being caught and punished. The major tool we can employ to help ourselves remain clear about the meaning of our activities is to continue to put our activities in a political perspective. If we are radical, we act in a deviant way by our mere presence and activity within conventional agencies. We live with a contradiction. Making confidential agency materials available to radical community groups is illegitimate only to the extent that we accept the legitimacy of the agencies in which we work. Rather than accept that legitimacy, we need to see these settings as locales for the larger struggle for social justice, not as the appropriate repository of our loyalties.

This guideline creates some dilemmas for workers and for the way in which a radical approach to social work is perceived by nonradicals. For workers it raises the issue of their commitment to a given agency and to a generally desirable norm, namely, confidentiality, which conflicts with their commitment to the larger process of human liberation. Confidentiality, as a general concept in practice, is not undesirable. At the same time, confidentiality as a protection for service users is too often used as an umbrella concept behind which agencies hide in their efforts to keep bureaucratic secrets, manipulate opinion, and control their opposition. Workers will need to make careful choices in these cases, keeping in mind their own security and seeking guidance on a case-by-case basis from their larger political commitments.

The suggestion that agency confidentiality might appropriately be breached also may feed impressions that the left is unprincipled in its efforts to create change. Obviously I do not believe this is so. To understand why, it is necessary to remember, once again, that social agencies are not politically neutral organizations. They do not keep "secrets" on behalf of the general political interest or the public good. They keep secrets for the sake of their own bureaucratic interests and ultimately for the class interests they uphold. Inasmuch as radicals working within such agencies are both part of and not part of those agencies, so too their response to agency confidentiality must be constantly assessed in the light of their commitment to the agency and to a larger morality and politics.

There are other ways in which we can serve community-based groups from within social agencies. In some settings social service workers with a planning or administrative role may find ways to siphon off agency resources to community groups by building a role for community groups into funding proposals. For example, when social workers are involved in developing community advisory boards to agencies or service review mechanisms by outside parties, they can work for the inclusion of community groups as part of these mechanisms and resist the kinds of self-serving peer review procedures that are more typical in such settings. At the more mundane level, and yet of potential significance, are the specific concrete resources that a creative worker can make available to community groups, even by providing office supplies, access to telephones, or part-time use of agency personnel. While the actual resources made available may be limited, even small amounts can be significant in helping to produce a newsletter or maintain a storefront walk-in center. The worker with a belief in the importance of such groups and a commitment to facilitating their growth is likely to find a variety of ways to coordinate his or her activities with the needs of these groups.

This kind of support is not at the level of sophistication that will ultimately be necessary; it continues to be somewhat primitive as a form of political struggle, since it involves individual workers, rather than workers organized together. However its importance should not be underestimated. It provides immediate support to service user groups. Less obviously, but potentially of considerable significance, it enriches the education and political growth of the service provider who begins to conceptualize his or her role as a political person and to act on it, first with hesitation and possibly guilt, and later with increasing clarity about such action as an expression of political commitments.

Short-Term Problem Solving

introduction

One of the most difficult areas for socialist analysts and practitioners to develop has been the linkages between direct service delivery situations, particularly those with a therapeutic intent, and strategies of socialist transformation. When a person comes to a social service agency for help, a great deal of the situation is already defined. Both worker and service user are constrained by many forces, including the desires of both to solve some immediately pressing problem in the most expedient manner. The possibilities for collective action may also be very limited at this point in the intervention process.

None the less for most social service workers, direct service delivery is the "point of production." It is the place where service workers put most of their energy. Further, even the minutiae of the casework or direct service intervention reflects the values, and consequently the politics, of the society. As a result they also become a locus for contesting dominant values, interpretations, and helping processes. While we can anticipate and acknowledge the political limits set by the parameters of the direct service dynamic, we can also find ways to extend those parameters and to operate within this situation with some degree of political consistency.

problem analysis

A socialist perspective can influence the immediate dynamics of a service situation by shaping the ways we look at a given problem, that is, the analysis we make of it; the ways we encourage an individual to look at a particular problem; the values we assume as we interact; and the kinds of alternative solutions we support. A socialist outlook influences our perception of the people with whom we work and may help focus our energies in the casework situation. These steps do not take the commitment to movement building very far. At the same time, they begin to distinguish the stance or context of radical practice from that of conventional practice and may represent the limits of "the possible" in a specific situation.

The first practice issue that confronts a worker in a service delivery situation is the assessment of the problem presented. There is always more than one way to look at a given situation, as is fully recognized in traditional casework practice with its concern for diagnosis. From a radical viewpoint the problem of diagnosis is no less pressing. A radical diagnosis will not necessarily discard the analytic tools of conventional practice. It will, however, modify the liberal view with a critical perspective on the society as a whole and an understanding of the impact of the society on individual lives. The radical view pivots on an additional dimension of analysis and reformulates liberal casework's understanding of the immediate situation. As Cloward and Piven have suggested,

> We have to break with the professional doctrine that ascribes virtually all of the problems that clients experience to defects in personality development and family relationships. It must be understood that this doctrine is as much a political ideology as an explanation of human behavior. It is an ideology that directs clients to blame themselves for their travails rather than the economic and social institutions that produce many of them. . . . This psychological reductionism—this pathologizing of poverty and inequality—is, in other words, an ideology of oppression for it systematically conceals from people the ways in which their lives are distorted by the realities of class structure.[9]

Radical diagnosis is based on the understanding that people do not live in social isolation. They live within the context of a given social order. Liberal casework has its own perceptions of this reality inasmuch as it rests on a theory that is aware that family, job, and community have an influence

[9]Richard A. Cloward and Frances Fox Piven, "Notes Toward a Radical Social Work," in *Radical Social Work*, eds. Roy Bailey and Frances Fox Piven (New York: Pantheon, 1975), pp. xxiii–xxiv.

on an individual's well-being or lack of well-being. However, liberal casework, by definition, does not rest on a critical analysis of the fundamental nature of the social order.[10] Because it takes that social order as a given, it cannot incorporate actively into its analysis a perspective on the larger oppression which people suffer. For example, a thoughtful worker would certainly be alert to the dynamics of an individual's job that were hurtful to that person and amenable to short-term amelioration. However, liberal caseworkers would not scrutinize the alienating conditions of work as a whole under capitalism. Such conditions would, in a sense, not be noticed since they are part of the social fabric that is taken for granted. If these realities were noticed, they might not be brought actively into the casework situation since, from a liberal perspective, there is nothing that can be done about them. They then become part of the social reality to which the individual must adjust.

This is not to suggest that there is no consciousness of forces like racism, sexism, and agism in mainstream social work. There is such consciousness, and it has found its way into some aspects of casework practice. However, it is necessary to distinguish a liberal from a radical perspective on these "isms." The liberal analysis examines these problems within the framework of capitalism. That analysis concludes that the abolition of racism, sexism, and agism is possible within capitalism. It also holds as the standard of success equal treatment of women and men, people of color and whites, and young and old, within the context of current capitalist arrangements.

Alternatively a socialist analysis leads to the conclusion that these forms of exploitation are functional to the maintenance of capitalism and generated by it. They are not anomalies, and they are not resolvable within capitalism. Further, even if they were, an adequate resolution to the exploitation of women can hardly be their equality with men in a pattern of systemic exploitation. We must go beyond these formulations. The current understanding of these issues within social work does not do this.

The liberal perspective is also inadequate in its conception of the possibilities for systemic change. The theories that inform traditional casework do not contain strategies for fundamental social change and have little faith in the ability of people to shape their own destiny in the larger sense. Pessimism about solving or approaching problems beyond those most amenable to psychosocial manipulation pervades the casework relationship so that individual problems requiring broader political and social solutions tend to be viewed as irrelevant issues in the casework process.

Radical analysis understands that oppressed people internalize their

---

[10]I have developed this theme more fully in Jeffry Galper, *The Politics of Social Services* (Englewood Cliffs, N.J.: Prentice-Hall, Inc., 1975), "Person-Situation: Casework as Politics," pp. 119–29.

oppression and that this needs to be examined if people are to become free enough to deal with oppressive social forces. A radical approach, even when it fully takes into account the realities of capitalism's impact on individuals, is still legitimately concerned with the ways in which people contribute to their own pain by misunderstanding reality and acting self-destructively. Radical practice is not antipsychological. However, it recognizes the social and political sources of personality formation, and it recognizes that the political and economic context of our society is critical in shaping who we are and how we respond to the world.

An example may help to make this discussion more concrete. A woman went to a sexuality clinic located in a mental health center for help in becoming orgasmic. The usual procedures in such cases involve psychological exploration to uncover the pathological roots of repressed sexuality, and couple counselling to discover and modify the dynamics of the primary relationship. After a period of initial discussion, the worker, herself influenced by an analysis of women's sexuality emphasized by the women's movement, took a nonconventional point of view. She felt that the problem, ostensibly one of individual pathology, was rooted in prevailing social conditioning which encourages women to deny and condemn their own sexuality and which deprives them of knowledge about their bodies and their sexuality. From this perspective the worker was able to conceptualize the helping process as a learning process. The learning involved a personal exploration of women's sexual repression. In this case the process was facilitated when the worker was able to refer the woman to a woman's self-help group oriented specifically to preorgasmic women. The premise of the self-help group was that preorgasmic women are experiencing sexual repression that has social roots. The therapy involved sharing with other women in similar situations. It focused on social and political discussion as well as intrapsychic dynamics and was rooted in a learning and consciousness-raising approach to self-exploration. By putting the issues presented by this woman in a feminist framework, the worker shifted what would have been the usual diagnosis and subsequent treatment, with positive outcomes for the woman. At the same time, she helped the woman to experience sharing with other women and to experience the power of feminist analysis. Consequently the worker helped that woman to link what had seemed to her to be an idiosyncratic problem with a larger dynamic of repression in the society.[11]

To summarize, the analysis on which a radical worker approaches a direct service situation differs from the analysis of conventional approaches in two respects. First, it locates individuals within the broad social context of their lives and analyzes their particular problems in light of their personality

---

[11]This example was provided by Barbara Julius, then a student at the School of Social Work, University of Pennsylvania.

structures, social-psychological environment, and in terms of the nature of the society as a whole. That analysis, rooted in a socialist critique, influences each aspect of the way a worker looks at a discrete problem. Second, a radical perspective is grounded in the belief that people have the power to change their circumstances when they understand them concretely and act on them in a collective political way. Radicalism is not pessimistic about the possibilities for change, and it understands that working people, acting together as a class, are the primary shapers of history. For a given individual the implications of this view may not be clear in the short run, but a radical analysis of a particular problem situation is necessarily the first step in formulating an action strategy.

empowerment

Radical workers should encourage service users to appreciate their own power and to develop the attitudes and skills that will permit them to engage more fully and actively in shaping the world. The creation of an equalitarian relationship with the service user, to the extent possible, facilitates this outcome. Caseworkers ought not use the generalized authority and prestige that may be attributed to them in ways that suggest that service users are not fully capable of making critical decisions. An important part of the political education that must occur in the society is challenging the myth that people are not capable of understanding the way in which their lives work or the way in which the society works. Social service workers have an obligation to demystify the helping process and the interventions which they make on people's behalf.[12] The "worker as expert" role must be downplayed in favor of the notion of the worker as colleague, political ally, and facilitator.

Some radical therapists have suggested that a group process is more valuable than a one-to-one relationship in pursuing these aims because it encourages sharing which is crucial when people confront their sense of isolation and their responsibility for causing their own problems.[13] However in some situations a one-to-one relationship may be the only format for intervention that will be helpful or possible. It is useful to think in terms of stages. Once the most pressing short-run strains are relieved, the individual has more freedom to take a deeper and broader look at the situation and to address the problem in a more fundamental way. To the extent that we develop a methodology of intervention that resembles a consciousness-

---

[12]For example, see Murray Edelman, "The Political Language of the Helping Professions," *Politics and Society*, 4 (1974), 295–310 and Paulo Freire, *Pedagogy of the Oppressed* (New York: Herder and Herder, 1971.)

[13]For example, see Claude Steiner, "Radical Psychiatry: Principles," in *The Radical Therapist*, ed. Jerome Agel (New York: Ballantine, 1971), pp. 3–7.

raising group as well as a therapy group, we will be able to be more helpful to the people with whom we work. Then we can explore the common ground of what looks at first like individual and unique problems, and through that process we can mobilize an appropriate anger at the institutions and processes contributing to the problem. That anger can find expression through people's use of their collective power.

The radical worker will not ignore the problems that arise in the helping situation for which there are no immediate solutions. Even if the solution to a particular problem points in the direction of a revolutionary movement, and that is obviously not on the agenda in the immediate future, it is still appropriate for the worker and service user to explore the meaning of the problem and the kinds of solutions that would be required. Just as we are trained not to underestimate the strengths and capabilities of the people with whom we work, so too from a radical perspective, we must not underestimate people's ability to develop revolutionary movements to express their political will.

To return to the case of the preorgasmic woman, some potential next steps are suggested by this discussion. The denial of the woman's sexuality can be analyzed as part of a larger dynamic in a society which oppresses women by encouraging them to deny their own power and vitality. Ultimately this is part of the process whereby women are socialized to accept the role assigned to them in society. Helping the woman involved to get in touch with her sexuality is important work. At the same time, it addresses only one of the manifestations of the oppression women experience. A viable socialist feminist movement, in the context of a larger revolutionary socialist movement, is the prerequisite for successfully challenging basic issues. Such a movement exists only in rudimentary form. At the same time, many women have found that their involvement with feminist services concerned with discrete problems, such as sexuality, divorce, physical abuse, or abortion, provides a point of linkage to the thinking, values, people, and organizations that define a broader movement. Given an appropriate political framework and some encouragement, the helping process addressed to the specific issue of orgasm can become a vehicle for exploring and attacking problems that previously might not even have been identified clearly as problems or as problems which could be influenced.

fighting social welfare bureaucracies

Thus far I have discussed some underpinnings of direct service in the immediate interaction of worker and service user. It would be shortsighted, however, not to recognize that the vast majority of social workers practice within bureaucratic social welfare structures in which casework interactions are decisively shaped by agency policy. Efforts to challenge agency policies on behalf of service users are one aspect of radical social work on behalf of individuals. In cases where collective worker and service user power do not exist as a basis for challenging agency policies, workers can none the less confront agency policies in ways which challenge agency oppression and which increase the likelihood of achieving immediate gains for people.

One thrust may be to question agency definitions of service users' problems when those definitions are based on conservative notions of problems. Workers can press for definitions of those problems that are grounded in people's economic, social, and political circumstances. This might involve helping to keep people from agencies altogether, as in the case when workers help people fight against institutionalization. It may mean supporting people in seeking the specific benefits needed to alleviate a particular problem. It may also be important to those seeking help that we reflect back to them a nonpathologized view of their problems and that we record that view in whatever official records we keep or in the conferences in which we take part.

Similarly we must be prepared to fight other agency personnel and agency rules when that is necessary to best serve people. A thorough knowledge of the rules and procedures of each agency and of the agencies to which we most frequently turn for collateral assistance is essential. Agencies, as we know, are not structured to serve people maximally. They respond to many other mandates first, and in the remaining space they may or may not attend in a logical and humane way to people's needs. Repressive and unreasonable agency policies must be challenged at every turn. The obligation to serve people must be taken seriously, and in the short run, fighting vigorously against agency policy may be one available tool for serving others. Once again in the case example I have been using, the worker had to refer the woman to the self-help group without the knowledge of her agency. Past experience had led her to the conclusion that the agency would not support the outside referral since that would not add to the number of "client contact hours" the agency could report. That would have a subsequent impact on its funding.

political education in the service delivery situation

When people request social services, they infrequently do so with a radical view of their situation, with the thought of being introduced to such a view, or with knowledge of the implications of that view for their lives. They come to social agencies with the range of political viewpoints and unformed ideas normally found among people. And they come to receive assistance with a particular problem. In a public welfare setting a radical approach to practice that attempted to introduce more explicit radical content into the casework interaction would hardly be effective. For example, a discussion of the role of welfare recipients as a reserve labor force in a capitalist economy would be nonproductive—not to mention the consequences of such discussion for the worker's survival potential in the agency. Political education in a service situation does not necessarily involve sharing an explicitly radical analysis with social service users.

On the other hand, it is entirely likely that a social worker in a residential setting for teenagers, for example, might legitimately be involved with facilitating relationships among the residents of an institution and might have responsibility for establishing procedures for the ongoing functioning of a residential cottage. In such circumstances, where principles of government and issues of collective management are part of the bread and butter of daily work, discussion about self-management, collectivity, mutual responsibility, and so on might be perfectly appropriate at an early stage of work with individuals. Similarly in working with a group of senior adults in a community center, the political questions which are often actively on the minds of seniors, for example, the costs of drugs, medical care, and housing can easily be raised appropriately as an ongoing part of practice.

The point of this discussion is obvious but sometimes lost sight of as people struggle to integrate radical political education with social work practice. We need to start, as social workers have known for some time, where people are, on the issues they experience as most pressing in their lives, and on ground they can understand. When people come to the agencies with pressing immediate problems, we must help them to deal with those problems. It may be that a person under great psychological stress simply cannot develop a larger perspective on that distress unless and until she or he experiences symptomatic relief. We cannot ignore that reality and that need, and we should not feel guilty or politically misdirected in addressing problems at that level.

At the same time, we have an obligation to make every effort to advance the situation beyond symptomatic relief, since we know that the symptoms are likely to reappear and that so-called normal functioning is normal only by the abnormal standards of our society. We need to move to the next level of political work in our practice, the level of introducing an explicitly radical analysis into our direct engagement with social service users.

Every intervention we make as social service workers is based on a political world view, whether or not we are conscious of that fact. The kinds of questions we ask of a person we are interviewing, the kinds of suggestions we make, the way we conduct ourselves in relation to others, all reflect our conscious, and more often unconscious, assumptions about the way the world works, about what is important to people, and about what can be expected from a given interaction. For example, there is no doubt that a world view that perceives women as homemakers and primary nurturers will find its way into social work interventions with women, just as a world view that sees women as whole and competent people, capable of full and equal participation in the world, will find its way into social work intervention.

Moreover just as we social service workers perceive the world through ambivalent and sometimes confused political lenses, so too do social service users. We all tend to internalize our experience of oppressive social conditions, and we all tend to believe ourselves to be at fault when our lives are difficult. At the same time, there is a part of all of us that rebels at the way our society is organized. To some degree we are aware that the society is not working in a way that supports our lives.

In our interactions with service users, we always make choices about the comments and perceptions to which we will respond. There is too much that comes our way for us to respond to it all. From a radical perspective we will look for and reinforce that part of the service user's perspective that is aware of social oppression. Rather than view the introduction of a radical perspective as injecting radical politics into an unwilling recipient, a preferable model is one of being receptive to, and supportive of, the already radical or radically inclined part of the people with whom we work, even when they may not see themselves that way. Political education occurs, not only apart from the normal events of life, but as a part of the everyday occurrences. As we become clearer about our own political position, we will find ways to communicate it more effectively with others.

In introducing radical content into our work, we must remember that our goal is to serve people. If introducing a radical view puts us in the position of aligning against those we serve, then we must reexamine the correctness of our theory and/or the way in which we are pursuing our political commitments. It may be perfectly appropriate to push people, to make them uncomfortable, and to challenge their views. However if we consistently find ourselves opposed to oppressed people, then we must reexamine the way we express our politics.

The art of radical social work is to develop ways to bring radical politics into practice in an integrated fashion so that radical work becomes a logical part of the service situation. Initially service recipients may view our attempts to facilitate radical collective action as an extra burden. If our analysis is a useful one, however, and our choice of points of intervention is well selected, the sense of burden will give way to a sense of satisfaction as people find ways to extend their problem-solving capabilities.

Thus far I have focused on some of the less complex ways of introducing a radical perspective to those with whom we work. There is also a role for more explicit political education, particularly as we take steps to help people put their specific problems into a larger perspective. The internalized sense of guilt, blame, and failure which many people carry is a very powerful force in preventing them from seeing and acting on a radical view. While psychologically sophisticated radicalism does not deny people's own con-

tributions to their pain and oppression, it is also grounded in a keen awareness of the real world conditions that limit our life possibilities and that are
the external source of the pain we internalize. When we help people feel
better by helping them alleviate the most immediate sources of their discom-
fort, we increase the possibility that people will be able to uncover the social
and political conditions that contribute to their dilemmas. At this stage of
people's self-examination, they may be ready to explore a more explicit
analysis of social conditions that pertain to the specific problems at hand. We
can be helpful by being willing to share explicitly the points of view we hold,
and by helping to make educational materials such as books, articles, and
newspapers available to the people with whom we work.

A Radical Approach for Community Organizers

There is a belief within social work that while casework practice often represents a more conservative side of the field, community organization represents a more progressive thrust within social work and so rescues social work
from charges of ignoring its commitment to progressive change efforts. Organizers and caseworkers tend to share this belief. In actuality conventional
social work community organization practice is as likely to serve a cooptive
role, or to function as a community-based approach to social control, as it is
to operate as a vehicle for progressive change.[14] It is necessary, therefore, to
give special attention to the ways in which community organizers can infuse
their work with radical politics, since such politics are by no means inherent
in that mode of practice. While there is less of a community-organizing focus
in social work than there was a decade ago, community organization continues to be taught in schools of social work, and social agencies continue to
hire organizers trained in social work for jobs in settlement houses, mental
health centers, community centers, and hospitals. Furthermore the principles which inform a radical community organization approach will be useful
to organizing work which any radical social worker might undertake, and
therefore these approaches will have wider applicability than does conventional training in the "professional specialization" of community organizing.

The problems facing radical social workers who are hired as community
organizers do not differ, in many respects, from those facing radical social
workers who are caseworkers. In neither situation will the employing agency
have a task in mind which stems from a radical analysis or points in a radical
direction. For the community organization workers, as for the caseworker,
radical work will involve simultaneously responding to the specific task that

---

[14]I have developed this critique more fully in *The Politics of Social Services*, pp. 111–
19.

is assigned and finding ways to infuse parts or all of that work with radical politics. For organizers the fact that community organization jobs often involve working with groups of people may facilitate pursuing radical commitments. Even for the community organization worker, however, part of the challenge will necessarily be to shape the work situation so that progressive organizing becomes more possible. For example, while it seems obvious that community organization jobs will involve organizing, many social work community organizers find that they are asked to use their community organization skills, not to organize constituencies for social change activities, but to facilitate direct service delivery, to help an agency meet externally imposed requirements for an advisory board, and so on. In these cases the challenge is to utilize a situation in which the official assignment involves coordinating a satellite service unit or staffing a harmless community advisory board in order to introduce radical political ideas and to bring people into more direct confrontation with existing instutitions and values.

The key task for radical organizers is to link immediate issues with longer range agendas and actions, that is, to connect short- and long-term agendas. Agencies do not conceptualize worker assignments to organizing projects in terms of long-run movement building and structural changes. However each specific project may offer numerous opportunities for linkage with broader political processes.

As an example, consider the case of settlement houses which have undertaken juvenile delinquency prevention efforts in their neighborhoods with grants from the Law Enforcement Administration Agency. Often one part of this effort involves developing jobs in the neighborhood and helping teenagers connect with them. Organizers assigned to such projects might typically undertake the task of canvassing local merchants to explore the possibilities of their hiring neighborhood teenagers for the summer or for after-school hours. The funding source and the agency are primarily interested in finding jobs for teenagers who might be potentially disruptive. The organizer must also be concerned with those jobs, both to satisfy the immediate requirements of the agency assignment and to provide a needed service to the community. Simultaneously that organizer must explore ways to make this effort part of a longer range politicizing and organizing campaign.

In this case the direction seems apparent though, of course, it may not be so easy to implement in any particular setting. The organizer must find a way to work with and through teenagers themselves. He or she might begin by organizing teenagers for that purpose. If the agency is conservative, an acceptable rationale for organizing might be that such a project requires a teen advisory board. If the agency is more progressive, the worker might solicit agency support for working with and through a teen council that focused generally on employment issues. Summer or after-school, part-time employment might then be one particular issue that gives focus to the larger concern.

Job issues are good ones on which to organize teenagers, and it would not be difficult to bring a group of teens together around that concern. As with any decent organizing effort, there must be some immediate payoff to the people who involve themselves. In this case the payoff is the possibility of a job. Neighborhood canvassing could be organized by the teenagers themselves. The effort might be structured through a teen-controlled job clearinghouse. In addition to a coordinating function, the clearinghouse could serve as a forum for discussion and decision making. It might be a place to raise and explore an analysis of the scarcity of jobs, the effect of competition for jobs or creative ways of organizing job sharing or rotation. Similarly working with and through an organized body raises the possibility of introducing collective and democratic working styles, and of training teens in self-management, canvassing, and other skills of use to them in the immediate project and as organizers of future projects. Most important, approaching this issue in the context of an organizing project sets the stage for developing the power that can enable people to demand jobs rather than request them as favors.

The organizer, as well as the teenagers, must be concerned with the immediate need for jobs. However if the project fails to move beyond this concern, it will be decisively shaped by its conservative political origins and so will serve as a cooling out, ameliorative mechanism to control working-class youth. The systemic issues must be raised, and appropriate analytic and action connections must be made between the immediate job situation and the larger dynamics of the society.

When working with teens, a radical analysis is often easier to communicate than when working with adults. Young people are well aware of the lack of opportunities available to them and are often less locked into traditional analyses of social phenomena. As part of a discussion session, a youth council with a focus on youth unemployment might make good use of radical literature that focuses on the national employment situation and that is geared to a general audience, for example, a document such as Popular Economics Press' *What's Happening To Our Jobs?* [15] Similarly the organizer might link some of the council members to regional and national efforts by radical organizations which give attention to unemployment issues from an anticapitalist perspective. [16]

---

[15] Popular Economics Press, *What's Happening To Our Jobs?* (Popular Economics Press, Box 221, Somerville, Massachusetts 02143), 1976.

[16] On the national level both the New American Movement and the Democratic Socialist Organizing Committee have engaged in political work on the issue of unemployment from a radical perspective. To the extent that the organizer is informed about these and other socialist

In a similar vein, a youth employment project could look more broadly at employment policies on a citywide level. The key tasks for the organizer would be to find ways to encourage the youths involved to challenge citywide employment policy. Typically they will discover that cities spend community development funds and other discretionary money in ways that benefit the already advantaged districts and classes within the city. They will find job-creation programs riddled with corruption and favoritism. They will experience the realities of urban politics when they try to approach appropriate city officials about their concerns and are dismissed or manipulated in one way or another. Raising the issues that need to be raised will necessarily bring the group into conflict with the established political and economic powers.

The radical organizer will never approach the assignment of job creation as an individual activity if there is a way to involve relevant constituencies with a progressive political potential in that effort. This is true even if the organizer believes (or knows) that the most "efficient" way to develop jobs, or health services, or whatever is to do it alone, on the basis of "professional-to-professional" negotiation. Similarly the radical organizer will look for ways to sharpen political issues through any particular encounter. A job-creation situation offers natural possibilities, as the larger economics of job creation in a neighborhood or city are investigated. The same process of enlarging and deepening understanding and involvement occurs as the organizer seeks linkages between a particular local project and broader citywide, statewide, and nationwide efforts to deal with the same issue.

Organizers do not always have the opportunity to choose the issues on which they will focus. When they do have the opportunity, or can shape their approach, it is important for them to work on issues that unify, rather than divide, people. This is especially important in neighborhood work where the potential of racial divisions is great. The organizer will look for issues that can bring people together in common struggle, rather than issues that can stimulate divisiveness.

In general the approaches a radical community organizer takes do not differ greatly from those a radical caseworker will take. In both cases, whether the worker can be up front working in a radical way or behind the scenes working in a more limited fashion will vary according to the particulars of the situation. The choice of issues will also be determined by several factors, including the official agency assignment; the short-term needs and desires of the constituency; the skills, interests, and political commitments of

---

organizations, there will be little difficulty in connecting with radical groups focusing on almost any of the issues that are commonly raised in doing community work, whether it be in the area of housing, medical care, schools, services for the aged, day care, or numerous others.

the worker; and the long-range potential for moving in a more radical direction. In both cases the goals are to build political power among powerless people, to encourage their movement in the direction of challenging existing sources of power, and to do so in a way that deepens their understanding of capitalism and heightens their awareness of the socialist alternative.

8

Social Workers
and Radical Unionism

Introduction

Radicals in the United States and other capitalist countries have a long-standing involvement with the trade union movement. This involvement is not based on a self-professed commitment by most unions to socialism. In fact in the United States, the trade union movement has sometimes acted with considerable hostility toward the left.[1] Nevertheless unions have represented one of the vehicles through which members of the working class of capitalist countries have banded together to fight for higher wages and for job security. Even when workers and union leadership have not viewed their collective activity as part of an anticapitalist struggle, unions have carried at least rudimentary anticapitalist sentiment by uniting workers, by fighting for a larger share of the wealth workers create and sometimes by demanding greater self-determination in shaping the conditions of production. While the

---

[1]For example, see David Dubinsky and A. H. Raskin, *David Dubinsky: A Life With Labor* (New York: Simon and Schuster, 1976) for an example of the antileft sentiment of one long time union leader.

conservatism of many unions cannot be denied, radicals continue to explore the potential of trade unionism for furthering the development of a socialist movement in the United States and in other capitalist countries.[2]

Unions do represent fertile ground for radical work and the unionization of social service workers should be given serious consideration as an arena for radical practice by social service workers. At the same time, if unions are to become an effective vehicle for socialist transformation they will need to move markedly to the left so that they can become self-conscious instruments for furthering the interests of the entire working class. Unions must view themselves as class-conscious, class-struggle, or class-conflict unions. These terms imply a point of view about unions and a role for unions that involve the defense of workers' day-to-day rights and interests, along with the advancement of workers' long-term rights and interests. From a socialist point of view, that rests on the abolition of the capitalist system. Class-conscious unions integrate their concern for the immediate protection and advancement of workers with a long-term commitment to the fight for socialism. Most unions today do not operate within this framework and are best identified as class-collaborationist unions. They protect the interests of a narrow segment of workers and operate within the larger context of the capitalist system. Since they do not challenge capitalism, they ultimately fail the very workers they were initially organized to serve. The concepts of class-conflict and class-collaborationist unions differentiate radical and nonradical unionism.

I begin this chapter by developing the case for social work unions and for radicals' involvement in helping to organize and advance those unions. Then I briefly describe the history of social work involvement with unions and update the story with a review of current developments in social work unionization, particularly, and white-collar and public sector unionization, generally. There has been a substantial tradition of social work involvement with the trade union movement in the United States, and I will point to the significant role radicals have played within social work by pursuing social work unionization as a contribution to more fundamental social change.

I suggest some criteria by which progressive workers can analyze alternative unions for possible affiliation, and I review some of the basic steps which workers in a particular agency must take to organize a union. Finally I discuss approaches to bringing a socialist perspective to bear on union work so that the union movement becomes a stronger ally in the struggle for socialism.

---

[2]Some useful pamphlets are *Class Struggle and Unionism* and *Fighting to Win*, both from the International Socialists, Sun Press, 14131 Woodward Avenue, Highland Park, Michigan 48203, 1975; and *The Trade Union Question: A Communist Approach to Strategy, Tactics and Program*, by the Philadelphia Workers Organizing Committee, Box 11768, Philadelphis, Pennsylvania 19101, 1977.

Unions for Social Workers[3]

Social workers have a history of union involvement that extends back almost fifty years. Unfortunately political developments in the late 1940s and 1950s interrupted what might have been an earlier and more rapid growth of progressive ideas in the country as a whole, took a toll on the union movement, in general, and in the same sweep, hampered the union movement in social work. The conservatism of that period was partially expressed through the suppression of the trade union movement. One of the effects within social work was a turning away from unionization as a means of protecting social service workers, and a turning toward increased professionalization as a (more conservative) alternative method for protecting social work jobs. This history has left many social workers with a residue of uninformed and ambivalent attitudes toward unions. While the number of social workers organized in unions has grown, as have the number and percentage of unionized public employees and other white-collar workers, some social workers continue to view unions as inappropriate for themselves or even harmful to themselves and to those they serve.

In general in North America unions tend to be somewhat denigrated, in contrast to prevailing attitudes in most other capitalist countries. In the case of unionization for social work, opponents offer several major criticisms. The first of these, though the least often stated explicitly, is the reluctance of social workers to see themselves and conduct themselves as members of the working class. Some social workers maintain that they are a cut above blue-collar workers in status and in other rewards and that their involvement with unions would aligned them with a less privileged segment of the labor force and would therefore tarnish their image as professionals. They believe that their designation as "professionals" protects them from exploitation and assures them continued opportunity for salary increases and other forms of advancement. They fear losing what they see as the special privileges accruing to them as professionals if they consciously and explicitly adopt the mantle of "worker" through involvement in unions.[4] For some social workers an associa-

---

[3]A number of progressive social workers with a strong commitment to social work unionization were willing to share their thoughts and experiences with me. I would particularly like to acknowledge the assistance of Dennis Brunn, LaSalle College, Philadelphia, Pennsylvania; Cheryl Feldman of 1199C, the Hospital Workers Union, Philadelphia, Pennsylvania; and Paul Neustadt of Boston, Massachusetts. In addition, Richard Fortmann, then at the School of Social Administration, Temple University, Philadelphia, Pennsylvania provided helpful case material and background information on the Pennsylvania Social Service Union.

[4]This mindset is represented in an analysis of public welfare work by John E. Horejsi, Thomas Walz and Patrick R. Connalloy. In a statement that characterizes a line of reasoning within social work, they write that "Collective bargaining, in our view, encourages polarization and a win-lose atmosphere. Distinct battle lines are drawn in disputed areas, making each side

tion with truck drivers, however distant, evokes sufficient status and class anxiety to prevent an objective examination of the realities of their situation.

Underlying these considerations is the notion that social workers can advance themselves more successfully by negotiating without a union structure than by negotiating through a union structure. This judgment stems partly from the fact that social workers have fought for acceptance as professionals. As professionals, in popular imagery, they operate primarily as solo practitioners, rather than as functionaries in large bureaucracies. Even though social work services have been delivered primarily through bureaucratic structures for over forty years, some social workers hold to a nineteenth-century vision of the conditions of their work. This is not a notion which employers have been particularly eager to challenge since negotiations with individual employees are far easier to manage and less likely to result in wage gains than are collective negotiations.

Similarly some have argued that social work unionization, by raising the cost of providing social services, can lead to a loss of social service jobs in the long run. In this respect social workers fear that they will face the problem experienced by some industrial workers in highly unionized sections of the country where industry is leaving to find nonunionized labor in the U.S. South or in other countries. In this same vein, particularly in rural settings or in settings in which a small number of social workers are employed in large offices consisting primarily of nonsocial work employees, social workers have sometimes worked out convenient arrangements with local political bosses, for example, county boards of commissioners, that seem to work for them, at least in the short run. In these cases the workers as well as the commissioners resist the introduction of collective bargaining in fear that such a process might disrupt long-standing patterns of mutual accommodation.

In the face of this kind of antiunion sentiment, the most telling prounion argument for most social workers is that unions are necessary for the protection of workers' jobs and salaries. Traditionally this has been the single most important function which unions have played. The idea that social workers individually negotiating for salary increases and other improvements in condi-

---

reluctant to compromise for fear of appearing 'weaker' than the other ... Antagonism is almost certain to be the byproduct. Then, too, collective bargaining is time consuming and fosters intraorganizational competition and maneuvering. . . . It is for reasons such as these that we prefer the approach of cooperative negotiation over that of collective bargaining. Administrators and workers alike would do well to search for alternative ways of affecting positive program change and improved working conditions. Cooperation can co-exist with the expression of protest and major disagreement as long as each side is committed to open negotiation. This, too, is a form of collective bargaining; yet the collective is not a professional union with paid leadership; rather it is the gathering of members from all levels of an agency, who meet to discuss goals shared both by workers and administrators in an atmosphere relatively devoid of coercion. Thus, it can be structured into a win-win situation." *Working in Welfare: Survival Through Positive Action* (Iowa City: University of Iowa School of Social Work, 1977), pp. 85–86.

tions of work can do for themselves what social workers acting together through a union structure can do is, in fact, a myth.

It should not be assumed, moreover, that social workers are uniformly hostile to unionism. While there is relatively little empirical evidence available about social work attitudes toward unions, a 1970 study in Detroit, historically a prounion city, found that 75 percent of the social workers questioned favored unions for social workers.[5] Further the official position of the National Association of Social Workers "supports the collective bargaining process between organized labor and management as one means of providing a rational and coherent method of solving problems inherent in employee-employer relationships."[6] Most important, the growing numbers of social workers who are actually involved in organizing unions and who are members of unions is testimony to prounion sentiment among social workers.

The well-being of individual social workers is linked closely with the fate of welfare state economics and politics. The forces generating the fiscal crisis of the state are very profound. In the short run, it may be true that unionization, by supporting wage gains, may stimulate some reduction in the number of social service jobs. However, the alternative is for social workers to exploit themselves by acceding to lower pay and thus contributing to the state's efforts to provide noneconomically viable services required by a capitalist economy. While unionization may contribute to the larger crisis of capitalism, it is capitalism itself that is at the heart of the problem. The crisis goes well beyond the higher pay gained by workers through unionization efforts.[7] With a union, workers have an organization to fight the forces that lead to job losses. Without a union, they have no protection. If workers allow the threat of job loss to impede their efforts to unionize, they will do themselves a tremendous disservice, by depriving themselves of what is at this time their single most effective weapon for fighting against job losses and pay cuts.

Social workers are workers. They do not own the means of production, and they work for salaries or wages. Further, even social workers who are among the elite in social work, that is, those social workers with higher salaries, more prestige, and work autonomy, find that their work increasingly resembles that of the traditional blue-collar working class in certain ways. They are given increasingly less autonomy in their choice of assignment, and

---

[5]Metropolitan Detroit Chapter, National Association of Social Workers, *Newsletter,* June, 1970, cited in Milton Tambor, "Unions in Voluntary Agencies," *Social Work,* 18 (July, 1973), 41.

[6]National Association of Social Workers, *Standards for Social Work Personnel Practices* (Washington, D.C.: National Association of Social Workers, 1971). See also National Association of Social Workers, *Standards for Social Work Personnel Practices,* 2nd ed. rev., 1973.

[7]Data supporting this argument are presented in Nancy D. Tomaso, "Public Employee Unions and the Urban Fiscal Crisis," *Insurgent Sociologist,* 8 (Fall, 1978), 191-205.

they have increasingly less discretion in the processes they utilize to accomplish their tasks. They are closely supervised and monitored in their work, more and more they are asked to punch time clocks, and they are held accountable to production schedules, as a measure of accomplishment. All of this is presented in the guise of management efficiency (Management By Objectives, Program Planning and Budgeting Systems and so on) which helps to cover the realities of increased control and speed-up with a more acceptable veneer. In addition all social workers are finding that, as are other members of the working class, they must fight simply to save their jobs and to win salary increases that keep pace with inflation.

Some social workers have viewed unionization as inappropriate for an occupation whose commitment is to human services. Unions for social workers, it is sometimes argued, are inimical to the best interests of service users. This issue is highlighted in the case of social workers serving dependent people since strike activity might have detrimental effects on institutionalized populations, welfare recipients, hospital patients, and so on. Similarly some social workers fear that union involvement in service situations would interfere with workers' freedom to pursue what they see as the best options for service users by narrowing the range of permissible activities for a given worker or class of worker. However, the reality is that unionization is one of the few means available to social workers in their fight for the right to provide adequate service to people.

There is also antiunion sentiment among some leftist-minded social workers, although their criticisms of unions are quite different from centrist or rightist criticisms. These leftists argue that unions are so hopelessly conservative that they are not useful for advancing radical movements. They see industrial unions as symbiotically tied to big business, and public sector unions tied to the state; they see little hope of interrupting that pattern. This assessment reflects the antiworking class analysis of the New Left, which emerged in the early to mid-1960s.[8] The New Left represented a student population and elements of the NWC. Initially it saw itself not only as a vanguard in making revolution, but as a sector that could fundamentally change society by itself. It saw blue-collar workers, and by extension, the unions with which blue-collar workers were involved, as opposed to many of the progressive stands taken by the New Left, as was indeed the case. The early "hardhat" opposition to the antiwar movement, to the women's movement, to the gay liberation movement, and to the civil rights movement left a negative impression of the trade union movement among some New Leftists of that period. One residue of that impression is antiunion and antiworking

---

[8]See Paul Buhle, "The Eclipse of the New Left: Some Notes," *Radical America*, 6 (July-August, 1972), 1–10 and James O'Brien, "Beyond Reminiscence: The New Left in History," *Radical America*, 6 (July-August, 1972), 11–48.

class sentiment in some sectors of the left, although these attitudes are changing.

It must be acknowledged that unions in the United States have not always been progressive in the stances they have taken on broader social issues, and they have not always been models of democracy in their internal practice.[9] Union leadership has sometimes been more aligned with the needs and interests of the capitalist class than with the needs and interests of the workers whom they are supposedly representing. At the same time, this is only part of the picture.

The larger class struggle taking place on a daily basis in the United States occurs within the union movement as well. There is a history of very progressive unionization in the United States. However the progressive unions have been attacked vigorously by representatives of more conservative trade unionism, who have often had the upper hand,[10] in just the same way that conservative political forces have dominated the society in other arenas. Time after time the more progressive unions have been expelled, first from the AFL and then from the AFL-CIO. Within individual unions, the more progressive people, who often have done the hard work of union building, are driven out as conservative leadership emerges. We are not well versed in the history of class struggle in the United States, since it is not reported to us as part of our own history, or it is reported in a distorted way. For the same reasons we do not know the full history of class struggle within individual unions and within the union movement as a whole.[11] Unions must be viewed, not only in terms of what they are now, and particularly in terms of what the top leadership is and represents, but also as another arena in which conflict occurs between radical and conservative forces, between forces representing the interests of the working class and those representing the capitalist class.

It is also helpful to distinguish between the top officials of unions and the rank-and-file members. In the last dozen years of U.S. labor history, the struggle between rank-and-file workers and the entrenched, bureaucratic union leadership has often been as fierce as the struggle between unions and

---

[9]For a discussion of the important question of the role of minorities in trade unions see Philip S. Foner, *Organized Labor and the Black Worker, 1619–1973* (New York: International Publishers, 1974), and "Organized Labor and the Black Worker in the 1970's," *Insurgent Sociologist*, 8 (Fall, 1978), 87–96.

[10]See Sidney Peck, "Current Trends in the American Labor Movement, *Insurgent Sociologist*, 5 (Winter, 1975), 23–40.

[11]Several sources of a more rounded history of the U.S. labor movement are Richard O'Boyer and Herbert Morais, *Labor's Untold Story* (New York: United Electrical, Radio and Machine Workers of America, 1955); Jeremy Brecher, *Strike!* (San Francisco,: Straight Arrow Books, 1972); and Alice and Staughton Lynd, eds., *Rank and File: Histories by Working Class Organizers* (Boston: Beacon Press, 1973).

employers. The level of wildcat strike activity has been increasing in the U.S. in this decade. These strikes have often taken place against the wishes of union leaders, and sometimes the union hierarchy resists them as vigorously as do the employers. The growth of rank-and-file caucuses and other militant worker factions within unions has been one of the optimistic political developments in recent labor history.[12] This is not to suggest that all union leaders are conservative and all rank-and-file union members are progressive. It is to say that the political tendencies and potentials of unions cannot be equated solely with the politics of union leadership or the official political position of a particular union. Unions often represent conflicting political tendencies. While the official posture of many unions remains essentially conservative, the underlying realities are much less placid and staid than they seem on the surface.

There are several reasons to view unions as potentially important organizations for progressive political work. It is necessary to take a broader view of unions than we obtain by looking exclusively at their day-to-day struggle for higher pay and job security, although we must not minimize the importance of these bread-and-butter issues. We need to look at some of the inherently radical potential of the trade union movement, for social workers as for all working-class people.

Unions, in and of themselves, are not socialist organizations. They do not raise the question of private ownership of the means of production by their very existence. In this sense they accept capitalism and even facilitate its smooth functioning. At the same time, they represent workers organizing as workers to challenge the power and ability of capitalists or in the case of social service workers, to challenge the power and the ability of the state to control wages and conditions of work. Therefore unions organize workers on the basis of their class position, that is, on the basis of their relation to the means of production. They take a step in facilitating workers acting together, as workers, on behalf of their own self-interest.

Even traditional unionism has political potential as a stepping stone toward the development of socialist consciousness and socialist forms of organization because unions provide a vehicle for workers to experience collective action and to fight for changes that are in their best interests. Also since employers often actively resisted unions, the union struggle helps workers to demystify the "one big happy family" concept endorsed by employers. Consequently unions help to sharpen political issues and the reality

---

[12]A useful case example is Mathew Rinaldi, "Dissent in the Brotherhood: Organizing in the Teamster's Union," *Radical America*, 11 (July-August, 1977), 43–55. Several cases are reported in "Essays on the Social Relations of Work and Labor," a special issue of *The Insurgent Sociologist*, 8 (Fall, 1978). See also Matt Witt, "Two Reform Groups Take on the Teamsters," *Working Papers for a New Society*, July-August, 1978, 10–14.

of class conflict, even when they are not consciously organized as instruments of class struggle.

For social workers, particularly, labor union involvement can be an important step in political education and growth. As social workers we internalize, in part, an anticonflict ethic. We are socialized into the belief that people of good will, acting together, can solve problems in a mutually satisfactory way. Despite the fact that reality does not often bear this out, since the reality is that different classes in the society have different, nonresolvable (contradictory) interests, many social workers continue to hold this view. Further we are queasy about conflict. We view it as impolite and as inconsistent with effective professional functioning. However, by the logic of the issues unions pursue, they lead to the necessity for drawing political battle lines, for being impolite at the least, and for taking strong, conflict-oriented actions. Unions can provide the experience of collective work, organizing, and engaging in political analysis. They can move workers to a more activist stance in relation to social and economic issues.

Unions can play another important political function, particularly unions whose members are involved in service work of various kinds. Union contracts and union structures provide ways of raising issues about the social policies that govern service delivery and the nature of service provision itself. These are real workplace, point-of-production material issues, they are not mystified, so-called professional ones.[13]

Most unions, blue and white collar, generally make demands beyond those concerning pay and fringe benefits. For industrial workers safety conditions and the right to take immediate remedial action when faced with unsafe conditions are often among the issues on which unions bargain. In the case of public service unions, like those of teachers and social workers, policy-related issues, for example, can be and sometimes are among the issues debated during contract negotiations. Unions can potentially bring up a wide variety of issues, and they are often the only vehicle for raising these issues consistently and with any hope of success. Rather than view unions as an impediment to high standards of service delivery, it is more accurate to see them as a means of fighting for decent service provision. The involvement of social workers in unions, therefore, while not guaranteeing that progressive policy issues will be raised, creates a means for more effective action than may otherwise be possible.

In considering the case for social work unionization, social workers must examine the alternatives to unionization and the implications of those alternatives. Social workers need job protection. Social work is not an especially popular or prestigious occupation. Further as a public sector activity, it is

---

[13]A helpful discussion is Paul Johnston, "The Promise of Public Sector Unionism," *Monthly Review*, 30 (September, 1978), 43–60.

subject to the economic squeeze created by the fiscal crisis of the state and exacerbated by the fact that social service work is only partially responsive to automation. Social workers, therefore, will and do seek ways to protect their jobs and their right to do their jobs in a decent fashion. If social workers do not involve themselves with unions, they will nevertheless involve themselves with self-protective associations and take other similar measures. Licensing and other efforts to strengthen social work as a profession are the primary alternatives to unionization. These alternatives are far more conservative and much less effective in their overall impact. They divide social workers from other segments of the labor force, and they align social work more closely with the state itself which then becomes, simultaneously, both the social worker's oppressor and protector. If we examine other occupational groups that have sought self-enhancement through increased professionalism, we will find little reason to be optimistic that this line of development will propel social work toward increased social activism or toward greater concern for the larger social and political factors that influence the lives of service users.[14] Unionism, therefore, serves as a counterideology to professionalism. While it is sometimes suggested that unionism and professionalism are not necessary contradictory tendencies, in actual practice, they have tended to be so in other occupational categories and are likely to be so for social work as well.

The political differences between unionism and professionalism emerge even more sharply when we examine these alternative possibilities for social work in the light of socialist strategies of change. Socialist strategies clearly require united action on the part of coalitions within the working class. This includes members of the NWC, blue-collar workers, and social service users who may be marginal members of the working class or temporarily displaced from the working class. Licensing, as one concrete manifestation of the drive toward professionalism, is based on several implicit political assumptions, including the idea that social problems can be effectively handled by "experts," whose competence is certified by the state, and that the state can, or at least might, address itself in a caring and effective way to the needs of working class people. Both of these ideas are highly suspect.

Alternatively unionism suggests that social change results from the large-scale political mobilization of ordinary men and women acting on their

---

[14]For elaboration of this argument, see David Wagner and Marcia Cohen, "Social Workers, Class and Professionalism," *Catalyst: A Socialist Journal of the Social Services*, 1 (1978), 25–54; John B. McKinley, "On the Professional Regulation of Change," in "Professionalism and Social Change," a special issue of *The Sociological Review Monograph*, ed. Paul Halmos, Keele, England, 20 (December, 1973), 61–84; Brian Heraud, "Professionalism, Radicalism and Social Change," in Halmos, "Professionalism and Social Change," pp. 85–101; Jeffry Galper, *The Politics of Social Services* (Englewood Cliffs, N.J.: Prentice-Hall, Inc., 1975), pp. 89–100; and Magali Sarfatt Larson, *The Rise of Professionalism* (Berkeley: University of California Press, 1977).

own behalf. Unionism, as a basis for organization, puts social workers into alignment with other segments of the working class. It clarifies for social workers that their target for political action, their employer, is the state. In this way it more closely aligns social workers with social service users who must also view the state as the target of whatever political activity they undertake. Whereas professionalism tends to position social workers against social service users in the assumptions it makes about long-term interests, unionism heightens the potential for workers and service users to clarify the common role that the state plays in their well-being, or lack of same.

To summarize, labor unions have not always been a model of progressive political activity and have not always conducted their affairs with high degrees of responsiveness to their membership. They are none the less the best hope that social workers have, at present, for meeting the immediate economic dilemmas of public service employment. Further from a socialist perspective, labor unions, in general, and social work unions, as well, have served as important schools for workers in the larger process of politicization and radicalization. Particularly for social service workers, they offer a way to express concern about broader policy issues as well as about immediate job conditions. Also of special importance to social service workers, whose own power when acting alone is not great compared to that of some key segments of the blue-collar labor force, unions offer a vehicle for building coalitions with other public sector and private sector workers, and with service users. This alliance is key to the formation of a successful socialist movement in the United States.

Social Workers and Unions: A Long Acquaintance

Historically social workers have considerable experience with unionism.[15] It is useful to trace this history, since the quiescent 1950s left a gap in the continuity of social workers' union experience with the result that unionization in social work seems like a new idea and hence more of a departure from social work traditions than it actually is.

Social workers were among the earliest public employees to unionize. Many entered the union struggle with an understanding of the relationship among job security issues for social workers, the needs of service users, and broader issues of social change. These efforts began in the 1930s. Many of those early union struggles and the rationale for those efforts were reported in the leftist social work journal of the day, *Social Work Today*, and so are

---

[15]To the best of my knowledge, no complete study of social work unionization has been undertaken. A brief historical overview is found in "Unions in Social Work," *Encyclopedia of Social Work* (Washington, D.C.: National Association of Social Workers, 1977), pp. 1559–63.

available to us as we uncover our own history.[16] In 1936 Mary Van Kleek, one of the better-known radicals in social welfare, made the case for social work unions during that period as well as anyone might make it for our own times. She argued as follows:

> Protective organization along trade union lines seems to me necessary for social workers for two reasons; 1. With the growth in the size of social agencies and with concentration of control over funds through central money-raising organizations, salaries and conditions of work are set for a whole group and not for the individual. Organization is necessary if social workers are to have any voice in determining what shall be their salaries and conditions of employment. 2. The environment in which social work is done is economic, and so are the conditions which give rise to the need for most of the activities included in social work. If, in addition to seeking to aid the individual, social workers are to exert a broader influence toward changing conditions which cause poverty, then organization becomes necessary in order to cooperate with other organizations with an economic program directed toward greater security of employment and higher standards of living. These are the purposes of the labor movement. Upon the labor movement devolves the responsibility for support of measures which social workers naturally advocate. By becoming part of the labor movement, they are strengthened in their advocacy, and they may in time broaden that scope and increase the effectiveness of the trade unions in the development of a social program.[17]

In a similarly direct statement, and one consistent with a line of reasoning which many social workers accepted, Howard Cullen argued in 1936 that he was

> definitely of the opinion that social workers, like all other workers, have a perfect right to organize along trade union lines. It has always appeared highly illogical for supposedly philanthropic and humanitarian organizations to attempt to evade responsibilities which even profit making industry today accepts. In the long run there can be no decent relationship between workers and their employers without adequate representation on both sides.[18]

Not only were such arguments common at that time, but many social workers pursued the same logic in actual practice. What was called the rank-and-file movement in the mid-1930s claimed 15,000 members, employed largely in public agencies. It did much of the ideological and organiza-

---

[16]Some history of the rank and file social work clubs that sponsored *Social Work Today* is found in Leslie Leighninger and Robert Knickmeyer, "The Rank and File Movement: The Relevance of Radical Social Work Traditions to Modern Social Work Practice," *Journal of Sociology and Social Welfare*, 4 (November, 1976), 166–77.

[17]Mary Van Kleek, untitled discussion in *Social Work Today*, 3 (January, 1936), 6.

[18]Howard S. Cullen, untitled discussion in *Social Work Today*, 3 (January, 1936), 7.

tional spade work that stimulated public sector unionization efforts among social workers.[19] In addition as early as 1931, workers in the private sector associated with the Jewish Federation in New York City organized the New York Association of Federation Workers and later conducted the first work stoppage in social work history.[20] Shortly after, in 1933 the first protective association in the public sector, the Federation of Social Service Employees, was established. Though it was not successful as an organization, it laid the groundwork for the idea of social worker trade unions in the public sector and led to the formation of a more powerful employees association shortly after. Specifically workers in the Home Relief Bureau of New York formed the Home Relief Employees Association in December, 1933. Its notable successes in raising salaries and improving working conditions led to a rapid spread of the social worker unions. Within a year similar organizations existed in Chicago, Cincinnati, Cleveland, Detroit, Minneapolis, Newark, Philadelphia and Pittsburgh.[21]

It is exciting to discover the level of political consciousness and degree of militancy that existed among these early trade unions. In issue after issue of *Social Work Today*, militant, and often radical, trade union activity is reported. The following example from the December, 1937 issue illustrates such action.

> The question, "Can social agency employees go on strike?" now has an answer. They did it. Not only did the organized social service employees of the Los Angeles Federation of Jewish Welfare Organizations call a 100 percent effective strike but they won their strike. The spectacle of a group of professional men and women parading on a spirited picket line in front of the Federation building for eight days from June 28th to July 7th, is one never to be forgotten by Los Angeles citizens.

> In protest against the arbitrary dismissal of three social workers with an average employment period of eight years in the Jewish Social Service Bureau (a private family welfare agency, which is a constituent of the Jewish Welfare Federation supported by the Community Chest), the entire staff of the J.S.S.B. walked out after weeks of fruitless negotiations and "conferencing" with their administration. The staff's determination to have the dismissed workers reinstated was wholeheartedly endorsed by their union, the Association of Employees in Jewish Social Agencies. Because the workers throughout the entire Federation believed that "insecurity for one means insecurity for all," it was only several hours after the Bureau workers walked out that they were joined on the picket-

---

[19]Jacob Fischer, "The Rank and File Movement, 1930–1936," *Social Work Today*, 3-(February, 1936), 5.

[20]Ibid., p. 6.

[21]Ibid.

line by workers from six other Federation agencies. The line included professional, clerical, and maintenance employees, and by the second day of the strike the entire building was deserted except for executives and emergency workers, authorized by the strikers to serve clients in need of emergency care.[22]

Similarly a February, 1938 article detailed the fight of the State, County, and Municipal Workers of America, which had organized public welfare workers in Pennsylvania, to maintain adequate welfare policies in that state in the face of political efforts to reduce benefit levels as the depression deepened.[23] As late as the early 1940s social work unions were continuing to battle for union recognition and for the right to participate in shaping policy issues in the social welfare arena[24] in the face of escalating domestic repression encouraged by World War II.

These early, promising developments in social work unionization met increasing resistance from the war years through the McCarthy period. In 1950 the United Office and Professional Workers of America, the major social work union of the time, was expelled from the CIO for alleged communist domination as were ten other unions.[25] Also expelled was the State, County, and Municipal Workers of America, one of the major unions to which social workers belonged. While exact numbers of social workers involved in these unions is not available, the United Office and Professional Workers consisted of approximately twenty locals in 1949, of which the best known was Local 19, New York City, the Social Service Employees Union (SSE).

The rate of social work unionization slowed in the intervening period. However in the most recent decade, social workers have been joining two major social work unions in increasing numbers. In the public sector the Service Employees International Union (SEIU) represents approximately twenty thousand social workers in California, Rhode Island, Connecticut, and Pennsylvania (out of a total membership of four hundred thousand people). Many social workers are also organized in local unions that are affiliated with the American Federation of State, County, and Municipal Employees

---

[22]Deena Merlin, "Los Angeles Picket Line," *Social Work Today*, 4 (October, 1937), 16.

[23]Jack Strobel and Nathan Newstein, "Pennsylvania Union Fights On," *Social Work Today*, 5 (February, 1938), 11.

[24]A review article on this period is "Social Work Democracy in Action," *Social Work Today*, 7 (December, 1940), 9–15.

[25]This history is reviewed in a very useful study by Leslie Alexander, "Organizing the Professional Social Worker: Union Development in Voluntary Social Work, 1930–1950," (Unpublished doctoral dissertation presented to the School of Social Work and Social Research, Bryn Mawr College, 1976).

(AFSCME). The total membership of AFSCME is approximately 1.2 million people.[26] Of the sixty thousand AFSCME members who are social workers, fifty thousand work in county, city, or state welfare departments, and ten thousand work in voluntary agencies.[27] It is possible, therefore, to account for at least eighty thousand unionized social workers, out of a total social work population in the United States of approximately a quarter of a million workers (according to BLS accounting of occupational categories.[28]).

The union experience of public school teachers in the United States may presage developments for social workers. For teachers the 1960s were a crucial period.[29] The level of teachers' union consciousness is now remarkably sophisticated, given the state of affairs ten or fifteen years ago. At that time many teachers were critical of teacher unions. Unions for teachers and typical union-like activities, for example, strikes, were viewed as contrary to the service ethic of the teaching profession, and in any case were often illegal. By the late 1970s the idea of unionization and the right, and even the necessity, of teachers to engage in trade union action was generally taken for granted both by teachers and by much of the rest of the working class. It is fortunate for teachers that this is so. In view of the consistency with which government is unable to fund public education, the unions are often the only political force that stands in the way of severe cuts in teachers' living standards. Similarly while no one can precisely predict the future of social work unionization, in terms of either the extent of unionization or the political direction that unionization will take, it is likely, given the similarities in backgrounds and situations between teachers and social workers, that social work will develop greater union consciousness and the political ideas that go with that consciousness in the near future.

Several forces propel the recent upsurge in public sector and white-

---

[26]In June, 1978, the Civil Service Employees Association of New York affiliated with AFSCME to raise AFSCME's total membership to 1,200,000. That made AFSCME the largest union in the AFL-CIO at that point, raising it from a position as third largest union in the AFL-CIO.

[27]Alexander, "Organizing the Professional Social Worker," p. 3.

[28]By this reckoning, approximately one third of all social workers are unionized. In contrast, 21.6 percent of the total labor force of the United States was unionized in 1974. Excluding agricultural workers, 25.7 percent of the labor force was unionized in that year. They were involved in 173 national and international unions. Of these, 111 were AFL-CIO affiliates. An additional 36 organizations are identified as professional and state public employee associations. Data are from U.S. Department of Labor, Bureau of Labor Statistics, *A Brief History of the American Labor Movement*, Bulletin 1000 (Washington, D.C.: U.S. Government Printing Office, 1976), p. 54.

[29]A useful review is Steve Leluck's *Toward Teacher Power*, Sun Press (International Socialists Book Service), 14131 Woodward Avenue, Room 225, Highland Park, Michigan 48203, n.d.

collar unionization. One of the most critical has been the shifts that have occurred in the composition of the labor force itself. Over 42 percent of all workers in the United States were white-collar workers in 1975 in contrast with 28 percent in 1960.[30] In 1974 one in six United States workers was directly employed by government.[31] In addition the pressure created by early efforts at public sector unionization led to some significant developments in public law that created a more favorable climate for such efforts, including John F. Kennedy's Executive Order on Employee-Management Cooperation in the Federal Service, issued in January, 1962, and similar legislation enacted by many states and localities related to collective bargaining. Growing unionization has also been a response to an awakening by the U.S. labor movement to these shifts in the composition of the labor force and has led to their subsequent unionization drives in the public sector. The influence of the civil rights movement, in addition to generally acknowledged unfavorable working conditions for public employees, were also important factors.[32]

Social work unionization, then, is taking place within a broad context of increased unionization in the public sector. The trend has been advancing for almost twenty years. Social workers are increasingly active in that movement. In becoming reactivated in the union struggle, social workers revive an involvement which began in the 1930s though it experienced a period of quietude for some twenty years. Now their involvement reemerges in response to the particular circumstances of the 1970s and 1980s.

Selecting and Organizing a Union

selecting a union

The process of introducing a union into a nonunionized work situation generally begins with the interest of one or several workers in an agency.[33] They begin to investigate the possibilities for unionization by talking with potentially interested workers, by educating themselves about the various

---

[30]*Pocket Data Book, U.S.A., 1976* (Washington, D.C.: U.S. Government Printing Office, 1977), Table 206, p. 164.

[31]*Pocket Data Book, U.S.A., 1976, Table 203, p. 163.*

[32]Brief History of the American Labor Movement, p. 47. The proportion of white collar unionists as a percentage of all union members in the United States rose from 12 percent in 1960 to 16 percent in 1970. Data are from Martin Oppenheimer, "The Unionization of the Professional," *Social Policy*, 6 (January-February, 1975), 34.

[33]It also sometimes originates with the union, which targets workers in an agency or group of agencies as potential affiliates. However, we are concerned here with worker-initiated activity.

unions with which the workers in that agency might affiliate, and by meeting with workers in unionized agencies to review the pros and cons of unionization. Relatively early in the process, the people most closely involved in the effort to unionize must make a choice about which union affiliations to pursue more seriously. Eventually a certification election will be held among the workers who would be included in the union. That vote will determine whether or not the workers want to join a union and may also determine which union the workers will join. Many unions organize workers from a wide range of occupational groupings. Therefore the workers in a given agency and the people who take the initiative in introducing the union idea may have considerable influence in the decision about which union best meets the needs of the workers in that particular agency. On what basis might the selection of unions be made when viable alternatives exist?

There are three primary considerations in selecting a union. The first is the extent to which a particular union has a history and structure supportive of democratic processes in the handling of union business.[34] In considering the relation of union work to the broader process of politicization, it is particularly necessary to give attention to whether union involvement encourages attitudes and skills among workers that foster further progressive political work. Therefore in selecting a union, it is important to investigate whether the union sees itself as facilitating the efforts of workers in the local agency to pursue the issues of particular importance to them or operates in a top-down, authoritarian fashion. Concretely this involves being certain that the union will support workers in local agencies in formulating their own contract demands and in voting directly to approve or not approve a contract, after full opportunities for review of the proposed contract language.

There are several other standards by which workers can assess unions' commitment to democratic processes. If the proposed organizing drive is of some magnitude; that is, if it involves a very large agency or a series of branches or deparments of an agency, the full-time or nearly full-time efforts of one or more organizers may be devoted to the project for a period of time. If so, does the local organizing committee have a say over who that organizer will be? Is that organizer responsible to the local committee or to the central union office? Are competing slates presented in elections for union office, and how well publicized are union elections and alternative platforms in those elections? How much authority and discretion do shop stewards and grievance chairpeople at the shop level have in acting on local issues? To what extent does the union involve shop stewards in conducting the overall business of the

---

[34]A useful discussion is Sherrie Holmes, "Beginning Clerical Organizing," in New American Movement, *Discussion Bulletin # 19*, 1977, pp. 7–11. A useful case illustration of some of the issues involved in selection of a union, and the stakes, is Judy Syfers, "San Francisco School Workers' Union Struggle," *Radical America*, 12 (March-April, 1978), 62–71.

union and in establishing union policy? Finally what proportion of members' union dues are kept by the local and made available for use at its discretion, and what proportion is sent off to the national or international headquarters?

A second consideration in union selection is the militance and political thrust of the union. Is the union a fighting union; that is, does it have a history of vigorously supporting and representing the interests of its members? What is its local and national history in supporting progressive issues and with how much vigor has it pursued these issues? Has the union organized broader coalitions with other public employee unions, blue-collar unions, and groups of service users and community people? To what extent does the union have a history of encouraging workers to bargain over a broad range of issues, including, in the case of unions whose members are social workers, those concerning social policy and the delivery of service? What evidence is there that the union will back workers' demands to include service issues and policy issues as part of contract negotiations?[35]

The third consideration involves the question of vertical as opposed to horizontal unionization. A *vertical union* structure is one in which all the workers in a given agency or institution are organized into a single union, regardless of their particular occupational category. A *horizontal union* structure is one in which a group of workers in a given occupational category are organized into a single union with workers from other agencies or institutions who have the same job or occupation. If the social workers organizing a union are employed in a large institution, for example, a hospital in which other employees are already unionized, there is a strong case to be made on behalf of the social workers joining the same union as their coworkers. This vertical integration of all workers in a single agency creates greater strength for each separate unit during contract negotiations. Vertical integration of this sort helps to make the union a potentially more powerful tool in the struggle against racism and sexism in the workplace. It allows for the possibility of addressing racism and sexism in a unified way. Alternatively when workers are organized into different unions and stratified by occupation, the more elite workers, who are likely also to be disproportionately white and male, are encouraged to look after their own interests, with less regard for the situation of women and minority workers.[36]

---

[35]There are a number of ways to obtain this information, including discussions with existing members of the union, a review of the union's contracts (which are available on file with the Department of Labor) and a look at newspaper clippings. For some unions, the *New York Times Index* will cite relevant news items.

[36]A useful case analysis is Jacqueline Bernard, "Organizing Hospital Workers," *Working Papers for a New Society,* 4 (Fall, 1976), pp. 53–59. See also Claudette Giroux, "The Role of Women in the Canadian Trade Union Movement." Independent Enquiry Project, School of Social Work, Carleton University, Ottawa, Canada, August, 1978.

If the union that is already involved at the workplace does not have a great deal of expertise with social service workers, a possible disadvantage for the social service workers might be the union's unfamiliarity with issues of particular concern to social workers, for example, those related to service delivery. This disadvantage would have to be weighed against the greater strength the social workers would gain by joining together with other workers in that agency. To the extent that the workers in a single agency are fragmented in their union representation, all are seriously disadvantaged, and this is an important consideration in such cases. Even then social workers should know that they are free to raise issues of particular relevance for them, though they may experience some pressure to pursue uniform demands in selected areas of contract negotiation.

On the other hand, if no other unions are involved with the workers in a particular agency, or if there are compelling reasons on other grounds not to affiliate with the union that is involved, social workers would have more reason to seek affiliation with a national or international union experienced with social workers. In such cases the workers in the agency will not necessarily bargain jointly with workers in other agencies. They will not be part of the same bargaining unit even though they are members of the same national union. This represents a form of horizontal integration. Since much policy affecting social workers in any particular agency originates at the state and federal level, strong statewide and nationwide unions of social service workers can have, and already have had, an important role in the political process.

While there are obvious advantages for social workers in joining unions experienced with social workers, and for social workers in joining unions involved with other workers in their workplaces, there can also be some advantages in joining unions primarily composed of blue-collar workers. For various historical reasons, some social workers are members of unions in which the majority of the members hold blue-collar occupations, such as public employee unions of sanitation workers, city engineers, and bus drivers. The clout of these unions can benefit social workers, who are less powerful. Also the social work voice in the councils of these unions, which tend to be somewhat more conservative in many cities (particularly at the leadership level), can be a positive influence, though generally a small one, on overall union policy.

organizing a union

The mechanics of the union-organizing process are not difficult to outline though they may be difficult to implement if there is resistance from the employer or if coworkers are not united in their commitment to unionizing. The union-organizing process begins with conversations with coworkers about their workplace concerns and about the role which a union could play in

responding to those concerns. Once the effort to organize a union is under-
way, it is useful for the individuals most closely involved to make that fact
known to the National or State Labor Relations Board[37] since certain legal
protections against firing and harassment are then in effect. This does not
mean that there will not be harassment and possibly firings if management
learns of the unionizing effort and is hostile to it. However opportunities for
legal redress exist in some settings. The National Labor Relations Act is
modified from time to time, though presently the protections for social
workers in some (not all) nonprofit organizations are not as strong as are those
for workers in other sectors of the labor force.

Once consideration is given to a union or alternative unions, contact
with those unions will bring the assistance of an experienced union organizer
with knowledge of the applicable laws. The goal of the effort is to sign up a
majority of the employees involved in the bargaining unit.[38] They must
indicate their desire to be part of the union on a union authorization card.

Once enough authorization cards are signed, the union will request a
certification election, monitored by the State Labor Relations Board or by the
National Labor Relations Board. In rare cases the agency will accept the
evidence of the authorization cards and not insist on a formal election. Typically a formal election is required. If the majority of the workers vote for the
union, a bargaining committee is chosen and contract negotiations are begun.
The committee will include a union staff negotiator.

The process, from the initiation of interest to the onset of bargaining for a
contract, may take as long as a year, or even longer. The organizers must be
prepared for this. During this period it is also important to continue to hold
union meetings, some of which will once more involve discussion of the basic
questions about unions and the rationale for unionization. Since staff turnover
in many social agencies is high, union organizers must attend to the orienta-

---

[37]The union activities of Federal employees and of social workers in private agencies are
under the jurisdiction of the National Labor Relations Board. Other public employees are under
the jurisdiction of their respective State Labor Relations Boards. Information on relevant labor
law is available in two accessible United States government pamphlets. They are *A Layman's
Guide to Basic Law Under the National Labor Relations Act* (Stock Number 3100-095:
Washington, D.C.: U.S. Government Printing Office) and *Electing Union Officers* (Stock
Number 2900-00212: Washington, D.C.: U.S. Government Printing Office.)

[38]The bargaining unit consists of those people who work in a "community of interest" in
performing a given task. The concept is loose, and the union can advise which workers might or
might not be allowed to be considered as part of the unit. If management contests the workers'
definition of the appropriate unit, which they may do if they feel it will help to defeat the union, a
hearing will be held by the Labor Relations Board, whose definition of the appropriate bargaining
unit must be adhered to in the certification election. The major strategies for avoiding a defeat on
these grounds are to check with the union beforehand as to their best judgment about the
appropriate bargaining unit and, most critical, to do the work that assures strong union support in
all segments of the agency so that the union has majority support regardless of the workers
included in the bargaining unit.

tion and education of new staff members as an ongoing part of the organizing process. At this stage a useful tactic is to prepare a written document for new staff members on why the union drive was organized initially. This can help to provide some continuity of shared understanding during the early, critical phases.

The organizers must also expect some workers to be fearful and resistant. There are no easy solutions to these problems. Fear is best combatted by realistically acknowledging the potentials and problems involved in unionization and by encouraging workers to share their questions and their support for the union with one another on an individual basis and in larger support meetings. If the initial interest in a union, which often arises from one or several people, is spread through creation of an organizing committee, and if the organizing committee involves other union supporters in the process, the ability of management to intimidate individual workers will be limited.

An important part of the organizing process is educating workers about unions. Many social service workers are not familiar with unions. They do not understand the union process, and they may have a variety of prejudices about unions. Initial contacts with workers, focusing on their feelings, complaints, and hopes about the workplace, are an important starting point in the educational process that must take place if the union is to be active and progressive. Workers with a commitment to unionization in a given agency must be prepared to take the lead in this task. Practically they cannot rely on the union organizer to have the time and commitment to undertake the required educational task.

It is also realistic to anticipate that agencies will resist workers' efforts to unionize and to be prepared for that resistance. Some executives may argue that the agency will lose support from private funding sources if workers unionize. They may try to head off the union by promising or actually delivering pay increases or benefit improvements prior to the election. They may harass, intimidate, or fire key union activists. In addition management is likely to publish and circulate misleading or distorted information about the union, its budget, its policies, and the control it will exercise over workers. Union organizers are well advised to take nothing for granted that emanates from management. They must be prepared to invest considerable energy in correcting and countering management propaganda.[39] The major defenses against these tactics are a commitment to the right and the necessity of social workers to organize, as solid a knowledge base as possible about the legal

---

[39]Some of the traditional union busting techniques in blue collar organizing, many of which have been adopted whole or in modified form by social welfare agencies, are reviewed in "Union Busting in the Midwest," *The Organizer*, Newspaper of the Philadelphia Workers Organizing Committee, February, 1978, pp. 8–9.

rights of workers to organize, and most critically, the support of workers in the agency who believe firmly in their right to organize.

Organizers can also anticipate direct opposition from some coworkers who may fear losing special privileges, who may have bought management perspectives about lay-offs as a consequence of unionization, or who may simply oppose unions on general principle. Again the response must necessarily be patient, ongoing educational work among those whose negative attitudes can be influenced, and active pursuit of endorsement and involvement among those who are already prounion.

Progressive Unionism

the importance of a political framework

What I have discussed to this point covers what is by far the easiest part of the job. Of course the effort to organize a union can be long and difficult, and sometimes these efforts are not successful. However in most cases, unionization can be achieved in social welfare settings.

From a radical perspective organizing a union is only the first step. Unfortunately the energy required to build a union is often substantial, and the ongoing commitment necessary to maintain union life is sufficiently great that even progressive people can lose sight of the larger political purposes involved. They become so enmeshed in the daily events that the broader political questions and the connections to socialist development are misplaced.[40] There is also an ongoing temptation to downplay more radical

---

[40]The Association of Social Service Workers is a radical social service workers collective in Toronto, Canada. Through the mid-1970s they directed considerable energy toward encouraging unionization among social service workers in Toronto, a project in which they were quite successful. Looking back on that effort, one of their members concluded that the socialist commitments that led to that effort were displaced in the struggle. See Peter Holland, "Organizing Social Service Workers," *Network, A Political Newsletter for Social Service Workers,* 1 (February, 1978), 13–14. Other radicals who have involved themselves in union work report similar experiences. A useful discussion of some of the tendencies to move too far in a reformist direction while involved in essentially nonradical mass organizations is Frank Ackerman, "Dare to Struggle: Dare To Influence People," *Radical America,* 12 (March-April, 1978), 56–61. Among the suggestions which radicals have made to counter these tendencies are that radicals put energy more heavily into the formation of a rank and file, or radical caucus, rather than allow themselves to be drawn into formal leadership positions within unions; that they focus on leadership roles centered around the grievance procedure particularly; and that they focus on the formation of citywide caucuses of radical social service unionists. While there is insufficient empirical evidence to suggest the absolute desirability of any one of these strategies, undoubtedly radical unionists will pursue many approaches and hopefully will find vehicles for making their successes and failures known to others.

unionism in the face of worker and employer resistance. Further the effort to maintain a radical commitment in union work is hampered at present by the absence of a strong socialist movement in society. Such a movement would facilitate more radical unionism through the political ideas it introduced to larger numbers of people and through the concrete support radical unions would experience as they found other groups of people organized to fight the same kinds of fights they were undertaking. The fact that the movement is not powerful at present makes the job of integrating radical politics with union work more difficult.

Since we are concerned about radical practice, it behooves us to explore ways in which the radical political commitments that initially inspired union involvement can continue to play a prominent role in our union work. As in other areas of radical practice, the starting point in this effort must be our willingness to assess our work as unionists using the criteria of our politics. To some extent we will be pushed along by the tide of events which sometimes moves spontaneously in a more progressive direction. In a more conservative period radical ideas and radical practice will not often appear spontaneously. We must, therefore, make conscious efforts to work from the perspective of our socialist commitments. This requires that we assess our union work in terms of its role in building broader coalitions among working-class people, spreading radical ideas more broadly, and developing the kind of organizations that will encourage militant class struggle in the society.

It is useful to keep in mind that organizing a union and working politically with and through a union are part of a continuing process. Too often union organizers, including those with radical inclinations, target the certification vote and the first contract as the culmination of their organizing work. In the present political climate, workers in a local agency situation cannot count on the ongoing involvement of a paid union organizer or of most workers. It is almost always up to the politically conscious workers in an agency to maintain a strong union local through their constant efforts. This means that union activists must strive ceaselessly to involve members in union affairs and to encourage members to unite for political action, not only at contract time, but on a continual basis on the issues that will inevitably arise. The union needs to become a vehicle for political education through the issues it raises, the way in which it conducts its business, and through forums, newsletters, and so on. Unions can also organize formal educational experiences for their members and for other workers, for example, through film presentations and through classes on unions, union history, union-organizing methods, and the larger political import of unionization.

When progressive workers help to organize a union and then abandon that effort, they may do a political disservice. Without ongoing organizing efforts at the local level, the union will not achieve strong contracts, and workers will not develop their appreciation of the power of collective efforts. A union which is weak in its ability to achieve what workers want and need and which becomes oligarchical will reinforce in workers' minds the idea that collective political success is not possible. Workers will feel cheated, left out, and angry that their issues are not being represented. They will be reinforced in the notion that only individualistic solutions to problems can help them.

Organizing a union and doing political work in a union are means to an end and not ends in themselves. They will not be effective unless they serve the immediate needs of workers. At the same time, unless the union is a means for the political education of workers, unless it pursues a class-conflict, rather than a class-collaborationist policy, and unless it pursues nonreformist reforms, it will fail in the immediate situation and in its contribution to socialism.

I will explore some possibilities for introducing radical perspectives in three areas of union practice. They are (1) the issues which the union raises about the immediate circumstances of the workplace and about larger political questions; (2) the way in which the union operates internally, particularly its commitment to union democracy; and (3) the strategies and tactics the union employs, particularly its militance and its willingness and ability to move in the direction of forming broader progressive coalitions.

choosing issues

In any union situation a variety of goals may be pursued. Even traditional union contracts can and often do take up many aspects of the work situation. Most commonly these include wages, hours, and working conditions; authorities and conditions for employing, suspending, and discharging employees; schedules and procedures for performance ratings; classifications of employees; seniority, promotions, and transfers; work schedules, overtime, holidays, vacations, leaves, and terminations; benefits, expenses, and clothing or uniform allowances where applicable; salaries; grievance procedures; provision for emergency services; contract duration and renewal provisions; as well as other items such as those related to the specific organization.[41] While these are areas that are commonly accepted as appropriate items for collective bargaining, there are actually no issues which workers cannot raise through their union. Their ability to win their demands will depend, of course, on the power they generate through their collective efforts to force concessions from employers.

Not all of the political efforts of progressive unions are directed toward achieving particular contract provisions. The union, as a vehicle for political work, may move in many directions within the agency and in the larger society. However much of the political work of the union will be directed

---

[41]"Unions in Social Work," *Encyclopedia of Social Work*, pp. 1561–62.

toward achieving progressive changes and improvements in the contract itself. Two areas that are often of particular interest to social service workers and that are beyond the usual scope of union contracts concern workplace democracy and service issues themselves. These concerns are often linked, since workers, in fighting for more input into agency decision making, often find themselves fighting in order to be in a position to make a progressive impact on delivery patterns.

In some settings workers have fought for worker involvement in policy-making bodies of the agency as a contractual right. These provisions may take various forms. In some cases they may involve worker participation in formal structures for reviewing the care given to service users. For example, in one case an agency with a middle- and upper-class clientele was known to give preferential treatment to people with personal connections to key staff or board members or who were generous contributors to the agency. Workers typically had little say about these matters, even in cases where the priorities assigned by the administration conflicted with workers' assessments of the needs of the people with whom they were working. A service review committee, formalized through the contract, provided a means for worker input into these matters. Similarly workers have fought for representation on boards of directors, as a formal contract provision. However, it is well to stress at the start that the power of workers to influence policy depends only partially on formal contract agreements. The willingness and ability of workers to act collectively and vigorously in pressing management at each and every turn is critical.

A decent, if conventional contract, vigorously pursued, can provide workers with a means of influencing service delivery patterns through their daily activity as well as through official participation in structured agency decision-making bodies. Social work unions, as well as unions in most sectors, have been actively resisted by management when they have sought greater involvement in areas management has typically reserved as its own bailiwick, namely, policy making. None the less the potential power of workers to agree to perform or not to perform any particular task, and to do so in ways that the workers view as consistent with their own best interests and those of service users, provides the workers with a great deal of leverage over agency direction. For example, social work unionists in New York City in the early 1970s refused to staff the experimental "Brownie Point System." Under this plan AFDC grants would have been cut to a rock bottom minimum, to be supplemented by the recipient who would earn "points" for various kinds of approved behavior. Points could be earned if the children in the family joined the Boy Scouts or Girl Scouts, regularly attended school and cooperated with their teachers, and if the mother made home improvements and reported bi-weekly on the whereabouts of a missing father. While resistance to the proposal extended beyond the union, the refusal of the union workers was crucial since their rejection of this policy would have made its implementation impossible, had it not been rescinded.[42]

In a similar vein, many public sector social work unions have bargained over the issue of caseload size. This issue is analogous to one which is frequently negotiated by teacher unions, namely, classroom size. Caseload size is important to social workers who are frequently not allowed to work with people as fully and thoughtfully as they would like. At the same time, the ability of the union to specify caseload size impinges on the agency's policy-making prerogatives since it helps to define an appropriate workload and subsequently influences budgetary planning.

An example of the kinds of issues that can be pursued by progressive social work unions was provided by the SSEU of the New York City Department of Social Services through the 1960s. The union was by no means completely successful in winning all the demands it raised, and it was not able to sustain its militant posture through a subsequent period of repression and internal conflict. However the issues it raised are exciting and illustrative of the possibilities. Through this period the union pursued, through its collective bargaining demands, the right to bargain for whatever matters were considered job related, including caseload, workload, and many aspects of the job generally viewed as managerial prerogatives; the elimination of multiple levels of approval for authorization for grants so that line workers could directly and speedily authorize welfare payments; participation in policy making; budget raises for welfare recipients to reflect cost of living; automatic clothing grants and telephones for recipients; the right of workers to determine the adequacy of housing accommodations without waiting for official action from municipal housing agencies; caseload reduction; and worker training programs including funding for university education in social work studies.[43]

Unions have also taken active stands as unions on issues not immediately and specifically related to them and encouraged their members to do the same. Many progressive unions have urged their membership to support other union struggles, for example by boycotting nonunion lettuce and grapes to support United Farmworkers Union tactics. Similarly union struggles with the Farah company, Coors beer, J. P. Stevens, and others received support

---

[42]See "Brownie Point Welfare," *Social Service Review*, 46 (March, 1972), 111–13 and "Relief Workers Reject Program," *New York Times*, November 23, 1971, p. 53.

[43]From Richard H. Mendes, "The Professional Union: A Study of the Social Services Employees Union of the New York City Department of Social Services," (unpublished doctoral dissertation presented to Columbia University, 1974), p. 364. Mendes' study is reviewed, and additional analysis of that same union offered, in George Silberman, "Professional and Oligarchical Tendencies in the Social Services Employees Union," Office of Training, Department of Social Services, New York, New York, 1977, unpublished.

from unions which encouraged their members not to purchase products manufactured by the companies involved. At the level of broad national policy, unions were active in the antiwar movement during the 1960s and frequently participated in political campaigns on issues such as improvements in social welfare measures, national health insurance, and fights against utility rate hikes. While progressive, not all of these demands are radical ones. Once again the job of the radical within a union is to push the union to take the most progressive stand possible on fundamental issues as they arise. For example, it is important that radical unionists make their influence felt in encouraging unions to oppose all antistrike and binding abritration laws, to oppose any future efforts at establishing wage controls, and so on.

An issue that is natural for social work unions and that combines the immediate needs and interests of social workers with a larger anticapitalist struggle is funding cut-backs in the public sector, in general, and in the social services, in particular. Some social work unions have played an active role in fighting such cut-backs. In New York City the SSEU Local 371 AFSCME won an important victory in this arena in 1977. Workers in the Department of Social Services refused to complete a detailed accountability form which management had requested of them as a tactic for justifying subsequent cutbacks in service. In the resulting confrontation and negotiations, the union was successful in raising the more basic issue of service needs and eventually in pushing the agency to rehire laid-off workers.[44] Similarly members of the Pennsylvania Social Services Union in Pittsburgh conducted a one-day wildcat strike in July, 1977, in conjunction with demonstrations planned and conducted by and with various community groups, which led to a rescinding of announced layoffs.[45] The radical British social work journal *Case Con* reported many cases in which social workers refused to perform the work that had been done by workers who were laid off and not replaced. This refusal had the backing of the union to which most British social workers belong and generated a national "Save Your Services" Campaign throughout England.[46] A tactic of this sort has the advantage of being hard to ignore since it brings the workers face to face with state policy and agency policy on a daily basis and so escalates the level of confrontation and militancy.

To summarize, social work unions can pursue many issues that raise

---

[44]This struggle was reported in "News: New York, New York," *Catalyst: A Socialist Journal of the Social Services,* (1, 1978), 109.

[45]"News: Pittsburgh, Pennsylvania," *Catalyst: A Socialist Journal of the Social Services,* (1, 1978), pp. 108–109. The political battles of this local were also reported by Judy MacLean, "The Union Is Us—A Rank and File Campaign That Worked," *Moving On,* the Monthly Magazine of the New American Movement, October, 1977, pp. 15–17.

[46]See "Ways to Fight," Derek Relf, *Case Con,* A Revolutionary Magazine for Social Workers, 23, 1976, pp. 14–15.

basic questions of concern to radicals. The union can provide a vehicle for worker efforts to achieve workplace democracy, to fight for adequate service provision, and to raise larger social questions with an indirect and direct bearing on service delivery. The situation facing the union radical is not different from the one facing the radical in other arenas of practice. It is to search out the issues and the approaches to those issues that stimulate people's willingness to become politically involved and that contain the potential for raising fundamental questions.

union democracy

Unions are like most other large organizations in the United States in their tendency to function in a top-down, hierarchical fashion. The struggle for rank-and-file participation within unions, that is the struggle to democratize unions, is an important focus for radical unionism for at least two reasons. First, without active rank-and-file involvement in the union, the more important demands which workers raise will never be achieved. Especially in difficult political and financial times, such as the present, only a mobilized, united, and fighting union can hope to represent workers' needs adequately. This kind of mobilization occurs only when the rank and file has consistently been actively involved and invested in union affairs. Second, without active rank-and-file involvement the union cannot serve as a "school for socialism," that is, as a vehicle for the political growth and development of union members. It is the experience of actively participating in a fighting organization, of organizing, of leading, and of engaging in politics that helps people to move forward politically. Passive observation will not do the job. The contribution which radicals make within unions to push unions to become a voice for the political expression of union members is an important part of radical work.

Union officials too frequently resist the efforts of workers at the local level to become organized as a powerful voice within the union. Union leadership often prefers a more passive membership, so that the union members can be "delivered" with a minimum of conflict when leaders work out various compromises with employers. This reflects the conservative direction which the United States labor movement has taken and the privileged position of union leaders vis-a-vis workers, which makes them less sensitive than they ought to be to conditions and needs of rank-and-file workers. The union hierarchy is likely to be as formidable an opponent as is the employer when it comes to efforts to encourage rank-and-file participation.

The job of encouraging union involvement at the grass-roots or agency level begins with the very first attempts to organize the union. Even at this point the participatory nature of unionism must be communicated to those involved. As the union is being organized, it must be emphasized that the union can be a useful conduit for workers to voice their grievances, to achieve more decent working conditions and recompense, and to express broader political concerns. The focus of initial contact ought not to be on what the union can do *for* the worker. The emphasis should always be on what workers can do for themselves—a process in which union involvement often proves helpful.

Once a union and a first contract are in place, it is important to continue to involve workers in union activities. There are a number of ways to approach this task. Regular union meetings can provide an opportunity for workers to express their concerns, both on matters covered and not covered in the contract. Specific contract provisions may provide a reason for tackling a particular problem. However when they do not, this should not inhibit workers from acting on their own behalf, using the union structure as a convenient channel if that will facilitate their efforts. Unions and contracts must be viewed strategically. If workers are prepared to act on an issue or want to press for an item on a future contract, union meetings can provide a useful mechanism for planning and organizing. Similarly such meetings can offer a forum for informing members about larger union issues and encouraging their participation in union affairs, for example, in running for union office.

Inevitably formal contract provisions will prove inadequate for resolving some grievances that arise. If workers are not organized in an active way or prepared to act collectively, outstanding grievances are likely to be resolved in favor of management. To the extent that large numbers of workers express their support for a coworker's issue through job actions and through other declarations of their sentiment to immediate supervisors and management, they will assure justice both in the particular case and in a larger number of cases, since management will have been forewarned that arbitrary actions on their part will be resisted vigorously by a unified workforce. Union meetings are an opportunity to share current developments on issues in dispute and to encourage workers to use their full grievance rights.

If the agency is large, a newsletter or newspaper at the local level can also help keep members up to date on issues and can provide members with a forum for expressing their own concerns in writing. Such newspapers should represent a diversity of political opinions, and should be seen as tools for educating and mobilizing membership. They should not reflect official union positions exclusively nor should they serve as a one-way medium of communication from union leadership to union membership.

Most unions are organized through a formal arrangement of shop stewards, that is, workers on the shop level who represent coworkers to management and to the union. It is important that stewards understand, or be made to understand, that their job is not only to represent workers, but to help workers represent themselves. Shop stewards must be encouraged to be active in pursuing rank-and-file concerns with management and within the hierarchy of the union. They must be involved with coworkers as the base from which their power and authority spring. This is true as well of the people who are elected or selected to be grievance officers for the workers. They too must see themselves as facilitating the membership. Only by being publicly accountable for their work can they continue to operate from a psychological and political stance as allies of their coworkers.

All union officials should be subject to recall by the membership. If this is not permitted in the union's bylaws, it might be a worthwhile target to pursue. Similarly some unions follow the practice of paying full-time union staff workers at the same salaries they would have earned had they continued as line workers. If this is not a policy, it might prove to be a useful organizing point when the struggles with the union itself become open. Similarly a useful demand might be that all full-time union workers spend some time at their previous line jobs, whether that be a part of each week or for a year, at given intervals. Provisions that would permit this can then be part of the demands raised at contract negotiations.

More progressive and democratic unionism can also be pursued through the creation of a rank-and-file or a radical caucus within the union. Conservative unionists will argue against such a caucus on the grounds that it divides the union and therefore weakens it in dealing with management. Workers cannot allow this argument to divert their energies if they are convinced that the official union position opposed progressive rank-and-file involvement. Members of the caucus must be clear to themselves and to coworkers and union officialdom that they do support the union, but that they do so critically. Their goal must be to push the union to live up to its highest potential as a representative of the workers by providing a channel for rank-and-file self-expression.

It is necessary and important to take up the struggle against discrimination. Racism and sexism, evil enough in their immediately destructive impact on the workers involved, have also been one of the major underlying sources of divisiveness within the labor movement. As such they have prevented workers from speaking and acting in a more unified and powerful way.[47] Rank-and-file caucuses can speak to these issues as independent bodies and can encourage the union to form agency-wide or shop-wide committees, specifically organized to monitor and pursue issues of racism and sexism within the workplace.

Rank-and-file caucuses often take on the struggle for union democracy as a major concern. They provide workers with a voice for expressing themselves within the union. This perspective was clearly advanced by one such nationwide caucus within a British public employees union which has fought for

---

[47]See Philadelphia Workers' Organizing Committee, "Three Thrusts of the Rank and File Movement," *Trade Union Question*, pp. 23–24, and *Racism and the Workers' Movement*, Philadelphia Workers' Organizing Committee, Box 11768, Philadelphia, Pennsylvania 19101, n.d.

open union elections and for full membership involvement in contract ratifica-
tions, and in various ways has "raised the principle of rank and file control over
the union bureaucracy and has put it in the context of a serious long-term
perspective on work in the union."[48]

Closer to home, a progressive caucus within the Philadelphia branch of
the Pennsylvania Social Services Union (PSSU) pursued a commitment to link
the issues facing the union with the issues facing service users and other union
members. They viewed their aim as building "independent progressive caucuses in each public workers' union throughout the city" and further proposed
that, to make their caucus representative of the workers, they were "seeking
to encourage more black and female participation in addition to all other
individuals who are concerned with their present situation and are willing to
work to improve it." Finally they stressed the necessity for a strong stand
against racism and concluded that a major part of their purpose was to "bring
to the attention of our own unions a wider perspective on issues they should
deal with."[49]

Creating a rank-and-file caucus is not an easy matter, particularly when
such a caucus is not likely to be supported and may be attacked through official
organs of the union. None the less it may be worth the effort if the official
structures of the union are inaccessible or if mechanisms for rank-and-file
involvement in union affairs do not exist. Such caucuses can build significant
power within their unions. Whether or not such caucuses become more
powerful in any given case will depend on the particulars of that case as well as
on the support which progressive organizations within the union receive from
the development of a left movement elsewhere in the society.

union stragegy

An important strategic guideline for radical unionism is to encourage the
union to be militant in its work. Some unionists argue that militance may
alienate potential supporters or reduce the possibilities of achieving an acceptable compromise. Radicals know this and must be prepared to act in a
nonmilitant way if that is tactically advisable. Nevertheless the radical understands that union work represents a piece of a larger class struggle and that
struggle will not progress unless workers are prepared to fight in a militant
way for their rights. The union effort is not concerned solely with working out
temporary compromises with employers, though that may be a short-term

---

[48]John Phillips, "NAG Grows," *Case Con,* 23 (1976), pp. 5–6.

[49]The Public Workers Action Caucus was organized within the Pennsylvania Social
Services Union, Phildelphia, The call for the caucus was issued in *Contact,* the newspaper of the
Philadelphia union, May 3, 1973, p. 2. Unfortunately, the caucus did not develop significant
organizational strength.

goal. In the long run employers are not able to grant workers all the demands they will legitimately raise. Doing so would challenge the essence of capitalism. Therefore unions must prepare themselves and their members for the more typical experience of fighting for what they want. If it is to be successful, the union movement needs to pursue militant action along class lines.

Progressive unionism is also distinguished by its efforts to create broader coalitions of several types. One of these is to forge links with other unions in the public sector. There are problems in building such links, although they are not insurmountable. In the lengthy 1975 strike of the PSSU the state was successful in limiting union gains because it was able to reach a weak agreement with AFSCME whose members work in the same agencies as PSSU members and who initiated a strike at the same time as did the PSSU. When AFSCME went back to work after several days of strike activity, it undermined PSSU's ability to bargain with the state from a position of strength. At the local level there are numerous instances of AFSCME and PSSU locals acting jointly on common issues.[50] At the statewide level these unions compete to organize the same pool of workers and do not always act supportively toward each other. When unified action is not possible on an official union-to-union basis, progressives at the local level need to make efforts to reach out to one another, share concerns, and plan their actions in a way that gives united strength. The necessity for unity among unions is great within the entire labor movement and certainly among public service workers unions whose power, acting individually, is limited.

In a similar fashion during the 1977–78 coalstrike many social service unions gave support to the miners by writing letters and telegrams, by contributing money and in areas where miners live and work, by engaging in special efforts to make food stamps and other public benefits available to miners and their families. In another case support flowed in the other direction, that is, from private sector unions to a social service union (though for workers in a private agency). In 1975 workers in the Big Brothers' Association of Toronto attempted to unionize and had in fact signed authorization cards with the Canadian Union of Public Employees. In a case which received considerable attention in Toronto, the agency fought against union recognition. Since there were few workers involved, and since the agency was in the private sector, was therefore somewhat removed from the mainstream of political life, and was employing a variety of legal and illegal tactics to break the union, the workers' struggle was not going well. Eventually the union won recognition and negotiated a contract. A critical factor in forcing the agency to negotiate in good faith was the threat of the Toronto Labour Council to

---

[50]For example, see the report by Judy MacLean, "The Union Is Us—A Rank and File Campaign That Worked."

withdraw financial support from the United Appeal, a key funding source for the Big Brothers' Association.[51]

For social service workers it is logical to think in terms of coalitions with social service recipients. In the case of the Phildelphia PSSU, progressive unionists made special efforts to maintain ongoing contact with representatives of the Welfare Rights Organization. The Philadelphia local consistently organized and agitated on behalf of service user-oriented changes in welfare policy. In turn the PSSU strike in 1975 received support from the Welfare Rights Organization and minimized the ability of the state to weaken the strike by pitting service users against workers. Similarly in one report unionized social workers in a day center fought successfully against a reduction in wages to handicapped service users in a sheltered workshop situation, and in another reported experience workers refused to relocate welfare recipients in single-room occupancy slum hotels.[52] In the long run there is little doubt that the fate of social workers and the fate of social service recipients are very much connected to the same larger political and social dynamics. It is important that coalitions be built between these two groups for both short- and long-term political work. Unions are a logical vehicle for creating and sustaining these kinds of relationships.

Conclusion

The transformation to socialism will require unity on the part of a large segment of the working class. The steps that have been outlined here may seem like small contributions toward that process. However, they are important ones. Simultaneously union work meets an immediate need in the short run and cannot be overlooked on those grounds.

Political work within unions needs to be understood as a process. On one level, the first contract negotiated by workers in an agency is unlikely to be as strong as subsequent contracts. Even in terms of the bread-and-butter issues, building a strong union and achieving a decent contract take time. There is no alternative if we are to protect our jobs, the right to do those jobs in a competent manner, and needed services.

From a socialist perspective the argument for involvement with unionization is also strong. Radicals in social work may not always choose to invest their energies in union work, and that may be a perfectly reasonable

---

[51]Claudette Giroux, "Collective Bargaining for Social Workers in Private Sector Agencies: A Case Study," Unpublished paper, Ottawa, 1976. The same case is discussed in Peter Holland, "Organizing Social Service Workers," in *Network: A Political Newsletter for Social Service Workers,* 1(February, 1978), p. 14.

[52]Relf, "Ways to Fight," p. 15.

decision, given the constraints and possibilities in any specific situation. In the long run unions may make an important contribution to socialist development. The steps that social service workers can take in the direction of progressive unionism are important. Social workers work in the public sector, and public sector workers stand at the juncture of one of the major contradictions of capitalism, namely, its inability to fund the public services which both the working class and the system-preservation requirements of the capitalist class require. The state will try to avoid these dilemmas by cutting services and particularly by making them less expensive through cost reduction measures, many of which will be borne by the workers themselves. Social workers can resist these efforts through progressive unions and can use that fight in a creative way to make the fiscal crisis of the state an opportunity to advance socialism. When put in a long-term perspective, even the small, unglamorous activities of daily union life have an important larger significance.

9

Social Work Agencies and Radical Social Work Groups as Arenas for Practice

Introduction

This chapter consists of two parts linked by their pursuit of the common theme of working with and organizing social service workers as a component of radical practice. The first half of the chapter explores some possibilities for bringing a socialist perspective to bear on the internal dynamics of social agencies themselves. In agency situations radical workers most commonly work with people who are not leftists. This challenges radicals to find ways to advance a socialist perspective without becoming isolated from nonradicals. We must learn to present a radical point of view in such a way that it falls within the range of experience and perception of nonradicals and stretches their thinking and action possibilities. At the same time, in our desire to stimulate political interaction with nonradicals, we must resist the temptation to conservatize our politics.

In the second half of the chapter I will examine the phenomenon of the citywide and statewide groups that leftist social workers in the United States and elsewhere are creating to express their political interests. In such groups social workers often find support for their radicalism, since these groups bring together like-minded people. These groups face some what different problems than do leftist workers in agencies when the radical groups pursue. Variations of similar problems do appear, for example, when radical social work groups extend themselves to the broader community in their political work. Nevertheless radical social work groups are one of the ways in which social workers can act on their radical sentiments and can experience working as socialists with other socialists. While this model of organizing generates its share of personal and political problems, that set of problems may be a welcome relief from the problems that arise from working in situations where there is little immediate support available from other leftists.

Radical Practice in Social Work Agencies

radical and liberal analyses of agency struggles

Social workers with a liberal perspective, as well as those with a radical one, make efforts to stimulate changes in the agencies in which they work. Particularly since the revival of social activism in social work that accompanied the 1960s civil rights movement, the New Left, and the War on Poverty, liberal social work commentators and theorists have encouraged social workers to work for changes in the practices and policies of their agencies. As would be expected, the goals, focus, and strategy of political work in social agencies stemming from a liberal analysis differ significantly from those deriving from a radical analysis. It is important to be clear about these differences since a pitfall for radicals working politically in social agencies is losing sight of their radical commitments in the face of the conservative pressures within those agencies. While a sound theoretical perspective is not a sufficient guard against conservatism, it is a necessary piece of the equipment which radicals must bring to such potentially compromising situations.

This is not the place for a full review of the political functions of social welfare agencies. However it is good to remind ourselves of the contradictory role played by social agencies. On the one hand, they operate as mechanisms of social control. They generally provide minimal service to people whose need is substantial. They attempt to cool out, pacify, and isolate potentially disruptive populations. They create and maintain artificial and divisive barriers between people. They manipulate and exploit the workers who staff the services.[1] On the other hand, they provide assistance to people who might be worse off without their help.

The existence of these contradictory impulses in agencies is a reflection

---

[1]This critique of social services is developed more fully in Jeffry Galper, *The Politics of Social Services* (Englewood Cliffs, N.J.: Prentice-Hall, Inc., 1975), see Chapter 4, "The Political Functions of the Social Services," pp. 45–72.

of class conflict in the society at large. The class struggle that is a constant and inevitable aspect of life in a capitalist society plays out in many arenas, including social agencies. The results of that struggle at any moment represent the relative strength of the contending class forces. While the capitalist class clearly has exercised the greater power, the ability of the working class to force concessions cannot be ignored. As I suggested earlier, social policies and social services represent the efforts of the capitalist class to shape reform efforts to meet the requirements of capitalism, and they represent the efforts of the working class to force concessions from the capitalist class.

This view of the political forces operating in and through social agencies underlies the radical analysis of social agencies as a potentially useful arena for radical political work. The social welfare establishment as a whole is entwined with the maintenance of capitalism and with challenges to capitalism; the minutiae of daily life in social agencies reflects similar dynamics. Efforts to organize and politicize social service workers in agencies and to challenge oppressive agency policies toward workers and service users have the potential to ameliorate immediate problems and to contribute to the larger process of socialist development by helping to expose and challenge an additional manifestation of capitalism's irrationality and inhumanity.

criteria for selecting issues

Not every issue, problem, or campaign which radicals might take up has the same long range political potential. It is important that we seek out issues with a greater likelihood of bringing workers together, rather than stimulating the divisiveness that too commonly exists among workers in many agencies. For example, a campaign against work speedups can unite workers at every level of the agency. Similarly resistance to job fragmentation, that is, to increasingly circumscribed job definitions, can provide a basis for unity in situations where minorities would be classified downward in a reorganization of job categories by virtue of having had less formal training. On the other hand, the efforts of more highly trained workers to free themselves for work they enjoy by passing routine tasks off to workers lower in the hierarchy is unlikely to encourage greater staff unity.

The educating and organizing work we undertake will necessarily focus on the immediate issues which people face. Social service workers have no shortage of grievances about the ways they are treated as workers and about the unwillingness of their agencies to involve them in decision making. They are frustrated by the limited resources available to do the job to which they are assigned and by the obstacles which the agency creates to their doing their jobs in a satisfying way. They are likely to have at their fingertips a long list of objections to the policies to which they must adhere. Each of these concerns potentially provides a focus for organizing people.

As we think about engaging a particular issue, we should be guided by a concern for the potential role of any single campaign in helping workers experience their collective power. Whatever projects we undertake should be selected with a clear eye on the long-term need to organize. Even when it is possible to make useful changes by ourselves, the gains we achieve tend to be swallowed up or minimized by attrition. However, even modest gains or modest changes in policy, if they simultaneously further the analyses, experiences, and collective power that can provide a stepping stone to the next engagement, will serve dual ends, as they should.

An additional goal for radical work in agencies is to make conscious efforts to help coworkers discover the links between particular agency issues and larger social dynamics. For example, we might facilitate increased staff self-determination by beginning with the modest aim of achieving more open and responsive staff meetings. As we formulate strategy about ways to achieve this end, and successfully alter the decision-making process of the agency, we can begin to raise the issue of worker and/or service user and/or community control of the agency. We can help workers parlay the insight and satisfaction that come from winning even modest victories in a perspective on the larger implications of worker involvement in decision making. For example, it might be possible to plan one or more study sessions on worker self-management, or to move the agency to legitimate the participation of service users and community representatives in agency meetings, or to assign workers to community activities as a regular part of their job. We may not achieve the more radical goals totally. However, each step contributes to even more basic political struggle as people question the role of social institutions, the locus of control of those institutions and their personal relationship to them. The point is, we start with the immediate issues, such as the desire of workers for greater input into staff meetings. We push those issues as far as we can in a direction that raises more fundamental questions and that raises the more fundamental demand that institutions be controlled by those most directly affected by them.

Finally it is critical to stress how important it is for radicals to develop as deep an understanding as possible of their particular agencies before they engage in political action. Too often, leftists have simply not done their homework about the particular situations in which they find themselves. They have relied on rhetoric, general political analysis, or ad hoc interpretations and have failed to map and unravel their agency, its history, and its connections with outside institutions and people, personalities, and points of vulnerability. Solid political action rests on solid analysis of both a larger theoretical nature and a concrete immediate nature. We must attend to both.

influencing coworkers

Frequently radical workers in agencies cannot identify other radical people in their workplaces. Finding themselves in this position, they may fear reprisal, feel isolated, and be unsure of how to proceed. Even in these difficult cases, it is possible to take at least modest steps to bring a radical perspective to the agency.

A first possibility is to consider the role that each of us can play in sharing radical views with other workers. This effort may be as modest as being more conscious of the informal discussions that take place about daily events. Even casual discussions of a particular case or a policy in the agency offer an opportunity to present a radical point of view, as do discussions of larger social and political issues that arise. For example, we could help to point out the conservative assumptions that are contained in a discussion of a particular case when the realities of racial, sexual, or economic exploitation are overlooked. We could support a coworker's tentative expression of dissatisfaction about his or her job. We could encourage a coworker to ignore or openly challenge agency policy on behalf of a service user whose situation clearly calls for such action.

In addressing ourselves to coworkers, it is possible to identify at least five areas for pursuing radical ideas and for encouraging greater openness to radical action.[2] (1) We can attempt to raise the consciousness of coworkers about left politics in general, for example, by presenting a socialist critique of capitalism, by elaborating the nature of socialism and the possibilities for its achievement and by explicating the relationship between social services and social oppression. (2) We can encourage the involvement of coworkers in political activity outside of the agency. For example, we can invite people with whom we work to join us at political meetings. We can make radical literature available and can introduce radical friends to coworkers, with an eye toward encouraging further discussion about politics. (3) We can attempt to influence the analysis and assessment of coworkers about the specific social agencies in which we work by raising questions about the agency's definition of the problem with which it deals, the role it plays with service users, and its treatment of workers. (4) We can try to affect the way in which coworkers do their job in the agency by making suggestions and criticisms and by being open when questions are directed to us. (5) Finally we can support other workers whom we know to be radical or radically inclined in order to alleviate the isolation we feel as radicals.

As with any effort to influence people's thinking on issues that have as much emotional impact as these do, we must be thoughtful about the way we proceed. The best strategy with nonradical people is to avoid presenting a fully elaborated radical analysis as a first order of business. It is important to understand the thinking of the person we are trying to influence so that our

---

[2]Paul Neustadt, "Radicals in Clinical Social Work: How Their Radicalism is Expressed in Their Practice," Master's Thesis Presented to the Graduate School of Social Work and Social Research, Bryn Mawr College, May, 1977, p. 41.

comments and questions can be addressed to areas where the other person feels in a bind and in need of a new way of looking at things.

To be strategic in talking with others about political issues is not to suggest that we dilute our politics or be unduly cautious about offending or alienating. It does mean that we need to be aware that the conventional points of view which people have internalized have guided their thinking for many years. The internalization of an alternative point or view is a process in which our influence may be small or large. In any case it be only one of the influences that must operate among many if the political perspectives of the person we wish to affect are to change.

Anyone who has attempted to influence the political thinking of others has certainly experienced frustration at the difficulty and slowness of that process. We may find some encouragement if we keep several ideas in mind. First, the people who now consider themselves radical generally did not consider themselves radical at some point in their lives. In the United States today there are very few born radicals, that is red diaper babies who were raised in a socialist culture. Those who are radical became so as a response to a variety of internal and external factors. When we are tempted to succumb to the fatalistic idea that none of our more conservative coworkers can or will ever become allies in radical struggle, it may help us to remember that someone once might have said that about us.

We should also keep in mind that even our modest efforts to present a socialist view will be noticed since so little is available to most people by way of a reasoned alternative to conventional analyses. Our lone voice is unlikely to be a decisive political influence in anyone's life. At the same time, since people want an alternative, even when radicalism may not seem to be that alternative to them, an actual manifestation of radicalism in the person of a familiar coworker can be an important influence in someone's political development. When people already experience frustration in their jobs, and know at some level of consciousness that conventional perspectives do not offer an adequate way to understand that frustration, a radical analysis will support ideas already alive in a latent or partially conscious way in people's minds. We are not working against people. We are supporting them in grasping and confronting the pain and anger they have.

Finally we can avoid setting ourselves up as experts to be challenged or debunked, and we can reduce our own fear and uncertainty by acknowledging to ourselves and to those with whom we work that we do not have all the answers. This is not a maneuver, disguised as false humility, designed to manipulate others. We do not have all the answers. If we did, we would be further along the path of socialist development than we are now. What we do have is a method of political analysis, an ideological framework, and a willingness to question and to challenge values, assumptions, and procedures that are often held inviolable. Armed with this equipment and with a willingness to put ourselves and our ideas forward in a process of engagement with others, we can be quite useful to coworkers in helping them acknowledge more fully that part of themselves that is ready to challenge some of the traditions and views they have accepted heretofore.

When we do not have the active support of others for presenting more radical ideas, we may still find opportunities for addressing larger numbers of people. For example, even in more conservative agencies, workers may have a degree of flexibility in developing formats for in-service training. In such cases, if a radical worker is a member of a staff training committee, it may be possible to invite radical speakers on issues of importance to coworkers. For example, in one case a worker in a child welfare agency, under the relatively innocuous title of "Dealing With Worker Burn-Out," invited a speaker to an agency to discuss the necessity for unionization. In another case a student placed in a large mental health agency created a multisession forum on homosexuality and bisexuality and their relationship to counselling. Her special status as a student allowed her to engage the agency on an issue on which the agency was known to have a conservative stand and to do so in a way that might not have been possible for the regular staff.[3]

Similarly the radical worker who does not have a support group may be able to raise issues through a strategy of research and eventually may be able to use that research as an organizing tool. The idea of initiating a research project may be sufficiently nonthreatening so that coworkers can be engaged in the project in an unofficial, official, or quasi-official capacity. The research itself can provide a mechanism for raising issues and organizing people, regardless of the specifics of the findings. For example, research on the impact of a service agency on service users is likely to produce disturbing findings which may be enlightening for workers who have not stepped back far enough to get a sense of the overall impact of their work. A project might be designed to assess community attitudes toward the agency and might utilize a few hours per week of the time of several caseworkers. Regardless of the specifics of the findings, the project provides an opportunity to introduce workers to the community and to community attitudes, and to create potential unity among the members of the research team. Other research topics are more loaded and might need to be conducted without agency sanction. For example, it might be possible in institutional settings to organize coworkers to investigate the sexual or physical abuse of residents. Similarly it is often easy to establish the fact that the people who sit on agency boards of directors, or who are county commissioners, or who benefit from the agency in various ways are the same people who in other capacities create the conditions responsible for the

---

[3]Barbara Julius, "Homosexuality and Bisexuality: The Report of a Social Change Endeavor," Professional Project prepared in partial completion of the degree of Master of Social Work, University of Pennsylvania School of Social Work, April, 1978.

problems those agencies address. For example, in rural areas it is often possible to trace the linkages between the farmers who want welfare recipients to serve as stoop labor during the growing season and the welfare directors who make policy concerning eligibility standards. As we engage in such research work, we should make every effort to help coworkers understand the larger significance of what is being uncovered. As part of a research project on the relation of welfare to local agricultural needs, for instance, it might make sense to encourage workers to read some politically progressive analyses of public welfare and to arrange for speakers on the political functions of social services, as background for the research.

We can also influence coworkers by the example we provide of alternative practice possibilities through our own activities. We are unlikely to influence agency policy simply by our analytic power or our insightful comments. At the same time, we may generate a range of spin-off effects by vigorously raising issues of service user and worker rights at staff meetings; by pressing supervisors to utilize mutual criticism and self-criticism, rather than traditional styles; or by questioning the conservative assumptions that are inevitably part of any staff meeting. Our effort to create a visible radical presence represents relatively little actual power in the short run. However, we can provide people with a rallying point, and we can raise questions in people's minds about the content of their work and about their experiences as workers and potential change agents. Similarly we can work with service users in ways that represent higher degrees of consistency with our political views. We can then share that practice with other workers, both privately and in public forums.

organizing coworkers

All of these modes of practice represent fertile possibilities. At the same time, their limits are apparent, since I have assumed to this point that the worker is acting without substantial support. However even when no other workers in the agency are explicitly radical or open to organizing around a clear commitment to socialism, it may still be possible to organize other workers into progressive collectives. For many radicals in agencies, therefore, the organization of a minority caucus, a women's caucus, a rank-and-file caucus, or simply the effort to achieve more worker input into policy making through increased involvement in regular staff meetings becomes an important intermediate goal. This kind of organizing does not have to begin in a grandiose way. It can start with something as simple as two or three people agreeing to meet over lunch every week to discuss issues of common interest. Such informal gatherings can provide a structure for engaging others and might eventually lead to such formal trappings of organization as a name and a willingness and ability to act publicly. Hopefully it will. Even if it does not, it can serve useful functions as a vehicle for political education and mutual support. If the agency is unionized, the value of forming additional worker organizations will need to be weighed carefully in terms of the relation they will have to work in and through the union. A collective of the sort described here might be the beginning of a progressive caucus within the union. If it does not seem possible to work in a progressive way through the union, workers might decide to create a worker's organization outside of the structure of the union, with an eye toward influencing coworkers and the union in that way.

Ultimately it may be possible to develop the strength of a worker's collective to the point where it can function as a quasi government in the agency. For example, as is already true in some industrial workplaces, social workers may be able to develop a stronger worker's culture to challenge management's idea that the agency is a unified "happy family." Such a worker's culture, perhaps operating through the formal mechanism of a Staff Policy Concerns Committee or a similar creation, could help workers to discover and legitimate their own point of view about the agency and their role in the agency. It could, for example, serve as a preunion formation within the agency, fulfilling some of the functions a union usually fills. It could offer an opportunity for workers to speak to the larger community so that a worker's perspective can begin to be differentiated from a management perspective in representing the agency to its various external communities and constituencies. Similarly it could become a haven for study, research, strategy planning, and defense of workers who are being harassed by management for their political leanings. It could prepare and distribute a worker-and service user-oriented newsletter. The potential range of action possibilities is virtually limitless.

some guidelines for radical practice in agency settings

Some situations and agencies inevitably will be richer than others in opportunities for useful political work. It is also true that every situation offers at least some creative possibilities. Radical work is not a matter of single, decisive events, for the most part. It is more an ongoing process of looking for opportunities to politicize and organize. Ideally our focus must be on creating organizations that keep up steady pressure in a number of areas, neither backing off because of our fatigue nor trying to push too quickly in response to our own frustrations. Every staff meeting offers an opportunity to raise questions, to challenge conservative assumptions, and to encourage coworkers to do the same. Every supervisory session provides an opportunity for political encounter as does every interaction with a service user and every contact with people outside of the agency on agency business. If we are alert to all of the possibilities, we will always be in a position of having some vehicle for expressing our political commitments through our work in the agency.

As in all political work we need to explore and utilize the various pressure points available to us. The organized activity of large numbers of workers and service users is a potentially powerful tool. We have other resources as well. One of these stems from the fact that agencies legitimize themselves to the community at large and to their financial backers on the specific grounds that they are providing a useful service to people. Therefore they are vulnerable to negative publicity, and negative publicity can be generated relatively easily.[4]

For example, a group of radical social workers in Toronto was effective for several years in raising questions about the conservative nature of the local United Way. Their publicity material, organized around the theme "I didn't give at the office," struck at a vulnerable point, for the United Way depends on a politically noncontroversial image for its success in fund raising. That modest effort made a contribution to a larger process occurring in many capitalist countries where more people are questioning the use of private charity, rather than public mechanisms, as a source of funding for necessary human services.

It is important for radical workers to protect themselves as they pursue their politics. Radical workers will be more vulnerable to personal reprisal when they raise difficult issues, agitate, and organize within agencies. There is no virtue, necessarily, in being fired. We need to consider our own survival needs. Therefore we must be alert to the fact that we will increase the risk to ourselves by being radical and take steps to minimize that risk.

The first step we can take is to do the best possible job that we can at our agency-defined assignment, consistent with our political principles. Radicals must be particularly careful not to give their agencies an opportunity to harass or fire them because they did not keep up with the requirements of their jobs or because they did their jobs in a sloppy way. Being good at your job can make you sufficiently valuable to the agency that it will tolerate somewhat more political deviance than it might otherwise be prone to do. Being good at your job can also be an important part of the radical's effort to resist whatever harassment might occur.

It is also important to know your agency and the people in it. Be open to friendships with other workers; learn about the agency's policies and its history. Know which supervisors and administrators are more likely to be supportive and which require cautious treatment. Before questionning and challenging the agency, know the facts of the situation so that you are not

---

[4]See George Brager and Stephen Holloway, *Changing Human Service Organizations: Politics and Practice* (New York: The Free Press, 1978), especially Chapter 2, "Economic and Political Forces in the Environment," pp. 39–56.

tripped up or made foolish by basing action on a lack of information or on misinformation. Be clear, to yourself and to others, that you are a part of the agency as well as in resistance to it. In so doing you will be better equipped to raise questions and to organize challenges.

Finally avoid adventurism and isolation. Throwing a brick through a supervisor's window may have a certain romantic appeal. As political strategy it is worse than useless. It leaves people with the impression that radicals are irrational and destructive, and it surely will increase the chances that the brick thrower will be fired. Militance, as a tactic of social change, is appropriate in situations where it can be understood or where it can serve as a rallying point, not where it can frighten or repulse the constituency to be mobilized. If we do not advance radical ideas aggressively, we will surely not be effective. However, if we act in individualistic ways or in ways that are too far removed from the comprehension of the people we wish to mobilize as allies, we will find ourselves isolated and ineffective, as well as more vulnerable to reprisal. The art of effective political work in nonradical settings is to find the middle ground between these two positions.

Radical Social Work Organizations

a reemergence

Since the mid 1970s, small groups of radical social service workers have been organizing on a citywide basis in a number of urban areas throughout the United States and Canada.[5] While the weaknesses of their groups are apparent, and while some have dissolved after a relatively short time, the very fact of their existence and the important impact some of them have already had are

---

[5]Not all of these groups have developed the written materials that permit easy access to them for those outside their immediate areas. However, the following leads may prove useful for those wishing more information. The Radical Alliance of Social Service Workers (New York City) can be reached at P.O. Box 70, Gracie Square Station, New York, New York 10028; The Social Service Workers' Network, an effort to develop a Wisconsinwide alliance, briefly published *Network: A Political Newsletter for Social Service Workers*. It can be reached through the University of Wisconsin-Extension Center for Social Service, 313 Lowell Hall, 610 Langdon Street, Madison, Wisconsin 53706. The Association for Social Service Workers (Toronto) is discussed by Peter Holland, "Organizing Social Service Workers," in *Network: A Political Newsletter for Social Service Workers*, 1 (February, 1978), 13–14. Other groups include the Union of Radical Human Service Workers (Boston); the Coalition for Human Service Alternatives (New Haven); and the Radical Human Service Workers (Philadelphia). Undoubtedly there are other such groups, as there are numerous radical caucuses and organizations of students in schools of social work.

For a number of years, Case Con, a national organization of Marxist social workers, flourished in England. It consciously chose to dissolve in the late 1970s in order to free members to put more of their political energy into the trade union movement. Their monthly magazine, *Case Con*, may be available in the United States in some libraries. The Case Con Manifesto, and

encouraging to those committed to the creation of a leftist presence within social work. The strength of these organizations does not match that of the rank-and-file movement that existed in the social welfare sector from the early 1930s to the mid-1940s.[6] However these groups are exciting and promising because they have sprung up during a conservative political period, because they often are overtly socialist, and because they are organizing in the absence of a supportive national network or national organization.

The emergence of these groups was anticipated in the late 1960s and early 1970s by the progressive Social Welfare Worker's Movement, which developed a local presence in several cities as well as a national structure,[7] and by a number of citywide, left-leaning, though not explicitly socialist, organizations with a concern for social welfare issues.[8] However, as would be expected, the current reemergence of radical social work groups reflects the political realities of this period which include, in contrast with the late 1960s, a lower level of political involvement in the society at large (a discouraging reality), a greater openness to a socialist perspective, and a fuller recognition of the necessity for classwide action, rather than action limited to the social welfare sector (an encouraging reality).

While there are different emphases among the groups, reflecting the personalities involved, the length of time the group has been together, and other local circumstances, there is also considerable overlap in the foci of the

some of the political thinking of the organization are available in Roy Bailey and Mike Brake (eds.), *Radical Social Work* (New York: Pantheon, 1975) and in several of the essays in John Cowley, and others, eds., *Community or Class Struggle?* (London: Stage 1 Press, 1977).

One group of radical social workers in New York City has focused exclusively on the task of organizing a socialist social services journal. Their efforts have resulted in the appearance of *Catalyst: A Socialist Journal of the Social Services*. It is available from the Institute of Social Service Alternatives, Box 1144, Cathedral Square Station, New York, New York 10025.

[6]A useful review article on the rank-and-file movement is Leslie Leighninger and Robert Knickmeyer, "The Rank and File Movement: The Relevance of Radical Social Work Traditions to Modern Social Work Practice," *Journal of Sociology and Social Welfare*, 4 (November, 1976), 166–77. The rank and file movement is relatively accessible to review since many social work libraries carry the journal it produced for over a decade, *Social Work Today*.

[7]To the best of my knowledge, the only published study of the Social Welfare Worker's Movement is Stanley Wenocur's "The Social Welfare Worker's Movement: A Case Study of New Left Thought in Practice," *Journal of Sociology and Social Welfare*, 3 (September, 1973), 3–20.

[8]Two of these can be explored through published articles which are based on their experiences. Robert Knickmeyer reviews some of the work of Radical Action for People (St. Louis) in "A Marxist Approach to Social Work," *Social Work*, 17(July, 1972), 58–65. Knickmeyer presents further discussion of Radical Action For People in "A Radical Critique of Political Activism in Health, Educational and Social Service Institutions," State University at Oswego, New York, June, 1975, mimeographed. Jeffry Galper and Barbara Hemmendinger assess the work of the People's Fund, an alternative funding project for radical community groups, in "The People's Fund: A Political Evaluation," c/o *The Journal of Alternative Human Services*, 3 (Summer, 1977), 17–25.

groups. They tend to base their work on a similar political analyses. With some variation, and with more or less explicitness and sophistication, they acknowledge the frustration experienced by social service workers in conventional social agencies. They make a socialist analysis of the roots of that frustration and develop a socialist perspective on alternatives both in accomplishing short term political work and in achieving more profound long-term changes in the society. In their statements of principles, these groups locate the dilemmas of social service agencies and the personal frustration of their members at not being allowed to be more useful to service users, in the inability and unwillingness of a capitalist society to provide adequate human services to people. They make a radical analysis of social agencies in that they relate the problems in those agencies to the larger dynamics of capitalist society as a whole.

In the words of the Union of Radical Human Service Workers (Boston),

> These [capitalist] values and institutions are maintained by a state apparatus which uses welfare programs to "patch up" some of the casualties caused by capitalism. In addition, these programs act as social controls which pacify legitimate anger that otherwise might be directed against the system in the form of conscious political activity. As human service workers we find ourselves in the often contradictory position of acting as agents of this system while genuinely wanting to ease the pain that it creates.[9]

In like fashion Case Con (England), in its "Manifesto," argued that

> the problems and frustrations we face daily are inextricably linked to the society we live in, and that we can only understand what needs to be done if we understand how the welfare state, of which social services are a part, has developed, and what pressures it is subject to. . . . The welfare state was set up partly in response to working class agitation and mainly to stabilize the upheavals generated by war time conditions. It was recognized that improvements in the living conditions for workers helped provide capitalism with a more efficient work force and could nip militancy in the bud. Furthermore, the threat of withdrawal of benefits, under certain conditions (being on strike or cohabitating, for example), could be a useful technique of social control.[10]

These groups relate their commitment to building a socialist movement to their activities within the social services. In the formulation of the Radical Alliance of Social Service Workers (New York City),

> "People's needs must be the highest priority and must be given precedence over profits for the large corporations and monopolies who now control the economy

---

[9]Union of Radical Human Service Workers (Boston), "Principles of Unity Statement," 1977, p. 1, mimeographed.

[10]"Case Con Manifesto," reprinted in Bailey and Brake, eds., *Radical Social Work*, p. 144.

and the government and all major institutions including social welfare. . . . Within the context of an anti-monopoly, anti-imperialist perspective, we will promote understanding and support for anti-imperialist movements as they relate to the social needs both within the U.S. and in countries oppressed by U.S. imperialism. We will provide channels for dialogue concerning alternate economic and political systems and will work to undertake to stimulate discussion about basic causes of social ills and effective strategies for change among as wide an audience as possible."[11]

Network (Wisconsin) is viewed in part as an effort to "support social service workers in utilizing their discretionary power both to help clients more effectively and build more consistently a constituency for 'non-reformist reforms' which confront the structural roots of inequality in our capitalist society."[12]

These groups express their political commitments in a number of ways and serve a number of purposes simultaneously. Typically the members of these groups experience a sense of isolation from other radicals in their workplaces and join a radical social work group for psychological support and for assistance in clarifying their political directions. Aside from undertaking projects, such groups also serve as a source of psychological support for their members, a sounding board, and occasionally defenders of group members whose politics have embroiled them in political controversy.[13] Some groups see themselves as a vehicle for the political education of their membership. In fact several of these groups began as study groups and subsequently expanded to become study and/or support and/or action groups.

Most of the groups also engage in direct political action related to social service workers, social service issues, as well as other more generally political topics. In its statement of purpose the Radical Alliance of Social Service Workers (New York City) included as part of its agenda a wide range of

---

[11]"RASSW's Organizational Structure," in *The Social Service Alternate View,* Voice of the Radical Alliance of Social Service Workers, 2(Summer, 1976), 1 and 3.

[12]"Manifesto for Politicizing Social Service Workers," Bob Griss, Madison, Wisconsin, 1978, mimeographed.

[13]The Case Con groups were especially active in defending radical social workers, as article after article in their magazine reported. A clear statement of the need for such groups to help alleviate the sense of isolation is found in *Network,* which presented as part of its rationale the "need to activate a social service workers' network to pierce the sense of isolation we feel, and to develop a political consciousness about the social forces which structure our work and shape our relations with clients, supervisors and co-workers. Many of us face similar problems of bureaucratic controls, alienation and meaningless tasks, and we want to learn how others have dealt with them. Others want to solicit support for their efforts to innovate, to challenge the system, or just to survive. Some of us want to share our understandings of the social constraints which we confront so that we can learn to avoid reproducing the problems we face, blaming our clients, or burning ourselves out. And many of us want to share our excitement about what we do." "Statement of Purpose," *Network: A Political Newsletter for Social Service Workers,* 1 (February, 1978), 1–2.

educational activities, applying a class analysis perspective to issues affecting social welfare; giving major attention to issues of racism and sexism; joining coalitions particularly with labor and minorities; stimulating coalitions within the social service sector; seeking to influence existing organizations toward more effective social action, and encouraging and assisting social service worker's efforts to unionize.[14] The Union of Radical Human Service Workers (Boston) focused on

> providing support for each other as we work to integrate our politics with our role in the workplace; educating ourselves about the role of social services in a capitalist society; educating other human service workers about a socialist analysis of human service organizations and social welfare policy; and supporting unionization efforts of human service workers. Along with this we will be addressing issues of raising our own class consciousness, including the issues of professionalism and working class identification; resisting cutbacks in human services and other policies and actions directed against working and poor people; supporting rank and file worker's movements; supporting the struggles against the oppression of women, gay people and people of color; and supporting international liberation struggles.[15]

The groups cannot give equal attention to all of these areas. None the less even the limited achievements of some of the groups have been valuable. The Toronto group, over several years, supported its members in facilitating social work unionization in that city. It helped its members to understand unionization more fully and to be more effective as union organizers, and it helped to educate social service workers about unionization in that city.[16]

As part of their educational efforts several groups have published newsletters on a more or less regular basis and have written and distributed position papers on topical issues as they emerged.[17] Many have sponsored

---

[14]"RASSW's Organizational Structure," *The Social Service Alternate View*, 2 (Summer, 1976), 2.

[15]Union of Radical Human Service Workers (Boston), "Principles of Unity Statement," 1977, p. 2, mimeographed.

[16]See Peter Holland, "Organizing Social Service Workers," Network: A Political Newsletter for Social Service Workers, 1(February, 1978), 13–14. A dilemma in this case was that the socialist objectives that originally gave rise to the organizing effort were put in a secondary role, given the pressures involved in the unionization drives. I dealt with this problem more fully in the preceding chapter.

[17]Case Con (England), the Radical Alliance of Social Service Workers (New York City) and Network (Wisconsin) have published newsletters as part of their activity. The New York group, the Coalition for Human Service Alternatives (New Haven) and the Union of Radical Human Service Workers (Boston) have been among the groups to prepare and distribute position papers. For example, the New York group developed materials opposing state licensing of social workers. The Coalition for Human Service Alternatives prepared materials exposing and challenging the

radical speakers, forums, and in several cases, day-long workshops on radical analysis and practice in social work. A number of groups are working to develop linkages among social service workers and among public service workers, as well as among workers in the public sector, social service recipients, and progressive community organizations. Toward these ends several of the groups have joined other groups to support progressive political activity in their cities, for example, to oppose funding cutbacks in the public sector.

Some of these groups have undertaken specific political projects in their communities. Radical Action for People campaigned on the issue of lead paint poisoning in St. Louis.[18] The New Haven group built a coalition which organized a shelter for battered women. The New York group publicized the denial of human rights in Chile under the Junta through a campaign to investigate the fate of radical Chilean social workers who disappeared following the overthrow of Allende's government.

Several of these groups have also attempted to influence existing mainstream social work organizations. At the local level the New York group pushed the New York City chapter of the National Association of Social Workers, as well as the national association itself, to take a clear stand on behalf of affirmative action in the Bakke case. The New Haven group enlisted the support of the Connecticut chapter of the National Association of Social Workers in fighting Title XX regulations which involved the violation of the civil liberties of service users. The Social Welfare Worker's Movement, to return to an organization of earlier vintage, was organized in response to the conservatism its founders experienced at the National Conference of Social Welfare. Similarly the St. Louis group and the Toronto organization both challenged their local United Ways on the elitism of their decision-making mechanisms and the conservatism of their funding priorities in their respective cities.

The relationship of the gay liberation struggle to the development of a socialist movement in the United States is not clear, although most of the left in the United States has been supportive of the gay liberation movement. However only a segment of the gay liberation movement has viewed itself as operating within the context of socialist politics. Nevertheless the growth of gay social work organizations, particularly the Association of Gay Social Workers, with chapters in New York City, Philadelphia, and San Francisco, is worthy of note. Gay social workers are an oppressed minority within social

---

data banks established as part of Title XX programs in the State of Connecticut. The Union of Radical Human Service Workers prepared materials opposing forced work requirements for welfare recipients in Massachusetts. The *Catalyst* collective devotes its efforts to preparing a journal. The journal features article-length analyses on social welfare and briefer reports on political struggles in and around the social welfare sector, from a socialist perspective.

[18]Knickmeyer, "A Marxist Approach to Social Work."

work, and gay social service users have frequently not received needed services in a fashion that respected their sexual orientation. The Association of Gay Social Workers has been relatively effective in generating a more visible gay presence within social work and within social work education. It has created an organized presence at several of the annual meetings of the Council on Social Work Education, has influenced the curricula in schools of social work, and has both fought and worked collaboratively with social service departments in several cities on specific issues of social service provision affecting gay people. Radicals may legitimately criticize the conservative aspects of the gay liberation movement within social work. At the same time, radical social workers must acknowledge the legitimacy of the gay liberation effort within social work and the examples of effective organizational work or the part of some aspects of that movement as a contribution to progressive change efforts.

a political perspective on radical social work groups

It is not coincidental that these groups are forming at this time. To develop a full picture of their meaning, impact, and potential, it is useful to examine them in light of the political environment in which they emerge.

The primary explanation for this mini-resurgence of radical political organizations within the social service sector is the growing difficulty faced by social service workers in doing their job in a satisfactory way. This difficulty, in turn, is based on the growing inability of the state to fund social services adequately. As a result human service workers are experiencing ever more difficult working conditions as they are being asked to do more work with fewer resources and are being pressured to act in an increasingly bureaucratized and routinized fashion.

The forces giving rise to this development are similar to those giving rise to increased social work—unionization. Many of the people involved in radical social work groups are also advocates of social work unionization, and are active in unions in their agencies. However, they function as isolated radicals within those unions or as part of a radical or rank-and-file caucus. This is important political work. At the same time, since most social work unions are not radical in their orientation, radical social workers cannot always find in union work satisfactory political support for socialist ideas, and so they look to outside groups to meet these political needs.

This development within social work reflects the current state of the left in general. Relatively few people identify themselves explicitly as socialists. However many people are disaffected with conventional ways of looking at and acting on social and political issues. While they are not presently at a stage of political development where they embrace socialism, they are open to alternatives. Some of these people are beginning to be attracted to radical groups, including radical social work groups. At the same time, those people who do identify themselves as radical increasingly are grounding their radicalism in a socialist perspective, in contrast to the looser theoretical and ideological foundations of the New Left in the 1960s. As a result the radical social work groups, like radical groups elsewhere in the country, bring together people who are angry and disaffected, but not socialist, with people who have developed a socialist perspective.

While the emergence of these groups is a promising political sign, it is also a measure of the relatively underdeveloped state of the left that radicalism in social work is expressing itself organizationally in this particular way. Radical social work groups have definite limitations as a form of political organization. Since they are geographically defined, they do not coalesce significant numbers of social service workers from any one workplace. They are not organized as a political party, since their base is limited to social service workers; therefore, they cannot function to provide general political leadership in their communities. At the same time, the full expression of radical ideas in social work is often difficult within the workplace, and a well-defined radical political party or organization at the national level, with which radical social workers might affiliate, is not available. Therefore radical social work groups make sense as one organizational channel for the expression of these political sentiments.

In a period in which there is much dissatisfaction and anger, and in which a radical perspective is not readily available to many people, even the modest work and modest voice of these groups can be, and often is, significant. Radical ideas within the social welfare sector appeal to a growing number of social service workers who have not viewed themselves as searching for a radical alternative. Their life experiences make them open to such a perspective when they become acquainted with it. The very existence of radical social work groups as a source of thoughtful alternatives to status quo analyses and strategies is often appealing to social service workers who discover that they are more radically oriented than they had acknowledged, even to themselves. Ultimately the political future and impact of radical social work groups will depend heavily on their ability to speak to the needs, interests, and frustrations of that large group of social service workers who are not radical, but who are potentially open to moving in a radical direction. The insistence of radical social work groups on being open to all social service workers and on not classifying, stratifying, or dividing on the basis of narrow job definitions, specializations, or academic degress makes them attractive to a potentially wide range of human service workers. Similarly while they have tended to be predominantly white in their membership, their strongly articulated challenges to racism may make them more attractive to minorities over time.

Many social service workers feel the need to develop a more systematic perspective on their disaffection from their work and from the society as a whole. Many feel a need to integrate their radical political commitments with their occupations as social service workers. At a future time a radical political party and class-conscious trade unions may provide a more effective vehicle for the expression of those sentiments. At the present time radical social work groups are serving as one useful substitute.

problem areas for radical social work groups

Such groups experience the same difficulties as do other radical groups in the United States. They receive relatively little support for their ideas in the larger society. They face a prevailing attitude of pessimism about the likelihood of changing society in basic ways. And they must combat establishment efforts to suppress radical people and ideas through explicitly repressive measures and through heavy doses of conservative ideological thought which obscures the alternatives available to people.

Radical social work groups experience their own versions of these problems. For example, some social service workers who are in a position to influence political thinking within the human service occupations advocate the pursuit of heightened professionalism and state licensing as solutions to the dilemmas of social service workers. Radicals in social work do not have to convince their peers that the status quo does not serve them optimally. They do have to challenge conservative alternatives to the status quo, such as licensing, which are presented by mainstream organizations and thinkers. This is a difficult task. It is not impossible, however, since many social workers are discovering, in the course of their own experiences, that only militant, class-wide organizations and activity can protect their jobs and allow them to provide adequate service. Nevertheless the ideological tasks facing radicals in the social services are formidable.

While many social service workers are open to contributing to social change efforts, the level of political sophistication within social work as a whole is not high. Many social workers cannot readily distinguish extended social welfare programming from the socialist alternative, and they resist acknowledging their own position as members of the working class.

Radical social workers must also confront the reality of the modest power of social workers. Anyone who attempts to encourage social change quickly becomes quite aware of the power of the opposition and of how little power progressive forces can now muster to challenge the opposition. While we typically assume that we have less power than we in fact do, none the less it is true that our voice is a small one. Further, regardless of how successfully radical social workers mobilize other social workers, it will still be necessary to form alliances with other constituencies, particularly with other public service workers, with service user and community groups, and eventually with even wider coalitions within the working class. At present, these alliances exist in a tenuous fashion, where they exist at all.

Finally radical social work groups must make difficult choices about the kind of work they will undertake, since the need is so great on every side. Some members want such groups to provide an opportunity for personal, psychological support and for discussion of their individual working situations, of radical theory, in general, and its application to social work, in particular. This need is understandable and reasonable. On the other hand, there is much need for outwardly directed political work. Radical social work groups, like many radical organizations, struggle to achieve an appropriate balance among these tasks. The problem is compounded by the fact that people join these organizations with varying degrees of political sophistication which, in turn, means that they have different needs which they hope will be met by the group.

some guidelines for radical social work groups

There is much to be gained by such groups acknowledging to themselves and to the wider community that they operate on the basis of an explicitly socialist perspective. It is not always easy for groups to come to this point since some members and prospective members are cautious or confused about socialism. However, there are several reasons why it is useful for such groups to operate within the context of a clear commitment to socialism.

As many radical social workers know, a socialist perspective offers a very useful analytic scheme for understanding the problems facing social services and for suggesting strategies and guidelines for pursuing changes. While this is not the place to review the importance of a socialist analysis in understanding capitalist society, from the perspective of those committed to facilitating fundamental social change, it is important to utilize the most effective body of theory and strategy developed to this point as we address these large tasks.

Putting forth an explicitly socialist perspective obligates a radical social work group to undertake certain tasks. The first of these is attending to the political growth and education of the group's members. There are small, but significant, numbers of people who are prepared to investigate what it means for them to view themselves as socialists and to join a socialist organization. They need opportunities to learn more about a socialist perspective in relation to the work they do and in relation to their personal lives and experiences. A radical social work group will need to give serious attention to the educational needs of its members and to those of new members who join after the core group has formed. The political education that is required will not occur through a single educational experience, but through an ongoing process of exploration. However this is not to be lamented. Furthering socialist ideas is an important part of the political work of such groups. If social workers are viewed as a significant political constituency and as potentially valuable allies in the larger process of social change, then it is important for us to direct our

political energies to ourselves as social workers. Such efforts are not preliminary or tangential to some more significant work that we will do at a later time.

When such groups put themselves forth as socialist, it will also be
incumbent on them to explore, with other parts of the left, alternative ways to
make the socialist position understandable and appealing to more and more
people. This will require that we find ways to help social workers understand
that socialism does not represent an alien possibility, but actually does express
more fully than other social systems the concerns and interests that many
social workers have for a humane and caring society.

If a radical social work group is clear that it means socialist when it uses
the term radical, it will be useful for members to prepare a statement of
principles expressing that fact. Such statements generally begin with a
rationale for the group, including the reasons for assuming a socialist perspective, what that means for the group, and what actions and directions the group
will take as a result. While such a clear statement of principles and directions
may alienate some potential members, it will provide a basis of unity among
those who do become involved, and so will help the group move forward more
purposefully. It is generally useful to ask that prospective members be in
agreement with the statement of principles, or at least sympathetic to it. At
this stage of development it does not seem productive to allow the group to be
completely open to any political influences members may bring, since that is
likely to lead to a rightward drift toward reformist practice, as disaffected, but
not yet radical, workers join, or to a sectarian leftward drift as members of
existing, sectarian radical organizations join the group with an eye toward
converting it into an organ for their own particular political outlook.

Most important, expressing the socialist basis of such a group makes it
incumbent on the group to act consistently with socialist politics. Among other
things this requires that the group focus on building a broader movement as it
undertakes specific projects on immediate concerns. It must undertake immediate projects, and it must do so in such a way that the ideologies and
political organizations required for a broader process of socialist transformation can be developed.

The first general principle for such groups, then, is to be grounded in
socialist theory and practice. The second principle is to maintain a series of
"balances" as the group organizes and proceeds in its work.

The first of these is the balance between focusing inward on support and
education of group members and focusing outward on external political work.
If the group is organized, exclusively and over a long period of time, as a study
and support group, it can rightly be challenged for failure to use the theory and
strategy developed to influence larger events. On the other hand, if the group
turns to action without having given attention to the development of theory,
there is danger that it will lose sight of its socialist commitments in the press of
conservative political influences. Socialist theory can help the group to remain

clear-minded about the larger objectives it is pursuing, the rationale for doing so, and the attendant strategies. At any one point the group may focus more on study and support or on action. Over the long run these are mutual needs and must be met equally.

A second and related balancing act is one well known to group workers and to students of group dynamics, namely, the necessity for balancing the group's task and maintenance needs. Too often leftist organizations have not paid sufficient attention to the personal needs of group members and to the group's need, as a group, to develop higher levels of trust and intimacy. On the other hand, social work groups have often been accused of being so concerned with process and feelings that they have failed to accomplish a great deal in the world outside of the group. Radical social work groups must satisfy member's needs to feel useful in influencing events in the world, and they must also provide a supportive and nurturing experience for participants. The political tasks that radical social work groups are undertaking are difficult ones. If the experience of being part of such a group is not rewarding in and of itself, few people will remain with the group on the basis of commitments to some distant revolutionary goal. Radical social work groups must "do good," and they must also "feel good."

Third, such groups must achieve a balance between a clear commitment to democratic processes and a willingness to use the skills and leadership abilities of their members. The group will not be attractive to members if it fails to provide people the opportunity to develop new skills and to express their views fully. At the same time, a commitment to democracy can be destructive if that implies hostility to leadership and to clear decision-making processes. If the Old Left of the 1930s can be accused of authoritarian practices, and the New Left of the 1960s, of inappropriate touches of anarchism, the left that is now emerging must achieve a better balance between the two tendencies. Similarly radical social work groups must balance openness to the political ideas of new members with a commitment to a well-thought-out set of political principles, so they simultaneously are open to new ideas and clear about their direction.

Fourth, such groups must balance a need to challenge existing mainstream organizations, thinking, and people with a willingness to work with and support such groups when that makes sense. A radical group will find itself in opposition to conventional practices and thought, and it will rightly criticize and pressure organizations of the status quo. At the same time, radical groups will find opportunities to form alliances with liberal organizations and people. Radical social work groups cannot operate on the basis of a rigid strategy that insists that any alliance with a liberal organization is selling out. Nor can they pursue alliances at any cost, simply to have more allies. Total political "purity" in forming coalitions guarantees isolation and subsequent ineffectiveness. On the other hand, indiscriminate alliances with liberal groups assures loss of the socialist vision as the group seeks to make itself acceptable to mainstream thinking.

Finally, such groups must achieve a balance between undue optimism and undue pessimism. If the group nurtures grandiose conceptions about its potential impact, its members surely become discouraged as they experience the slow pace and frustration of political work, particularly of radical political work during a nonradical time. If the group is not realistic about what it can accomplish, members may be tempted to try to short circuit the slow organizing and building process that is required through grandstand activities that are likely not to be effective as political strategy.

On the other hand, the group must resist undue pessimism. Even small efforts will have an important impact. There is so little in the society that offers encouragement about the possibilities of significant political struggle that a well-formulated and well-presented analysis and strategy will be an eye opener for many people. It is also good to remember that political change takes time. As radical social work groups come to understand the particular role that they can play in politicizing even one small segment of public employees and in raising another voice against the uses to which the state puts public service programs, they will better learn how to assess the impact of their own work. If they look solely to some ultimate revolutionary outcome, they will be discouraged. But if they recognize the importance of their efforts in organizing and politicizing and in carrying forth a tradition of radicalism within social work, within the public sector, and within the working class, they will have a more rounded basis for appreciating their own impact.

The reality is that the work of such groups has already had an impact on the thinking of some social workers, on specific areas of social policy, and on the reemergence of a leftist current within social work. Two general factors will determine the future impact of such groups. The first of these is the skill, ability, and energy of leftist social workers in organizing such groups and in moving them forward effectively. The second is the fate of the left in the United States in general. If a radical movement emerges more strongly in the relatively near future, then radical social work groups will receive much encouragement and support for their work as they locate themselves within the context of this larger movement. If such a movement does not emerge, then a radical presence within social work will be much more difficult to sustain—though not impossible. While I cannot predict the future of the left in the United States, current efforts to build radical social work groups are important, regardless of the larger political climate, and will be our own small way of contributing to the humanizing of the public sector and to the building of the larger movement that is required.

10

Research and Writing for Radical Social Work

Personal Choices

The majority of social workers do not take an active role in social work research, either as producers or consumers.[1] In fact their disengagement is sufficiently pronounced that I suspect some readers may be tempted to bypass this discussion on the grounds that research and writing as arenas for expressing radical commitments in social work are neither interesting nor important. I urge those who react this way to read the chapter anyhow. Hopefully it will make the tasks of research and writing sufficiently approachable that increasing numbers of people will be encouraged to investigate the contributions they can make. Research and writing can be pursued at many levels of sophistication and complexity. If radical social workers are to have available the range of literature they need in order to work as effectively as possible, it will be necessary for many of us, including those with little training in research and writing, to contribute in a variety of ways.

The need for widespread participation in research and writing is greater

---

[1]Some of the issues are reviewed in Stuart A. Kirk, Michael J. Osmalov and Joel Fischer, "Social Workers' Involvement in Research," *Social Work*, 21 (March, 1976), 121–24.

from a radical perspective than it is from a conventional perspective. The development of a radical presence in social work and in the society at large requires the involvement of many more people in the process of reexamining ideas they have held and in taking responsibility for and control of their own circumstances. Radical analysis and strategy must be presented in such a way that they speak to the deeply felt experiences of people. If research and writing are left to academicians and to those with the ability to generate government and foundation monies, they will only partially reflect and advance the realities of rank-and-file working people, regardless of the politicial commitments of the researcher.

Conservative politics, on the other hand, are concerned with the needs and preservation of the status quo. They do not and need not reflect a working-class perspective. Conventional research, therefore, depends less on working-class participation. It is conducted by "experts," and it is undertaken in order to serve political purposes other than those of radical change. Our research must reflect a working-class perspective and working-class needs. Radical academicians can play a useful role. Alone, however, their research and writing will only partially reflect and serve a working-class movement. Social service workers involved in the day-to-day work of service delivery must also become invoived. The purpose of this discussion is to suggest some ways in which they can do so.

The Purposes of Radical Research and Writing

Ideas and theory are critical in effectuating revolutionary change.[2] In their absence, as revolutionaries have argued since the turn of the century, bourgeois ideology imposes itself on the thinking of the people in capitalist society. In fact ideological control has become as formidable a mechanism of repression as has naked police power (though ideological control is buttressed by the ever present potential of physical coercion). Further, theoretical development, while circumscribed by the level of revolutionary struggle in a given period, can also serve to clarify issues so that the accompanying political struggle can proceed more effectively.

Specifically research and writing can play a number of roles in helping to build a radical presence within the social services. In many of the same ways that conventional research supports conventional practice, radical research can support radical practice. The development of radical practice needs a

---

[2]A brief and useful discussion that summarizes a number of the key issues is Jerome Karabel, "Revolutionary Contradictions: Antonio Gramsci and the Problem of Intellectuals," *Politics and Society,* 6 (1976), 123–72. Also useful is Erik Olin Wright, "Intellectuals and the Working Class," *Insurgent Sociologist* 8 (Winter, 1978), 5–20.

fuller, more elaborated knowledge base in several areas, including the formulation of fundamental theory and the presentation and discussion of case or practice material. We have only begun to understand and elaborate socialist analysis and practice as they apply to the social welfare arena. Sound practice will require sound theory, and sound theory will be developed only as the result of conscious efforts on the part of many people. As radical theory becomes more fully developed, it will stimulate more effective practice. Recorded and shared examples of radical practice, in turn, will provide a basis for the further elaboration and refinement of theory, and so on.

A second function for radical research and writing in social work is to communicate what we are discovering and accomplishing so that we can learn from one another and be encouraged by one another. Both the explicitly radical and the radically inclined people in social work operate less effectively than they might otherwise do because they feel isolated from radical ideas and from other radicals, and indeed they are. Radical literature cannot substitute for immediate collective support. It can be a useful tool to reduce the sense of isolation often experienced by radicals. Writing about our experience is a valuable way of speaking to like-minded people, encouraging them in their work, and stimulating their practice.

A third function of radical research and writing is to support particular political projects. When we think of organizing on an issue, we most commonly think in terms of mobilizing people, planning strategies, confronting obstacles, and other actions. These efforts can be strengthened by appropriate research and writing. The facts and relationships we uncover can become a strategic tool in our work. For example, research which documents the procorporate spending policies of a municipal government might provide useful ammunition for sustaining the efforts of public workers in their fight for better wages during a contract struggle. Research can also play a role as an organizational tool in particular political projects. It is sometimes possible to bring people together to engage in a research project and to use that collective enterprise, as well as to analyze, interpret, and disseminate the resulting findings as a stepping stone to further collective work.

A fourth function of radical research and writing is to create greater visibility for radical ideas and radical approaches among nonradical people. Written materials will reach people we cannot reach face-to-face. By themselves they will not radicalize people. However, they can contribute to creating an awareness that an alternative point of view and alternative organizations and approaches do exist. They prepare the way for future involvement by making radical ideas more familiar. When they reach people at an appropriate time in their political development, radical materials can be a catalyst for rapid political growth.

Finally our work as researchers and writers will help us to develop our own analytic capacities. We will develop them through practice. Initially we will undertake modest research tasks and accept and confront our uncertainties about our abilities to make a useful contribution in this way. Research and writing are only part of what is needed in the development of a radical movement. They can be a useful part. It will serve us well to prepare ourselves to make the contributions we can.

Making Research Radical

Radical research can be defined as research which derives from radical, or Marxist, theory and which serves the end of socialist revolution. It is research that contributes to building a socialist movement, either directly or indirectly. In relation to social work specifically, radical research is research that contributes to the building of radical social work theory and practice.

In a number of ways it is possible to demonstrate the absolutely critical impact of the theoretical outlook and the political commitments of the researcher on the formulation, conduct, and utilization of a given piece of research. Political perspectives decisively shape the framing of research questions themselves. The questions we choose to pursue are necessarily influenced by the theory we hold about the nature of reality. This is true, regardless of whether or not we are conscious of holding that theory. Because the real world and its parts are so complex, we must develop orienting guidelines to help us sort out the way it works.[3] Otherwise we would be hopelessly lost amidst a barrage of disconnected stimuli. Research questions, designed to add to our knowledge of the world, are formulated from the perspective of the larger world views we already hold, since those larger world views, in fact, shape our perception of reality. To the extent that we are guided by theories that are rooted in liberal and conservative interpretations of reality, the research questions we ask will necessarily be framed within the logic of liberal and conservative ideology. Our findings will not enable us to question that ideology, regardless of their particular content, since they do not question those views but assume them as a basis of the specific research questions and findings will be formulated within that framework. There is nothing wrong with this procedure and, in fact, there is no alternative to it. Our ideology always determines our approach to research questions. Unlike liberal-conservative research, however, radical research makes no pretense of being value-free or politically neutral. It is consciously self-reflective and openly committed. It becomes, simultaneously, less subject to control by unconscious or hidden political factors.

---

[3]See Alvin Gouldner, *The Coming Crisis of Western Sociology* (New York: Basic Books, 1970), especially Chapter 2, "Sociology and Sub-Sociology," pp. 20–60.

The only circumstance in which this creates difficulties and obscures the meaning of our work is when we are not aware of, or when we deny, the political commitments that underlie the formulation of research questions. Clarifying the inevitably political nature of research can require some theoretical detective work. The political theory that informs conventional research is the theory that dominates capitalist society. This is true even when we are unaware of the conservative biases of what we consider "common knowledge." Like the air we breathe, conservative assumptions are so much a part of our reality that we stop noticing them. For example, some commonly held conservative biases that are frequently taken as universal verities are the ideas that competitiveness, rather than cooperativeness, is an inherent human trait or that capitalism itself represents the final and highest stage of social evolution. Radicals, then, have the dual task of formulating alternative research questions based on a socialist perspective and of clarifying the fact that we are actually pursuing the same logic as are liberals and conservatives of basing research on preexisting theoretical and ideological foundations.

Each of the major understandings of Marxist social science, when contrasted with perspectives on the same social dynamics as viewed by conventional social science, highlights ways in which research is formulated according to the political thought which it represents.[4] Marxist theory leads to the framing of radical research questions while non-Marxist theory, which in the West is most commonly grounded in the structural-functionalist school of sociology, leads to the framing of procapitalist, that is, liberal or conservative, research questions. Several examples follow.

Marxist social science views the struggle between the classes as the primary dynamic of social change. From the liberal or conservative perspective, social change is the result of a series of adjustments which a society makes over time to achieve greater harmony of its component parts (not classes). These competing perspectives represent contrasting views of social change and of the creation of new social inventions. The way in which the emergence of social work is assessed illustrates the impact which differing analytic schemes have on findings.

Marvin Gettleman is one of several historians who have examined the emergence of social work from a Marxist perspective.[5] Because he approached the issue of social work's origins from the viewpoint of class analysis, he was led to explore, among other things, the class background of the people who

---

[4]A useful discussion is John Horton, "Combatting Empiricism: Toward a Practical Understanding of Marxist Methodology," *Insurgent Sociologist*, 3 (Fall, 1972), 24–34.

[5]Marvin Gettleman, "Charity and Social Classes in the U.S., 1874–1900," *American Journal of Economics and Sociology*, 22 (April-July, 1963), 313–29, 427 ff.

helped generate the first social work agencies in the United States, their stated motivation, the political dynamics surrounding the emergence of the early social welfare agencies, and the political content of the casework that was practiced at that time. He discovered that members and representatives of the capitalist class were, in fact, directly responsible for the emergence of social work, and he discovered that they were quite explicit in understanding that their purpose was to pacify an unruly, exploited urban proletariat through encouraging them to accept their class position as morally just. Alternatively from a liberal perspective, and in the view found in the majority of social work texts which touch on its history, social work is seen as a caring society's response to the misery of its poor. Its motives are assessed not as class control but as benign assistance. The radical view leads to an analysis of the class origins and class functions of social work. The conservative or traditional view does not acknowledge or minimizes the role and impact of class struggle and leads to a perspective which sees social work as a manifestation of society's growing concern for human welfare.

As a second example, liberal thought and socialist thought begin with differing views of the role of the state in capitalist society and use these alternative conceptions to analyze some of the issues surrounding social service provision.[6] From the Marxist perspective, the state is understood primarily as an instrument designed to serve the requirements of the capitalist class. It does so in a variety of ways, some of which address the economic requirements of capitalism and others of which address the need to legitimate the existing social order. The state, in this view, is also a locus of class struggle and does not serve in a simple, linear fashion to do the bidding of the capitalist class. However since the capitalist class has thus far dominated the class struggle in the United States, the predominant weight of the state apparatus has favored the interests of the capitalist class over those of the working class.

In the conventional conception, the state is understood as a neutral arbiter of competing interests. From a more liberal vantage point it is argued that the state apparatus unduly favors "big business" or other special interests, and from a more conservative vantage point, it is argued that the state unduly interferes with the freedom of capital to maximize profit. Regardless of the direction of the bias, both the liberal and conservative views rest on a belief in the fundamental independence of the state in relation to class alliances. If the state favors the poor too heavily through social welfare measures, as the conservatives see it, or if the state favors the rich too heavily through advantageous tax arrangements, as the liberals see it, the conventional view inter-

---

[6]See Peter C. Findlay, "Theories of the State and Social Welfare in Canada," Forthcoming, *Canadian Journal of Social Work Education*, for an explication of competing views of the state and the relevance of these views to social welfare practice. Also excellent in the Canadian context is Leo Panitch, ed., *The Canadian State* (Toronto: University of Toronto Press, 1977).

prets this as an imbalance among competing interests rather than as a reflection of a fundamental class alignment of the state.

These alternative perspectives lead to quite different analyses of social welfare issues. From the conventional perspective the various problems of the social services mirror an "imbalance" in the state's arbitration of competing interests. Solutions are therefore found in righting that balance so that those served by social welfare programs are served more adequately. From a Marxist perspective the problems reflected in the social services exist because their existence is functional to the capitalist class.

Therefore in analyzing low welfare benefits, liberals point to the minimal political power of the poor and disproportionate government largess to the rich through devices such as tax shelters. They advocate building an alliance of interest groups to push for higher benefits. Radicals, on the other hand, critique the functional nature of low welfare benefits in maintaining capitalism by disciplining the low-income sector of the labor force. This low-income sector might be tempted to pursue welfare benefits, rather than to remain at low paid work if welfare benefits were higher (more nearly approximated the wages of low income workers). Accordingly, low welfare benefits are complementary to and supportive of the exploitative wage structure generated by capitalist enterprise. Therefore inadequate welfare benefits merge with the issue of labor market exploitation and consequently emerge as an issue that requires a socialist solution.

In similar fashion the unavailability of day care services, from a conventional perspective, is viewed as a consequence of government's insensitivity to the needs of women, particularly low income women whose involvement in the work force is essential to their economic survival. From a class-conflict perspective the availability of larger numbers of women to enter the labor force, an availability that depends on the provision of adequate day care, would result in an exacerbation of the existing unemployment problem. Therefore Marxists understand that the limits of the state's willingness to provide day care are set by the inability of a capitalist economy to provide full employment and by the subsequent necessity to create mechanisms to deter additional people from seeking employment.

Some readers may fear that the objectivity of research will be compromised when it is influenced by clear political commitments and when it is rooted in a specific ideological framework. The term radical research suggests that perhaps the researcher will slant findings in order to make the research outcome more consistent with a predetermined position or analysis. This is not what is meant by radical research or by the emphasis on the role of political commitments in research. To understand this, it is necessary to explore further the central role which values always play in research, despite the continuing claims of some conventional researchers and research literature that properly conducted research is "value-free."

Research cannot be politically neutral, and it cannot be value-free.[7] At the most obvious level the decision to pursue any research represents a decision to preclude undertaking some other research. Choosing to undertake one research endeavor rather than another is, in large part, a social choice. It is defined by social or political factors.[8] An example from the arena of medical research will illustrate this point. The question might be asked, What politics are involved in research on human organ transplants? Surely the issues involved in such research transcend, or at least skirt, the class struggle or class biases. However the money and human resources available for research are always limited. Therefore the decision to engage in this area of research circumscribes the potential for research on other problems. In this case the other problems might be any of the numerous medical problems that are widespread and destructive but which are uninteresting from a medical or a research point of view or which do not have high potential for leading to substantial rewards, that is, profits, fame, and prestige. For example, given the United States' unconscionably high infant mortality rates, research on infant mortality might pay off more fully than research on organ transplants in terms of a greater increase in health and well-being for a larger number of people. Obviously one kind of research has greater appeal to funding sources and researchers than another kind, for a variety of reasons, only some of which have to do with the human suffering that is involved.

To translate this understanding to the social welfare field, consider the ongoing interest in doing research on the number of people who receive welfare who might be shown to be technically ineligible to be recipients. On the one hand, we can argue that such research is politically neutral, in and of itself. The findings stand on their own. They either provide ammunition to conservatives by demonstrating the existence of large numbers of "welfare cheaters," or they neutralize conservative attacks on welfare by demonstrating that a small number of people receive welfare inappropriately. On the other hand, consider the fact that there is virtually no research investigating the number of people who do not receive welfare and who actually meet the requirements to be recipients. We can now begin to understand that the choice of research question is significantly influenced by political considerations. Whatever is discovered about the extent of ineligibility among welfare recipients, the outcome is likely to be greater hardship for welfare recipients. Alternatively findings about "unenrolled eligibles" could fuel a movement to

---

[7]Alvin Gouldner has been one of the better known sociologists to argue this point consistently. For example, see his *The Coming Crisis*, especially Chapter 1, "Introduction: Toward a Critique of Sociology," pp. 3–19 and Chapter 2, "Sociology and Sub-Sociology," pp. 20–60.

[8]A vivid portrait of this dynamic is Thomas J. Cottle's "Show Me a Scientist Who's Helped Poor Folks and I'll Kiss Her Hand," *Social Policy*, 4 (March-April, 1974), pp. 33–37.

expand welfare roles. Government-sponsored research is not likely to support such activity.

In discussing the characteristics of radical research, I have thus far suggested that it is distinguished by its commitment to serve the interests of the working class, which is to say that it serves the cause of socialist transformation. I have also suggested that it does this through the choice of questions it pursues and the ways in which it pursues them. Radical research has an additional critically important quality, namely, its commitment to investigate points of intervention for change through the mobilization of working-class people. It asks, as one underlying concern, How do these discoveries or findings suggest ways to facilitate radical change? The political purpose of uncovering points of working-class intervention is revolutionary change. The theoretical orientation that alerts us to this question is our understanding that change is the basic reality of systems. The essence of systems is their dialectic quality, their imperfect integration of contradictory forces. This is a particularly important understanding for socialists in a capitalist society. As we experience our daily circumstances, we can fall into the trap of observing reality as conservatives would have us observe it, which is as essentially stable and unchanging. Marxist theory suggests that what appears as stability actually represents only the most temporary and imperfect resolution of antagonistic forces. Therefore in assessing a given area of social policy, even one that seems well-designed to serve the political purposes of control and repression, we will look for ways in which the class struggle that lies underneath the apparently calm surface can be reactivated. This is exactly the approach which Cloward and Piven took in their important study of public welfare. They assessed not only the control function of welfare, but the potential use of public welfare as a political tool in the hands of poor people.[9] Similarly in exploring manifestations of conservative attitudes and practices of social workers, we must also explore the frustration and anger that many social workers experience and the potential suggested by those experiences for their political mobilization. A socialist approach to research encourages us to stay attuned to the dialectic nature of social conditions and to the potential for change inherent in situations.

Content Areas for Radical Research

The content areas appropriate for radical research are numerous and varied. We will choose among them in a given situation on the basis of many criteria,

---

[9]Richard Cloward and Frances Fox Piven, *Regulating the Poor* (New York: Vintage Books, 1971). Elsewhere I have assessed several inherent sources of instability in the welfare states of capitalist societies. See Jeffry Galper, *The Politics of Social Services* (Englewood Cliffs, N.J.: Prentice-Hall, Inc., 1975), Chapter 9, "Counterforces," pp. 153–69.

including the political needs of the moment, our own skills, interests, goals, and motivations as researchers; and the resources available. I have organized some potential foci for radical research into four categories: the nature and functioning of the existing social order, radical social work practice, the organization and ideology of radical social work, taken as a whole, and the construction of appropriate theory for radical social work. There are numerous additional possibilities. The goal of this discussion is not to offer a comprehensive listing. Rather it is to stimulate thinking about the wide range of useful work that radical social workers can undertake in their capacity as researchers and writers.

An important area for research is the development of base line data on the following. What is the impact of existing social policies and social services on various populations, including service users, workers, potential service users, and the larger community? How is the system changing? What forces underly these changes? What points of intervention are created by these changes? Who benefits from various policies and services, and who loses?

A specific category of research of this kind focuses on the ways in which social welfare services achieve their political objectives. A socialist understanding of social services suggests that they function, in part, as mechanisms for preserving existing social arrangements. They also influence the immediate circumstances of service users. Studies of specific services, formulated with this perspective in mind, have already proven useful to many social welfare workers in their efforts to understand both the immediate and longer range impact of their work. In understanding the relationship of public assistance to control of the working class, the work of Cloward and Piven comes to mind, as an example of radical research which has had a very broad impact on social service workers and on a larger concerned population.[10] David Gil's work on child welfare services;[11] Betty Reid Mandell, on the private welfare sector;[12] Alexander Liazos, on juvenile justice;[13] and Katherine Ellis and Rosalind Petchesky, on day care[14] provide similar examples in other fields of service.

---

[10]Cloward and Piven, *Regulating the Poor.*

[11]David Gil, *The Challenge of Social Equality* (Cambridge, Mass.: Schenkman 1976).

[12]Betty Reid Mandell, "Who Rules the Social Services?" in *Welfare in America: Controlling the Dangerous Classes,* ed. B. Mandell (Englewood Cliffs, N.J.: Prentice-Hall, Inc., 1975). There are other excellent essays in this book that help to uncover the latent functions of various social services.

[13]Alexander Liazos, "Class Oppression: The Functions of Juvenile Justice," *The Insurgent Sociologist,* 5 (Fall, 1974), 2–24.

[14]Katherine Ellis and Rosalind Petchesky, "Children of the Corporate Dream: An Analysis of Day Care As a Political Issue Under Capitalism," *Socialist Revolution,* 12 (November-

Another type of research on the functioning of existing services investigates populations whose needs are not being addressed or whose needs are addressed in an unhelpful or a destructive way. The social service needs of gays is an area which has not received sufficient attention.[15] Similarly the problem of battered women and battered wives is only starting to come to light as a result of the work of the women's movement.[16]

These suggestions for research into the nature and functioning of the existing social order only scratch the surface. For example, how are social agencies changing in their patterns of organizing the work of social service providers? How are agencies responding to the growing unionization of social service workers? What techniques are being developed to stop union organizing or to compromise union politics? How are social agencies responding to the fiscal crisis of the state? How is the state responding? What opportunities for radical organizing do these responses create? What are the major costs of the service cut-backs that are taking place? The list of possibilities is virtually endless.

A second general area for radical social work research is the actual practice of radical social workers. Many people who consider themselves radical, or who consider themselves partly radical, are attempting to develop approaches to their practice which reflect their political commitments. However, they do not consistently share their attempts with others. If all of the instances of radical practice, including those which were more successful and those which were less successful, were known to all those social workers with an interest in developing a radical approach the impact might be significant. While that kind of sharing is unlikely to occur completely under the best of circumstances, even modest additions to the literature would be valuable.

Each facet of the work of radical social workers is potentially useful to record. For example, there is relatively little written material available about the efforts of radical social workers to organize coworkers, particularly from the point of view of the organizers themselves. What have radical social workers experienced and learned, in terms of the political process in which they have engaged and in terms of their own reactions to that process? There is some literature on efforts to practice therapy in a radical way, although relatively little of it is written by social workers with a specific focus on the

---

December, 1972), 8–28. A version of the same analysis is presented by Ellis and Petchesky in "The Politics of Day Care," *Social Policy*, 3 (November-December, 1972, and January-February, 1973), 14–22.

[15]See Don Milligan, "Homosexuality: Sexual Needs and Social Problems," in *Radical Social Work*, eds. Roy Bailey and Mike Brace (New York: Pantheon 1975), pp. 96–111.

[16]For example, see Bonnie E. Carlson, "Battered Women and Their Assailants," *Social Work*, 22 (November, 1977), 455–60 and Marcella Schuyler, "Battered Wives: An Emerging Social Problem," *Social Work*, 21 (November, 1976), 488–91.

needs and practice of other social workers.[17] A good deal of work needs to be done to assess and record the efforts of social workers to democratize their agencies and to push their agencies toward greater responsiveness to people's needs. Relatively little has been written about the ambivalence that social workers are making to become more clear-minded about their radicalism. The process of radicalization, the support that is needed in and received in that process, and the meaning for social workers of their changing political consciousness are all important areas for research.[18] For those radicals involved in teaching social work, a good deal needs to be researched and written about approaches to radical teaching in terms of both content and process.[19] Radical educators need to learn more about conceptual approaches to radical education in discrete areas of social work curriculum as well as in the total process of social work education so that we can help make radical ideas more accessible to larger numbers of students. We also need to learn more about teaching methodologies that are most consistent with radical political values and that exemplify those values in the practice of teaching.[20]

A third area for radical social work research and writing concerns the development of a radical movement in social work as a whole. Useful areas to research include the progress of unionization, particularly class-conscious or

---

[17]Two accessible examples from the social work literature are Philip Lichtenberg, "Radicalism in Casework," *Journal of Sociology and Social Welfare*, 4 (November, 1976), 258–76 and Anne Sparks, "Radical Therapy: A Gestalt Perspective," *Catalyst: A Socialist Journal of the Social Services*, 1 (1978), 91–99.

[18]An especially valuable account is Bertha Reynolds' autobiography, *An Uncharted Journey* (New York: Citadel Press, 1963). Also see Harvey Finkle and others, "Social Work Practice as Collective Experience," *Journal of Sociology and Social Welfare*, 4 (November, 1976), 277–83.

[19]Some examples of work in this area are Anatole Shaffer, "Community Organization and the Oppressed," *Journal of Education for Social Work*, 8 (Fall, 1972), 65–72; Philip Lichtenberg, "Introduction of Radical Theory and Practice in Social Work Education: Personality Theory," *Journal of Education for Social Work*, 12 (Spring, 1976), 10–16; Jeffry Galper, "Introduction of Radical Theory and Practice in Social Work Education: Social Policy, *Journal of Education for Social Work*, 12 (Spring, 1976), 3–9; and Geoffrey Pearson, "Making Social Workers: Bad Promises and Good Omens," *Radical Social Work*, eds. Roy Bailey and Mike Brace, pp. 13–45.

[20]In the late 1960s and early 1970s an organization of socialist educators and graduate students, the New University Conference, developed some useful materials on radical teaching. Some libraries, particularly those with "contemporary culture" collections or some similarly oriented specialization, may have materials from the New University Conference. I am not aware of NUC materials about radical teaching that are accessible in published books or mainstream journals. Some of the journals published by radical teachers or caucuses of teachers contain useful examples of radical teaching approaches. For example, see the several volumes published to date of *The Radical Teacher*, sponsored by the Radical Caucus in English and the Modern Languages. *The Radical Teacher* is available from P.O. Box 102, Kendall Square P.O., Cambridge, Massachusetts 02142.

radical unionization in social work;[21] the nature and impact of the variety of citywide radical social work organizations in the United States and in other countries;[22] the history of radical people and organizations in social work;[23] the work of radical social workers in those capitalist countries in which social work has been significantly influenced by Marxism;[24] and the efforts of radicals in social work to affect the process and progress of grass roots community organizations.[25] There are important current and historical examples of radical movement building and action within social work in this country and elsewhere. Many people in social work, including many radicals, are not familiar with these efforts and so do not have the opportunity to learn from them. Even when there are not tremendous successes to report, assessing and reporting what work is being done can be very helpful for the building of a stronger radical commitment in social work.

---

[21]A useful discussion is Leslie Alexander, "Organizing the Professional Social Worker: Union Development in Voluntary Social Work, 1930–1950," Unpublished doctoral dissertation presented to the School of Social Work and Social Research, Bryn Mawr College, 1976.

[22]*The Social Service Alternate View* is "The Voice of the Radical Alliance of Social Service Workers" (New York City). It can be obtained from the Radical Alliance of Social Service Workers, P.O. Box 70, Gracie Square Station, New York, New York 10028. Many libraries carry issues of *Social Work Today*, the publication of the rank and file social work organization in the United States of the 1930s. Some also carry *Case Con*, published in England until the late 1970s by a radical social work organization with the same name as its journal.

[23]Some examples are Bertha Reynolds, *An Uncharted Journey*; the issues of *Social Work Today*; Leslie Leighninger and Robert Knickmeyer, "The Rank and File Movement: The Relevance of Radical Social Work Traditions to Modern Social Work Practice," *Journal of Sociology and Social Welfare*, 4 (November, 1976), 166–76; and, Christopher Rhoades Dykema, "Toward a New Age of Social Services: Lessons to be Learned From Our History," *Catalyst: A Socialist Journal of the Social Services*, 1(1978), 57–75.

[24]A few suggestive comments on this development are found in Katherine A. Kendall, "Dream or Nightmare? The Future of Social Work Education," *Journal of Education for Social Work*, 9 (Spring, 1973), 13–23. See also Harold Lewis, "Analogy, Animation, Conscientization: Implications for Social Work Education in the USA," *Journal of Education for Social Work*, 9 (Fall, 1973), 31–38; Luis Araneda Alfero, "Conscientization," from *New Themes in Social Work Education: Proceedings of the XVIth International Congress of Schools of Social Work*, The Hague, the Netherlands, August 8–11, 1972 (New York: International Association of Schools of Social Work, 1973), pp. 72–81.

[25]For example see John C. Leggett and Frances V. Mouldner, "Integrated Cooperation Within A Grass-Roots Movement: The Class Emphasis," *Journal of Sociology and Social Welfare*, 4 (November, 1976), 283–98; Miriam Galper and Carolyn Kott Washburne, "Maximizing the Impact of an Alternative Agency, *Journal of Sociology and Social Welfare*, 4 (November, 1976), 248–57; and, Madison Foster, "Black Organizing: The Need for a Conceptual Model of the Ghetto," *Catalyst: A Socialist Journal of the Social Services*, 1 (1978), 76–90. Issues of the journals *Working Papers for a New Society* and *Social Policy* frequently publish reports about progressive community organizing efforts. So too does *Just Economics*, newsletter of the Movement for Economic Justice and Acorn.

A fourth area for research and writing in radical social work is theory building. There is a significant amount of useful literature on socialist theory and practice, in general, much of it directly applicable to theory building for radical social work. However the linkages between socialist theory and radical social work theory need to be elaborated considerably. For example, there is a useful body of Marxist literature on the role of the state. This literature can be very helpful in explicating the nature of social work, inasmuch as social work is one component of state activity. Similarly Marxist understandings of the nature, process, and potential of socialist transformation provide a useful framework for developing radical practice within social work. However we have a long way to go toward developing the theory that will be required for radical social work practice. We need to develop more precise analytic schemes to assess social welfare policy.[26] We need clearer conceptions of the nature and process of social change and of social work's relationship to it. Each area of radical practice is fertile ground for developing relevant supporting and orienting theory.

Outlets for Radical Research and Writing

While there is no shortage of potentially useful topics to occupy our research energies, radicals have some difficulty in publishing and distributing radically oriented material in social work outlets. Most of the mainstream journals accept very few, if any, articles that fall outside of the boundaries of conventional thought or that are based on other than liberal or conservative perspectives. Typically they reject these articles without comment or with references to unsubstantiated assumptions contained in the article.[27] None the less radical articles do sometimes find their way into nonradical journals. In addition there are several journals in or related to social services that are more accessible to radical ideas.[28]

---

[26]One attempt to develop an explicitly radical paradigm for policy analysis is David Gil, *Unravelling Social Policy* (Cambridge, Mass.: Schenkman, 1973). In the British context, a relevant analysis is Vic George and Paul Wilding, *Ideology and Social Welfare* (London: Routledge and Kegan Paul, 1976).

[27]Of course it is true that radical material contains unsubstantiated assumptions. There is no way to present any analysis without making such assumptions since substantiating the assumptions would require a presentation and defense of basic socialist theory and analysis. Even if this were done (and it could not be done within the confines of a single article or even a book), liberal and conservative readers would not be convinced that the article was other than rhetorical. Articles written from a liberal or conservative view also contain unsubstantiated assumptions, as they must. These assumptions do not tend to offend reviewers since they are not perceived as assumptions but rather are accepted as reflections of the way the world actually works.

[28]Among these are *Working Papers for a New Society; Social Policy: The Journal of Sociology and Social Welfare; Catalyst: A Socialist Journal of the Social Services* and c/o, *The*

These outlets will come to mind fairly quickly and, of course, they should be utilized to the extent possible. In addition there are other outlets and audiences for our work. One outlet is the presentation of papers at conferences, both of mainstream social work and social welfare organizations and of radical organizations in and out of social work. Some of the radical social work organizations also publish newsletters. While they reach a small audience, the people they do reach are often among the people we would most like to address. However it is clear that in the long run we will need to develop additional journals, newsletters, and the like for radical materials.

We should not overlook several other distribution channels for our research. In a local organizing situation in which we are utilizing research findings in relation to a particular project, we may have access to television and radio, through news spots and public service announcements, and to public hearings. We can also make good use of written research materials with a more select audience, for example, the workers whose strike activity we are supporting or a local community with which we are engaged. In addition some radical social workers have developed informal networks among themselves in which articles, papers, and even incomplete segments of writing are distributed to interested individuals for sharing and commentary. Radicals who are students or teachers in schools of social work can also circulate their written work among colleagues within their schools. In general many radicals have found that it is not as easy to distribute and publish radical materials in social work as it is to distribute and publish nonradical materials. At the same time, if we produce useful material, it will often find an appropriate outlet.

A final note on the distribution of radical materials concerns the basis on which we determine which outlets will be most appropriate for circulating our work. We need to decide who ought to be the readers and potential readers of our material and be guided in our choice of outlet by that decision. If we are writing in a way that assumes familiarity with radical ideas, or assumes identification with socialist commitments, we should target our material to radical people or to people who will be open to radical ideas. An alternative possibility is to reach nonradical people with such material but to do so through a forum that allows for reaction, discussion and clarification. Extended workshops at conferences fall in this category. On the other hand, if the purpose of our writing is to raise questions in the minds of nonradical people, then a different set of outlets for our material would be desirable. In either case we must present our material in ways that will make it most accessible to the audience we have in mind. This does not mean that we should

---

Journal of Alternative Community Services. A number of radical journals not specifically related to social work also publish social welfare articles occasionally. Among these are *Socialist Review, Radical America, Mother Jones, Monthly Review,* and the newspapers *In These Times* and *The Guardian.*

dilute our analysis for a more conservative audience. That will not serve our political purposes. It does mean that we must be alert to assumptions that should be elaborated or not elaborated, to our use of Marxist terminology, and so forth, in light of our intended readers or listeners. If we keep these considerations in mind, we are likely to discover an ever enlarging role for radical writing and research in social work.

Conclusion

Radicals in social work have produced relatively little written material specifically about and for radical social work practice. We have not systematically assessed and recorded our experiences, analyzed the facets of radical practice, or elaborated the underlying theory that informs a socialist approach to social work. This is not to say that no useful research and writing about radical practice is available. Some excellent material has been produced and distributed. Clearly, however, we are still in the early stages of conceptualizing and reporting. Further most social workers are not familiar with the literature that does exist since it is infrequently made accessible through social work educational and training programs and since it is filtered out of mainstream social work journals and newsletters. If the ideas and approaches embodied in radical social work practice are to influence growing numbers of people, a critical aspect of practice for radical social workers must include attention to research, writing, and theory building and to the wider dissemination of the written material that is developed. This chapter has attempted to lay some of the groundwork, in theoretical and operational terms, for the developments that are necessary.

11

Social Work Schools as an Arena for Socialist Struggle

There's No Place like Home

It is likely that many of the people reading this book are students or teachers in schools of social work. The purpose of this chapter is to encourage people in such settings to explore the implications of a socialist perspective for their work as students and teachers. One of the central themes of this writing has been that every situation contains possibilities for working from a radical perspective and for integrating a concern with the immediate needs of the moment with the process of building a socialist movement. Social work education is no exception.

Many practitioners are first exposed to social work in schools of social work. While the ideas and activities which students experience will not necessarily mold them decisively, they are often an important influence on their thinking when they begin full-time practice. To develop a radical presence and radical activity within schools of social work is to reach people who will be full-time social workers at a time when some of them are more open to exploring critical political perspectives. This setting offers an opportunity to reach people before more of their political thinking is solidified. This is not to say that people come to schools of social work with no previously developed ideas and political ideologies. It is to say that there is sometimes more openness at this point in their lives than there is later on.

Social service workers without formal social work training are also influenced by the political currents that emerge from social work schools. The ideas developed in these schools spread out into the field, through graduates, through writings of students and teachers, and through the impact of students' and schools' perspectives on the social agencies that provide fieldwork training. It is important not to underestimate the influence of the schools on the ideological tone of social work.

Developing a radical presence within schools can also be significant for those students who view themselves as radical or who are open to radicalism. Those people who begin to experiment with the meaning of a socialist perspective in school often find the school setting a useful arena for developing the ideas, attitudes, and skills that support them when they enter practice.

There are as many ways to express radical political ideas and to bring radical political agendas into schools of social work as there are facets of the educational process. Each facet represents an opportunity. I will explore some of the ways in which radical sentiments can influence classroom practice, fieldwork, and processes of internal school governance. Of course it is not possible for any one person to work on all fronts simultaneously. However, at whatever stage of radical commitment we find ourselves, there will be a way to move from that place to the next. This is true for faculty as well as for students.

The Political Functions of Schools of Social Work

A useful starting point in developing approaches to radical practice in social work schools is analyzing the political functions of those institutions. This is not a difficult task since that analysis follows so closely on an analysis of the political functions of the social work field as a whole. Elsewhere in this book I have cited or reviewed several useful discussions of those functions.[1] The key element of that analysis centers on the role which social work plays as a mechanism of both class control and class mediation. As we become clear that

---

[1]For example, see Marvin Gettleman, "Charity and Social Classes in the U.S.: 1874–1900," *American Journal of Economics and Sociology*, 22 (April-July, 1963), pp. 313–29, 425 ff; Christopher Rhoades Dykema, "Toward a New Age of Social Services: Some Lessons to be Learned From Our History," *Catalyst: A Socialist Journal of the Social Services*, 1(1978), 57–75; Jeffry Galper, *The Politics of Social Services* (Englewood Cliffs, N.J.: Prentice-Hall, Inc., 1975), Chapter 6, "Social Work as Conservative Politics," pp. 88–110 and Chapter 7, "Community Organization and Social Casework: The Containment of Change," pp. 111–39; and Chris Jones, *The Foundations of Social Work Education*, Working Papers in Sociology, No. 11, University of Durham (England), Department of Sociology and Social Administration, November, 1976. Available from the Department of Sociology and Social Administration, University of Durham, Elvet Riverside, Durhman, DH1 3JT, England.

the role of social work has been to serve as an instrument of the needs of the capitalist class, and yet has simultaneously been a field through which the competing interests of the classes have played out, we will have little difficulty in specifying the particular nature of the accompanying educational process.

Schools of social work initially were creations of the social agencies. They were organized to serve as training centers for those agencies. To that extent they have served to transmit accrued knowledge, rather than to develop a critique of society at large and the social work enterprise, particularly. Later in the development of social work, the schools became incorporated into universities. That incorporation helped to liberalize them to a modest degree. While they are obviously still tied quite closely to social agencies, they have also been influenced by the world of academia. And while that world is also tied closely to corporate interests, it has maintained some commitment to the notion of academic freedom. For that reason, schools of social work in the last twenty years or so have been somewhat more progressive in the political ideas they have represented than have the social agencies. Schools of social work have served the conservative political interests of the field as a whole, and they have been one of the places where some more progressive thinking has entered social work.

For many students in social work schools, the development of a radical critique of the educational experience does not require historical analysis of the political functions of social work or social work education. Nor is there need to spell out the existing connections between schools, agencies, and the corporate structure. Whether or not students make any such formal analysis, the political functions of social work are impressed on them through their experiences as students. For many students formal social work education is not a positive experience. They find their experience joyless and demoralizing. Their aspirations to be of service to people are not nurtured. They sense that all is not well with the field they have chosen, and yet they are not helped to develop the analytic tools that would enable them to understand their circumstances. Students who criticize their education and become aware that social agencies are not doing what they say may be told that they lack professional maturity. Some schools continue to try to "casework" the dissidence out of students. Others deal with radical awareness or critical analysis by ignoring it. The experience of being a student in a school of social work is often disheartening. While that discouragement does not often take the form of searching for an explicitly radical alternative, it does create some of the preconditions that lead to an openness to radicalism.[2]

---

[2]In the course of preparing this chapter I recalled that I had written some articles for the student newspaper at the Columbia University School of Social Work when I had been a student there in the M.S.W. program between 1963 and 1965. Since these articles spoke to my own experience at that point in my social work career, I dug them out of an old pile of papers and reread

It is sometimes painful to watch the progress of social work students as they move through a course of social work study. It is possible to observe the energy and enthusiasm actually drain out of students as they advance toward their degrees. Students are taught to settle for what is, rather than to explore what might be. They are not encouraged to consider socialist possibilities or even to consider fundamental alternatives to the present system. Their radical aspirations, when they have them, are too often evaluated as immature, unrealistic, and unprofessional.

At the same time that fundamental alternatives are either ignored or criticized, students are offered large doses of a troubling world view. They are encouraged to acknowledge some of the dilemmas of the society, although these dilemmas are not analyzed from a socialist perspective. In many schools they learn about the inadequacies of the service delivery system, the exploitative aspects of the society, and the existence of racism, sexism, and agism. Since the perspective developed about these issues is not socialist, and so does not point to revolutionary strategies, there is no way for the schools to suggest alternatives other than the conventional ones which are often, in social work schools, social service solutions. Students fail to find answers to problems.[3]

---

them. While it was not until eight or nine years later that I came to understand the role of a Marxist perspective in giving shape, coherence, and direction to my personal experience, I was interested as I reviewed that dusty material, in finding out the extent to which the gut reactions I now have to social work education were similar to the feelings and ideas I had when I was first a social work student.

The following comments, which appeared in *The Process: Student Association Publication of the Columbia University School of Social Work* (October, 1964), pp. 8–9, are presented in a less sophisticated and less theoretically informed way than I might put the same issues today. However, the spirit and general political direction reflect my current thinking and, I believe, the thinking of many social work students then and now. I wrote, "Of the faculty members I know, and of those I've talked about in bull-sessions, three and maybe four are honest about personal relationships with students and are the same ones who are asking the basic questions about where social work is going, what it has meant, and what our education is supposed to be giving us. Those teachers who are supposedly teaching methods of social change seem to be the most rigid concerning acceptance of the concepts of change. Their analysis of current events reveals what sometimes appears to be terror of any change but the most gradual, planned, and controlled. It has often been my impression that the objective of most of our faculty has been to indoctrinate my classmates and me with the fundamentals of the social work ethic—to make me a professional—rather than to do their best to teach me to make a better world.

The students, for their part, raise no great hue and cry over this. One reason is the generally dishonest atmosphere which preaches openness and the value of constructive criticism, while at the same time closing the doors to such an approach by the lack of openness and by the negative response to honest attempts to talk. The second is a widespread belief among students that criticism automatically will be seen as a personal problem on the part of the student, and therefore the solution is to be seen not in terms of any change in outside circumstances, but in terms of helping the student to work through his aggressions and insecurities, to achieve a healthier outlook or to better cope with his feelings."

[3]This analysis is developed nicely in Geoffrey Pearson, "Making Social Workers: Bad Promises and Good Omens," in *Radical Social Work*, eds. Roy Bailey and Mike Brace (New York: Pantheon, 1975), pp. 13–45.

They see the problems; they sense at some level that they do not have a way to deal with or understand them; and yet their survival and their self-esteem rest on their supposed ability to deal with them.

I have not seen empirical studies which assess the reactions of social work teachers. My impression is that they experience a version of the same dilemma as students do. Most social work teachers are not radical, and often they are not conversant with a radical perspective. They have been around long enough to know that neither they nor mainstream social thought has an adequate way to respond to the problems. And yet they are charged with the responsibility of preparing generation after generation of social workers.

None of us wants to function without knowing what to do. As a result many faculty members deny their own confusion and cynicism and verbalize a positive view of the value of social work and social work education. The internal contradiction created, even when the contradiction is not consciously acknowledged, diminishes their vitality. While it is true that some social work educators oppress social work students, the oppressor role is largely generated by despair and confusion. Social work educators are threatened by the radical aspirations of students, and even by the nonradical, but lively, posture of some students, because the students call into question the very serious compromises educators have made with their own commitments to progressive ideas and to a rich encounter with the real issues of the world.

If these are some of the dilemmas, wherein lie the solutions? It will come as no surprise when I suggest that socialist politics within schools of social work is the direction that we need to take. Radical students and faculty members in schools of social work will not be fully successful in radicalizing their schools, given the political climate of the times. However, the effort to bring radical ideas and approaches to that sector has the potential to make an important impact in several ways. A radical approach to social work education can bring vitality and clarity to the educational experience, and it can help make that experience part of social work's contribution to building a socialist movement. In the remainder of this chapter, I will explore specifically some of the ways in which this can happen.

Curriculum Issues

the confusion of liberalism

In some schools of social work, the curriculum stresses social change as well as the traditional delivery of social services. It also includes descriptive material on some of the more obvious problems of the society. Paradoxically curricula in these schools can confuse students even more than does the curriculum in schools of social work that make no pretense of concern about larger social issues. In the more progressive schools, students become some-what aware of the contradictions within social work and the society at large. They experience the problems of the society, they are partially supported by faculty in developing a critical social analysis, and they are presented with some ways to think about alternatives. However the analysis is not congruent and ultimately leaves students confused.

That lack of congruence is the product of liberal thought. The liberal analysis recognizes the problems and yet limits the range of possible solutions by operating within an acceptance of the essential elements of the status quo. For example, alternative solutions to social problems are contained within a discussion of possible variations of service delivery patterns or within the framework of more or less welfare state provision. The differences between welfare statism and socialism are not made clear. The societal context is not examined critically.

Students and faculty need to sort out the differences between a liberal and a radical analysis. Unfortunately many students and faculty are not clear that a political perspective is inherent in the curriculum. As a general rule, when classroom content seems not to represent a political position, it is reasonably safe to assume that it does in fact represent a political perspective and that political perspective is a conventional liberal one. We do not notice it since the assumptions it contains are the assumptions we have accepted about our society. They become part of our unconscious ideological framework and so are less available for scrutiny. A starting point in clarifying the confusion created by liberalism is the assumption that there is no apolitical curriculum content in a school of social work.

To clarify the politics of classroom content, we must turn to the funda-mental theoretical perspectives of Marxist analysis. Each dimension of that analysis generates a series of questions we can ask of content. For example, to what extent is any material about social work theory and practice analyzed in relation to the class structure of society? Are personality theory, social work history, methods, and so on, placed in a framework that is historical, mate-rialist, and dialectical, or one that is ahistorical, idealist, and one-sided? What point of view is presented or assumed about the role which the state plays in capitalist society? To what extent is the role of the state in capitalist society a topic of consideration when the nature and role of social work and social policy are analyzed? What theories are presented about the nature and possibilities of social change? How is "helping" defined? These kinds of issues, and the alternative perspectives on them that are derived from competing political analyses, can help to clarify both the inherent and explicit political content of particular facets of the curriculum.[4]

---

[4]A useful discussion is Howard J. Stanback, "Teaching for Radical Social Work Practice: Radicalizing Students in Schools of Social Work," Paper prepared for presentation at the Council on Social Work Education, Annual Program Meeting, 1977, Phoenix, Arizona, mimeographed.

curriculum content as an arena of struggle

Radical students and faculty and nonradical students and faculty who are dissatisfied with the confusion that exists about the directions and implications of their work have a big job to do in clarifying the politics contained in the ideas advanced in social work schools. A primary task is to develop perspectives and teaching materials that can help to clarify the radical alternative. As the discussion and the footnotes in this book make clear, there is written material available from a socialist perspective on every area of the curriculum. Part of our job will be to find it and to share it and to develop whatever additional resources are needed.

How can we structure our work on this project? In some schools of social work, groups of students have joined together to form radical study groups or radical caucuses. One of the projects which some such groups have undertaken independently is the development of a radical perspective on curriculum content. Alternatively some groups have developed the political capacity to demand an exploration of radical content in conventional classrooms. One strategy is to develop radical perspectives outside of the classroom, present them in class, and/or demand that the class jointly undertake the project of learning about radical alternatives. Part of this effort ought to include bringing pressure to bear on the individuals and committees responsible for library acquisitions so that socialist journals, newspapers, and books are available in the library.

In some cases students have targeted certain areas of the curriculum as priorities for ideological struggle, and in other cases they have worked on the creation of alternative or elective courses in which radical perspectives can be pursued. Each approach has strengths and weaknesses. By pushing for inclusion of radical material in conventional classes, radical students can help to introduce nonradical students to new ways of looking at things. Dealing with the concerns of nonradical students and teachers is important political work. That process is also useful to radical students in developing greater clarity about their own ideas, in refining their thoughts, and in learning to communicate more clearly with others. However working with nonradical students makes the job of moving further and deeper with a radical analysis more difficult, since the basic questions which radical students may have already resolved will need to be addressed again. On the other hand, developing a course that is explicitly radical allows students and teachers to move more rapidly and with more sophistication. Also students working to develop a course which is explicitly radical can solidify their mutual bonds so that they may then be in a position to work together over time on various projects, sometimes extending past graduation. Several radical social work groups originated in the efforts of their members to develop radical educational content during their years together as students. The disadvantage of working on special radical courses is that radical students and curriculum content can become isolated. Ideally it would be useful to develop these approaches simultaneously.

An exciting illustration of some of these possibilities emerged from the work of a group of students in the Masters of Social Work program at the School of Social Work, University of Pennsylvania, in the years 1976–78.[5] Part of the collective work of this group of radical social work students was to prepare a master's paper reporting on and analyzing their experiences as a radical collective in the school. In this way they left a record of their accomplishments from which others can learn.

These students joined together on the basis of their dissatisfaction with the content and process at their school. They did not begin with an explicitly radical analysis. Over the course of a year of meetings, readings, and consultations with radical people, they recognized that a radical analysis and radical practice would allow them to seriously come to terms with the problems they were experiencing. In their second year they moved into an action phase. They solicited the assistance of a faculty member who was willing to sponsor a student-led class on radical theory. In that class they developed a deeper appreciation of the fundamentals of radical thought, sharpened their critique of the conservative outlook and experience school, made a commitment to integrate their emerging radical analysis with appropriate practice, and undertook action projects on several levels. They involved themselves and much of the school of social work in support work for the efforts of campus housekeepers who were then engaged in union conflict with the university. They introduced radical perspectives into many of their conventional classes. They arranged for radical speakers to come to the school to speak to increasing numbers of students and faculty on radical themes. They brought a radical perspective to the school in several ways: They influenced nonradical students and faculty, contributed to larger political struggles that were active around them, and helped to make their educational experience a lively and vital one, instead of a deadening and demoralizing one. As they wrote in the closing words of their report,

> Our group's process during the past two years has been characterized by a positive movement from diffused frustration, a disjointed and ambiguous conceptual analysis, and feelings of powerlessness, toward more focused and purposeful activity, increasing conceptual clarity, a more refined political-economic analysis, and greater consciousness and confidence in our use of praxis and power. In the early stages, our group and radical activities were supplementary to the traditional educational process. We have taken the school's rhetorical

---

[5]Kathe C. Balter, Peninah A. Chilton, Marsha R. Ellentuck, Eileen M. Gilkenson, Sharon A. Jachter, Tenley K. Stillwell, "Radical Social Work: An Experience in Praxis" (Submitted in partial fulfillment of the requirements for the Degree of Master of Social Work, School of Social Work, University of Pennsylvania, May, 1978).

commitment to the concept of "students as the center of their own learning" and have made it a reality. It is our hope that others will join us in this struggle, and in so doing we will liberate ourselves, the schools of social work, and our profession, so that we might collectively build a new society.[6]

The possibilities for the radical student acting alone are always somewhat more restricted than for radical students acting together, since the isolated individual can never develop the power necessary to bring about change. None the less, useful work can be done, even when the radical student is isolated. One possibility in such cases is to undertake the intellectual task of clarifying the nature of radical thought and its application to social work. There often is choice in the subjects students investigate in the papers they write and in the discretional reading they do. This can provide an opportunity for studying radical material. In one case a student pursued a master's paper which involved explicating the inherent political content of the major courses she had taken in two years of social work school. She discovered, to no great surprise, that even seemingly apolitical content had been serving to reinforce conservative ideas about people, social work, and social change.[7] In other cases social work students have used the requirement to prepare a master's project as an opportunity to investigate the practice of social workers in the field who were already operating on the basis of a radical perspective or to develop their own best understanding of the nature of radical practice.[8] Students in schools of social work who feel the need to bring some political coherence to their educational experience provide excellent examples of research on radical approaches to social work.

To summarize this part of the discussion, an important role for radical students and faculty in schools of social work is bringing the conservative politics inherent in most social work education to greater awareness and helping other students and faculty to become familiar with the radical alterna-

---

[6]Balter and others, "Radical Social Work: An Experience in Praxis," p. 23.

[7]Linda Cherrey, "The Political Ideology of Social Work Education" (A Master's Degree Project, presented to the School of Social Administration, Temple University, in partial completion of the requirements for the degree of Master of Social Work, 1973).

[8]See Carol Angell, Julie Kenny and Alan Sherer, "The Concentric Model: A Model for Radical Social Work Practice" (An essay presented to the Faculty of the School of Social Work, San Diego State University, in partial fulfillment of the requirements for the Degree of Master of Social Work, May, 1977); Paul Neustadt, "Radicals in Clinical Social Work: How Their Radicalism is Expressed in Their Practice" (A Paper presented to the Graduate School of Social Work and Social Research of Bryn Mawr College, in partial fulfillment of the requirements for the degree of Master of Social Service, 1978); Carolyn Kott Washburne, "Social Work After the Revolution" (Presented to the School of Social Work of the University of Pennsylvania, in partial fulfillment of the requirements for the Degree of Master of Social Work, 1971), and Susan Eileen Sherry, "Building an Alternative Model of Social Work Practice" (Submitted in partial satisfaction of the requirements for the degree of Master of Social Work, San Diego State University, May, 1978).

tive. The ideological content of social work education is the ideological content of social work as a field. The classroom is one arena for addressing some of the political confusion that is rampant in the field, for presenting radical alternatives, and for making political and ideological struggle an ongoing part of all course discussions.

Radical Teaching

A common source of frustration for students in social work schools is the contrast between some of the ideas presented about social work practice and the style in which the material is communicated in the classroom setting. At the same time that the subject matter of a class discussion might focus on the importance of involving service users in agency decision making, students have no say over classroom content, requirements, or teaching approaches. At the same time that social work values about the inherent worth and dignity of the individual are being elaborated, students experience devaluation of their worth by faculty. While the benefits of developing contracts with service users is discussed, students are presented with a predetermined plan of study when they begin a new course. When the value of equalitarian relationships between workers and service users is stressed, the faculty members call students by their first names and establish a climate in which students are discouraged and punished when they attempt to influence school policy. Clearly radical students and teachers need to wrestle with ways to make the educational process as well as the content more consistent with socialist principles of equalitarianism.

The classroom needs to become a place in which interested learners, whether faculty or students, can come together to plan and execute a course of study that will satisfy their objectives. Students can have input into what they want to study and how they want to do it. At the same time, in the name of radical equalitarianism this process cannot deny the special expertise and experience that some faculty have. The desirability of encouraging full participation must be balanced against the desirability of making the maximum possible use of the special abilities of each person. One school of social work which is committed to this process expressed the issue in this way.

> There is a clear link between the attempt to develop theory and practice of social work and the attempt to work out the philosophy and practice of teaching of the department. Just as there is a rejection of the idea of social workers imposing things on clients, so there is a rejection of the idea that teachers pass on to students what they need to know. Both students and staff have been trying to overcome the contradictions inherent in the traditional teacher-student roles, and to engage in mutual dialogue. But these efforts are in permanent tension with the need to provide educational continuity, and to build on work done by previous course members in specific areas of theory and practice. One of the

contradictions we cannot escape is that by making available material which has been prepared in advance of the course, and by making at least initial choices about content and teaching methods the staff, past students and fieldwork teachers have made judgements about what are key issues, and so exercise power and influence, being pushed back to some extent into more traditional educational roles.[9]

Perhaps there is an inherent dilemma here. At the same time, we can take some steps to minimize that dilemma. One of these is to plan periods of feedback and criticism about each course, the content, the instructor and the assignments. Ideally such processes will become integrated into the ongoing life of the course. At the least several sessions explicitly designed for feedback and for a modification of aspects of the course can be planned. In cases in which the course is student-led or student-initiated, there is a good deal more room for equalitarianism to develop in the classroom relationships.

Evaluation and grading are difficult areas. Schools require grades, and even radical faculty experience dilemmas about how to deal with grades. In some cases, it is possible to discuss the grading question openly in class and to arrive at some mutually acceptable procedures. Some options include peer evaluation leading to peer grade assignments, agreeing on a single grade for all members of the class, grading on the basis of predetermined and mutually determined contractual agreements about what work will lead to what grade, and determining grades jointly in a student-teacher conference. In cases in which a stronger left exists in the school, it may be possible to use the grading issue as a rallying point for political struggle, for example, by publicly announcing that in a given class students will grade themselves, or that everyone will receive a "pass" grade. These strategies make sense only when students and faculty view them as a clear political statement and are willing to back them up with the ongoing work that will make the grading issue part of a broader political project.

In the 1960s some student radicals took the position that any faculty evaluation of students ran counter to the equalitarianism demanded by radical commitments. However, there is nothing politically inconsistent in radical faculty and radical students engaging in an evaluation process. Ideally the criteria for evaluation should be mutually agreed on by students and faculty or at least mutually understood and accepted as a basis for a working relationship. Students should have as full an opportunity as they desire to attempt to influence the evaluation statement and to attach any dissent they wish. In addition students should have a full opportunity for evaluating faculty. Ultimately the ability of students to influence who teaches and how they teach will rest on the success of students in winning a larger role in the overall process of the school. In some schools students prepare their own evaluations of faculty

---

[9]University of Warwick (England), *Social Work Education at Warwick,* Course in Applied Social Studies, 1977–78, Department of Applied Social Studies, pp. 1–2.

and distribute them to other students in advance of registration. Even in cases in which there is no bureaucratically sanctioned channel for student evaluation of faculty, as Cloward and Piven have suggested, "No faculty member can survive an empty classroom."[10]

Perhaps the single best way to develop a classroom that is consistent with radical commitments is to address the issue of classroom practice directly, in the classroom itself. We will never develop perfect models of radical pedagogy within nonradical schools. However we can make some progress in that direction.[11] Faculty must be prepared, in that process, to be open to challenging the authoritarianism that seems to be fostered by the teaching role and to giving up some of the control they maintain over the classroom. At the same time, students must be prepared to assume a good deal more responsibility for their learning in the classroom than they have typically done in the past. The requirement that teachers and students develop a politically consistent learning environment is demanding but exciting.

Fieldwork Possibilities

There are several ways in which radical students and faculty can express their political sentiments through the fieldwork component of social work education. Most obviously the various forms of radical practice already explicated are options for students in their placements, as well as for full-time workers in their regular jobs. In fact student status can provide social workers with protection that can, in some circumstances, allow them to go politically beyond what otherwise might be possible.

Students do not often receive faculty support for their efforts to develop radical practice in their agencies. That is a real problem, though not an unexpected one. In such situations, students must deal with two problematic institutions—their agencies and their schools. To the extent that radical faculty can be supportive in terms of complementary classroom material and appropriate fieldwork advising, radical students will be in a better position to develop their practice.

---

[10]Richard Cloward and Frances Fox Piven, "Notes Toward a Radical Social Work," in *Radical Social Work*, eds. Roy Bailey and Mike Brake, p. xxii.

[11]Some helpful resources are *The Review of Radical Political Economics*, 6 (Winter, 1975) which is devoted to the subject of radical approaches to teaching; Paulo Freire, *Pedagogy of the Oppressed* (New York: Herder and Herder, 1971); Roger Harrison and Richard Hopkins, "The Design of Cross-Cultural Training: An Alternative to the University Model," *Journal of Applied Behavioral Science*, 3 (1967), 43–60; and Michael Rossman, *On Learning and Social Change* (New York: Vintage Books, 1972). From the social work literature see Mary "Ski" Hunter and Dennis Saleebey, "Spirit and Substance: Beginnings in the Education of Radical Social Workers," *Journal of Education for Social Work*, 13 (Spring, 1977), 60–67.

For some students, fieldwork with radical community organizations, trade unions, or alternative agencies of various sorts is a desirable option. Some schools permit this. Many do not. Radical student groups and radical faculty can press to maximize the extent to which students are free to choose their own placements, or at least to have a significant input into the choice of placement. These placements might include women's groups, community organizations, gay counselling services, alternative services, and so on. In some schools this will require challenging the idea that only a supervisor trained in social work or only a social worker trained in the same school of social work can supervise those students.

Radical or alternative agencies will not provide an appropriate placement for all radical students, however. Most radical graduates of social work schools will take jobs in conventional social agencies, by necessity and because of their political commitment to bringing radical politics into mainstream social welfare settings. In traditional agencies there are two ways in which the development of students' radical practice can be fostered. First, it is helpful for students with a radical perspective to seek placements together in conventional agencies. They will then have each other as a source of support, stimulation, and feedback. Second, both students and faculty can make conscious efforts to influence the political perspective of the fieldwork supervisor. While we can have few illusions that most supervisors will understand and encourage a radical perspective, we cannot assume that supervisors are automatically in the opposite camp, anymore than we can assume that for any social worker. We can recognize that supervisors are not sympathetic to radicalism, in most cases, and can view them as another appropriate target for our political efforts. Radical student groups can plan educational seminars for their supervisors, can provide appropriate reading material, and in other ways can follow the various guidelines suggested earlier for working with nonradical colleagues.

In one case, a group of radically oriented students at the University of Connecticut School of Social Work developed their own combination group living and/or field work situation. In their words,

> Five years ago, a student developed the idea of a group of students living together in the community and acting as a "Link" between the School of Social Work and the community. [He] talked five faculty people into putting up some cash to buy a house in an integrated neighborhood four miles from the school. Other faculty donated furniture, a washing machine and a freezer. For several years, the people who lived at Link became involved in the Blue Hills Civic Association, developed field placements in the community and found other ways to participate in the community.[12]

---

[12]"Link, Inc.," in *Voice, The Student Paper of the School of Social Work*, University of Connecticut, West Hartford, Connecticut, Spring, 1975, p. 11.

Subsequently, the successor cohort of students at Link held a series of seminars on radical political economy at their home. A number of them went on to help form a radical social work group in their local area. In other cases, students have developed free-standing field work assignments. These assignments do not link with existing agencies, but rather represent the efforts of students to develop an independent project. For example, in the mid-1970s, a group of social work students at Carleton University, Ottawa, Canada, established a committee to abolish the training schools that are part of the intermediate world between the criminal justice and social service systems. They consciously chose not to present an alternative to the training schools. Rather they raised important questions about the human and political impact of the training schools. The project was originated and supervised from within the social work school, which gave the students, in this case, more flexibility and support than they might otherwise have had.

As a final suggestion, student social workers might consider exploring more fully the special power they have by virtue of the fact that so many different social agencies are represented in a given school and even in a given classroom, through students' involvement in field work settings. The possibilities are exciting. Students working with grass-roots community groups might be able to make good use of information concerning relevant issues that students placed in conventional agencies could provide. For example, students serving in the Department of Housing and Urban Development (HUD) might find ways to be useful to students working with community groups involved in the squatters' movement, or Walk-In Homesteading, as it is sometimes called. In some cities, squatters target and occupy housing formally under HUD's jurisdiction. HUD's planned response to the squatters, their decisions concerning use of local media and police, and their willingness to negotiate on a part of the squatters demands could be invaluable to a community group in its efforts to plan appropriate strategy. Similarly a student placed in one of the trade unions involved with organizing social service workers could receive potentially valuable information from other students situated in various agencies about the openness of workers to unionization, key workers to approach, likely management responses, and critical issues to stress in the organizing drive. Many possible linkages of this sort can be envisioned. It is even possible for social work students, in preparation for second year placements, to consciously plan linked placements to facilitate progressive political work.[13]

---

[13]As at several other points in the discussion of practice, questions of confidentiality and of loyalty to an agency as opposed to loyalty to the people with whom we identify, are raised. Rather than repeat the basis on which I defend these suggestions and argue their appropriateness, I refer readers to the discussion of working within a social welfare bureaucracy to aid groups of service users, as it was developed in Chapter 7.

Student Input into School Policy

One of the areas in which radical students and radical student groups have been active in social work schools is internal administrative decision-making processes. The Council on Social Work Education requires some student participation in the schools' decision-making processes as a condition of accreditation for the schools. How far students go with this right, and the direction they take with it, cannot be mandated. Typically students exercise their collective power within schools in a modest way. Often they organize student governments as one expression of their desire for a formal organizational presence in the school. However these governments do not tend to represent a radical point of view, or even to fully represent a student point of view. They often serve a cosmetic function or assist in socializing incoming students. Similarly when students have been part of school committees, they have not always developed and aggressively pursued a student perspective. Formal student participation has too often been more coopting than challenging.

Student involvement in school policy making and politics is important for several reasons. Even when faculty members and administration have the best interests of students at heart, and they by no means always do, many forces prevent that sentiment from expressing itself in ways most beneficial to students. For example, faculty members must respond to the mandates of the larger college or university in which the school of social work is located. If faculty members want to preserve their positions, in the face of the financial difficulties of universities, they will opt for larger class size, and hence each teacher will generate more tuition, despite the desirability of smaller classes for enhanced learning. Organized student activity can possibly block such moves and preserve manageable class size. Also faculty members, like all participants in formal organizations, are subject to a process of goal displacement which moves them away from a student perspective. For example, every faculty member believes that his or her content specialization is critical. Very few faculty members challenge the centrality of another's content area since the tables can easily be turned in the next round of curriculum revision. As a result every content area is included in the curriculum, and the freedom of students to select their own content and to plan student-run electives is curtailed in the face of increasing numbers of required courses. Finally faculty members are not students. However well meaning they may be, they do not occupy the same position as students and cannot speak from a student perspective.

In order to make a student perspective heard, students must represent their own point of view. Making student rights a central issue in school politics also provides students with the opportunity to experience political activity and to experiment with social change strategies. In cases where students are isolated in their agencies and so cannot work easily toward social change objectives, school politics can provide a valuable learning arena. Particularly when radical students lead and influence these struggles, as they often do, they can present and implement radical positions in ways that will not be so easy or so possible in a more fragmented post-graduate situation.

It is important that radicals in school settings push beyond traditional student involvement in faculty committees and develop independent forums for students to meet together to develop their own positions and issues. When students participate in faculty meetings, they are too often asked to take a position on alternatives that do not represent a student perspective. The issues that faculty members raise and the ways in which they raise them will not necessarily include a student point of view. Students must meet independently to clarify the issues that are of importance to them, and they must bring those issues aggressively before the various committees of which they are a part. For example, a goal for students might be full and equal participation with faculty in determining school policy. It is unlikely that faculty will raise the issue of a student role in faculty hiring and firing, in selecting new students or in decision making on the distribution of scholarships and grants. These issues will arise only if students aggressively pursue them. And they will not pursue them unless they have leadership from within their ranks that can raise consciousness about those issues and help develop appropriate strategies.

As with any arena of radical practice, it is necessary to work on problems that link the immediate concerns people have with larger issues. For example, in some schools students are rightly fearful of the subtle process by which they can be "counselled out." The lack of simple civil liberties and the coercion involved in this counselling-out process can be a rallying point for student organization. Dealing with this specific issue can enable organizers to raise questions about other issues in which student rights and student input are undermined. Similarly addressing student concern about a particularly authoritarian teacher can provide an opportunity for raising issues about student involvement in classroom decision making and in student evaluation. This in turn can lead to an exploration of the possibilities for student involvement in hiring and firing faculty.

Some student groups have found it useful to push the issue of making the job of staffing student government a field work placement. Faculty members have a great deal of time each week, in addition to the power which comes from their longer tenure in the school, to help assure that their interests are represented. Students are at a disadvantage in this way. A strategy is to work for the right of students to select an applicant for this field work position from among interested candidates. The student so selected would then be charged with any of a range of responsibilities. That student could attend meetings held during periods when students are normally in their agencies. He or she could organize a student newsletter; provide linkages with the National

Federation of Student Social Workers (NFSSW); staff a variety of student committees, for example, women's rights, minority issues, or curriculum; organize speakers and other special organizational forums; and help the student social work government link with other student groups in the university. Supervision could be organized as a collective endeavor by student government leaders. Alone these steps will not move a radical agenda forward. However to the extent that a radical caucus is active within the school, such staffing makes possible a great deal more progressive activity and education than might otherwise be possible.

Radical students in schools of social work are faced with the same problems of fragmentation that exist among the ranks of social service workers in social agencies. Many schools separate the Associate Arts students, the Bachelor or Social Work students, and the Master of Social Work students from one another. Faculty may or may not overlap, in cases in which a single school grants more than one of these degrees. However students typically do not have a great deal of contact with each other. They do not attend the same classes, they do not sit on the same committees, and they often organize separate student governments. As a result, their ability to deal with the faculty, administration, and larger university from a position of strength is weakened. Radical students may find it useful to address these issues by organizing formal and informal mechanisms for students at various levels to meet together, develop common agendas, and plan common strategies. Even in cases where the faculty and administrative structure are not organized on a cross-degree basis, an aggressive student organization representing the interests of all student social workers can pressure the faculty and administration to deal with common problems collectively.

In the arena of building wider coalitions of students, the relationship of individual student groups to the NFSSW ought to be explored. The NFSSW has shifted in a more conservative political direction over time and has not grown as a powerful force in schools of social work as it might have. It has had some influence in pushing for increased student participation through its efforts with the Council on Social Work Education, and in this way it has served a useful role. It has also held annual conferences which have brought together hundreds of social work students from across the country. These conferences have served some useful functions, particularly in providing an opportunity for students to compare notes and in bringing progressive speakers, workshops, and ideas to a broader cross section of students than might have been exposed to these influences in their separate schools.

However the NFSSW conferences have tended to duplicate the process and content of mainstream social work education, and the role of the NFSSW has increasingly become one of socializing students to the culture of traditional social work conferences and organizations. Some students who have been heavily involved in that organization have viewed their involvement as a first step toward their full integration into mainstream social work organizations and jobs.

At the same time, the potential of the NFSSW to represent a student position aggressively once again and to represent a more progressive perspective within social work is great. A strong student federation, on the national level, could find a variety of ways to lend support and encouragement to the struggles of individual student groups, and it could have some influence on the conservative direction that is taken by most mainstream social work organizations. To do so, however, it will need to develop considerably greater clarity about its political position.

Radical students could do some important political work in and around this organization. The organizational strength of the student federation, its leadership, and its short range agendas tend to change rapidly, reflecting the turnover in the student population. However some continuity in the organization's ability to do political work and to serve as an influence among social work students could be achieved if a group of radical students undertook the project of developing a coherent political direction for the organization and provided some leadership. To the extent that radical students understood the role of social work schools in training a compliant social service labor force, and linked that analysis with a radical analysis of the nature of social services, they could develop, through the NFSSW, an organization with some capability to represent a dissenting voice and a radical voice. The power which a nationally united student body of social workers could have is potentially significant.

Conclusion

Similar political currents and tendencies circulate among student social workers as they do among practitioners, although there may be somewhat more openness to radical thought among students than among practitioners, in general, Many people enter schools of social work wearing political blinders. They are not open to radical ideas in social work school, as they are not open to radical ideas, in general. They are concerned about preparing themselves to become valuable commodities so that they can sell themselves effectively in an increasingly tight job market. Many have strong upwardly mobile status drives. At the same time, in social work schools, as in the society at large, there is a significant minority of students who are open to radical ideas. Some of the people in this group are consciously radical, having developed a political framework before coming to school. Others become more radical through encounters and experiences in schools of social work.

Most people do not enter school or leave school with a radical perspective, but they do complete their educational program with a disturbing sense that they are less clear than they once were about the overall meaning of social work, in general, and their role within social work, in particular. This is true even when they are not clear that their confusion is a political confusion. In fact students are more likely to graduate believing that their primary deficit is not political, but is their inadequate development of practice skills. Social work schools do have problems helping students develop adequate skills, and students have a legitimate concern about that issue. However the basis of the concern and the self-doubt is actually a political one, rather than a technical one. Students do not have a clear sense of what it means to be a social worker. This will come as no surprise, since social work is so contradictory in the political purposes it represents, and students are not helped to sort out the contradictions or to take a position on them. Students try to compensate for lack of direction by developing a stronger technological repertoire.

Each of these three types of students—the already radical, the emerging radical, and the confused and concerned nonradical—can profit from the fuller development of a radical presence within schools of social work. The radical students can solidify their understanding of what radicalism means, and the nonradical students can become acquainted with an alternative perspective which might have greater appeal to them, later in their lives even if it does not influence them significantly while they are still in school. A radical student presence can also be a positive influence on those faculty members whose sentiments are progressive but not explicitly socialist. Finally a radical current in schools of social work creates ripples in the larger social work world, to the extent to which it is coherent and well organized.

Social workers tend to feel relatively powerless as a group, and student social workers tend to feel even more powerless. Student social workers carry with them the sense that they cannot influence their immediate political environment or the larger political environment. This can become a self-fulfilling prophecy. And yet student social workers, like all of us, have more power than they realize. An important role for radical social work students and faculty is to help themselves and others experience a personal sense of power and ability to influence the world.

Social work schools are not the most critical institutions in the world. At the same time, they clearly connect with social work itself and, as I have argued, social work connects in a variety of ways with significant institutions and dynamics of the society. For these reasons, the ferment that radical people in schools of social work can create is potentially of significance in influencing the immediate environment of the schools, the process that occurs in those schools, and the impact of radicalism in the social service sector as a whole.

12

Starting and Staying

Introduction

This chapter explores the question of how we can sustain our efforts as radicals over time in the face of the multitude of forces opposed to radicalism. To examine this critical issue, I will develop a framework through which radicals can evaluate the impact of their work. Then once again I will look at the important question of the risks that people face when they express their radical commitments. Finally, I will discuss the balance we all must achieve between meeting our own immediate and personal needs and meeting our needs to pursue a socialist commitment.

Evaluating the Impact of Our Work

To the extent that radicals look to conventional standards of political success for validation of the usefulness of their work, they will find relatively little encouragement for pursuing their commitments. Even at the height of the left's electoral success in the United States at the turn of the century, relatively few socialist officials held elective political office. Nor has there been a major left political party in the United States to which a majority of people, or even a near majority of people, have given their allegiance.

This fact understandably discourages many leftists and would-be leftists and weakens the ability of the left to organize people toward socialist objectives. Whether we think in terms of the role of radicalism within the social service sector or elsewhere, few people have been willing or able to engage in political work that can promise what seems to be such modest payoff.

Leftists pursue their political beliefs for many reasons. They feel they must take some action in the face of the systemic inhumanities around them. They are moved by their moral commitments, by an analytic perspective which suggests that the dilemmas of capitalism must lead to systemic change, by an understanding of the long-range futility of reformism, and by an awareness that radicalism enables them to experience greater consistency between their analysis and their actions. All of these motivations are legitimate. They do not substitute for tangible results. Unless and until the left can make more of a difference in our social and political lives, it will be caught in a cycle in which the anticipation of political marginality fosters disengagement from radicalism, in turn limiting the impact of socialism as a viable force in our lives.

This evaluation suggests the necessity for continued experimentation with ways of developing a socialist analysis and socialist strategy that can speak to the needs, pains, and aspirations of a majority of people. That is the task to which this book has been devoted, with special reference to the social service sector.

At the same time, without denying the limitations of the left, we must also take credit for the role that the left has played, even in that hub of imperialism, the United States. The left does play a role, and sometimes a significant role, in the social dynamics of this country. However leftists are not always aware of the ways in which they influence political dynamics and certainly nonleftists are not aware of the impact of the left. There are several reasons why this is so.

First, the role of the left is written out of the official histories of this country. When our own experiences are reflected back to us in history books, in newspapers, or in the speeches and pronouncements of politicians, they are presented in a way that stresses the role which the elite has played and plays in shaping history. For example, we tend to understand the history of the New Deal in terms of the activities of Franklin Roosevelt, rather than in terms of the role of the labor movement and the left in mobilizing millions of people to demand changes. The New Deal programs were, in part, a result of the far more radical demands raised by the left in the decade preceeding their initiation. Only a reading of the news of that day or of left literature today can remind us of how close establishment forces felt this country was to a revolution. In fact the organization, ideology, and ferment generated by the left seemed significant and was one of the forces contributing to the changes that occurred. Those changes were not fundamental, in the sense of challenging the long-term prerogatives of capital or in terms of substantially improving the lot of the working class of the United States. That they were not is a reflection of the fact that, after all, the left was not able to sustain a revolutionary momentum. At the same time, the changes did help to make life more bearable for millions of people. We will search vainly for reports of statements by Roosevelt or other political leaders of the day which acknowledged the role of the left in creating a climate leading to those changes.

We can make the same argument for other political periods, in a similar fashion. The War on Poverty is credited to the initiative of John Kennedy, and no analyst of that period would deny the importance of his role. At the same time, it is no coincidence that those reform efforts followed on the heels of the civil rights movement. Similarly neither the establishment political forces nor the center stream political constituencies that dominated the antiwar movement in its later phases formally credited the role of the left in stimulating the antiwar movement through the 1960s.[1] It is instructive to recall that some of the earliest organizing against the war stemmed from the Students for a Democratic Society (SDS). SDS was viewed widely at that time as a disreputable fringe element. When the United States finally withdrew from Vietnam, defeated both by domestic dissent and by an opponent with more strength than that of the United States, liberal and conservative forces, as would be expected, did not publicly acknowledge the role of the left.

In general as we analyze the various social and political changes that have occurred in this country, we will frequently find that the left has played a significant role. The women's movement, while not predominantly radical in its present form, owes much of its early development to leftist women. Social welfare measures, compromised though they are, would not exist even at the level they do if the left had not been involved in organizing for more fundamental changes. The existence of the labor movement might have been forstalled without a powerful commitment on the part of the left to labor organizing. In general the left has played an important role in raising issues and in organizing for change in many of the critical political developments of this century.

A first step for us, therefore, in evaluating the importance of the left in our lives, is to understand the contribution the left has made historically in the United States. As we would expect, conventional sources will not often acknowledge our role. History is necessarily written within the framework of a

---

[1]The more astute observers within these groups, however, are fully aware of the significant role played by the left. While the public proclamations of non-radical groups and people ignore the contribution of the left, the acknowledgment of the role of the left is signaled by the tremendous panic generated by the left among establishment forces each time it achieves organizational significance.

larger political perspective. The political framework which informs most historical research and writing is one that takes the major assumptions of capitalist society for granted. As leftist analysts reexamine the political life of the United States, they and we learn more about the significance of the left. That history can encourage us to understand that our present work also is likely to influence the directions we take as a nation.

A second reason why we tend not to be fully aware of the impact of the left is that we evaluate the role of the left on the basis of nonradical criteria, and on those bases we have not been important. For example, in conventional political analysis, the role of a political party is judged on the basis of its success in the electoral arena. On that basis, with the exception of a brief period at the turn of the century when socialists achieved some electoral victories, the left has not been successful. However that standard of political evaluation is not one that is rooted in a socialist perspective. The left has not operated primarily through electoral mechanisms to this point in this country. It has focused on workplace and community organizing. Its success or failure needs to be evaluated in terms of its work in those arenas.

Similarly if we were to conduct an opinion poll of a cross section of people and ask their assessment of "the free enterprise system" as compared with socialism, we would record answers that suggested that a leftist perspective was not widely shared. On the other hand, if our opinion poll were to explore people's attitudes toward the role which big business plays in the society or the larger political purposes government plays, we would discover that many people do hold radical ideas although they do not conceptualize their ideas in those terms. This point is similar to one I developed when I explored the theoretical basis of radical research. Social and political theory influence the questions we ask of the world. From a socialist perspective, we investigate political life in terms that are different from a liberal or conservative inquiry. We look for different kinds of development since we have a different understanding of political process. On that basis we discover a more significant role for the left than we otherwise would.

Finally we undermine our appreciation of our own importance when we fail to think in terms of historical processes. Our impact as leftists is not defined by our work in any single period, divorced from preceding and subsequent periods. This is especially important to keep in mind during a more conservative time, such as the present is. Each generation of leftists plays a role in maintaining a legacy of leftist thought and action. Even if a given period is one in which a more visible and powerful leftist movement is not possible, the leftism of every period helps keep alive a sense of struggle, a sense of an alternative, and a culture of resistance. Each reemergence of a more active left is just that—a reemergence—and not a totally new discovery of the socialist alternative. We are playing our role now in helping to maintain that current of political life.

It would certainly be exciting for all of us if we had the historical good fortune to be born in a period of more advanced political struggle, and even more so if we were born in a period in which society had progressed to the point where its primary business was fostering human welfare. That is not our lot in life. We cannot define or choose the historical circumstances of our lives. At the same time, when we have come to terms with the realities of the historical period into which we were born, we can begin to think about the role which our generation can play to facilitate a longer range historical process with the potential to create a more humanized society. Part of our role is to influence the fate of future generations. In knowing that we are doing this, we can take heart even during frustrating political periods and evaluate our own role in the political development of society more positively.

Risk

One of the first issues that is raised in people's minds as they consider moving in a more radical direction is the question of the risks they take in jeopardizing job and career. Certainly there are enough cases illustrating the harassment and persecution of radicals in the social services, as elsewhere, to give some credence to this concern. Without minimizing the realistic dangers that radical work can entail, there are several ways to look at this issue that may cast the question in a somewhat more manageable light.

First, it is useful to remember that the risk radicals face from engaging in radical work is the risk of retaliation by forces of the status quo. These are the very same forces whose propaganda heavily conditions our thinking about the question of risk. We develop a reaction to the dangers involved and subsequently a perspective on risk as a result of our exposure to establishment thinking about risk.

What follows from these understandings is that it is in the best interests of the establishment to magnify the risk involved in trying to change the social order. Without underestimating the significance of the repression that does occur, it is also reasonable to say that the risk involved in radical work may be less or different than we are programmed to believe by conventional perspectives on the question.

There are a number of ways in which we can protect ourselves against the danger of harassment or firing. We can be certain that we do our jobs as well as possible so that we reduce the opportunity we give to agencies to fire us on distorted charges of incompetence in our work. We can work collectively when we raise more risky issues. We can plan our strategies in a way that assesses the tolerance of an agency to being pushed without creating unacceptable levels of retaliation.

At the same time, most of us actually operate well on the safe side of the point at which further resistance would lead to self-destruction and less resistance would imply acquiescence. Our unwillingness to expose ourselves to risk has made most of us act in a more conforming way than need be, even allowing for our concerns about safety. Certainly we should be alert to the point at which a more explicit expression of our radicalism will be self-destructive. However the reality is that we have a good deal more room to maneuver than we generally use.

Many people have an unrealistic notion of what is involved in radical work. We conjure up stereotyped images of bomb throwing and individualistic grandstanding acts of resistance to supervisors and the like. These are largely establishment created images of radicalism, perpetuated to dissuade people from exploring the possibilities for themselves of engaging in radical political work. They are partially effective in making radical work seem unreasonably dangerous. As a result many people, contemplating this image of radical work, conclude that it is unacceptably risky and are discouraged from beginning. These are, in fact, not realistic images of radical work. Radical work, to be effective, cannot go too far beyond the experience of a majority of people, since it will fail to move them if it does. To the extent that we stay within reach of the majority, we increase the chances that others will join us in both radical work and in defense against repression.

We can also make strategic decisions about directions and activities that are too risky for us. We might decide that particular projects could result in our being fired. We might not be willing or able to pay that price at a given moment, or we might decide that the gains are simply not worth the costs. On the one hand, we need to be alert to the danger that we will so fear taking risks that we will never express our radical political commitments in the real world. On the other hand, it is perfectly reasonable for us to assess the risk involved in any given activity and include that assessment as one of the considerations that informs our actions.

The issue of risk taking can be analyzed in light of several other considerations. First, we must weigh the risks we take when we pursue a radical commitment against the risk we take when we pursue business as usual. We normally do not think of the question of risk in conventional social work practice, and yet we run considerable risk when we operate according to the established rules. For example, like many other social workers who have not pursued radical analysis and practice, we will become cynical, despairing, and burned out. Conventional practice asks us to deny our awareness of the enormity of the social problems we address. It asks us to accept a role for ourselves and an approach to our work that cannot allow us to be fully effective in helping others and that requires that we devote ongoing energy to denying much of the social, economic, and political reality around us.

We normally do not consider these responses as falling in the category of "risk taking." The traditional social worker, who has, in fact, been defeated by years of engagement with the social welfare sector, is not considered "at risk" but rather is considered to be a mature professional. Defeatism is not defined as a danger, but as a part of normal socialization. In order to appreciate the costs of conventionalism, we need to examine our own inner experience. When we have made that self-inspection, we may decide that the risks of radicalism and the risks of conservatism are simply two kinds of risks. Put in this light, the risks of pursuing radical politics may, in fact, seem like the better choice.

In a similar fashion, we need to weigh the risks we take as radicals against the benefits we experience from pursuing radical politics. As radicals we cannot hope to address all the problems that face us and all the people with whom we work so effectively that they no longer oppress us. However through pursuing radical politics, we will have the satisfaction of knowing that we are addressing those problems head on. We will be able to experience greater congruence between our theory and our practice. We will also have the experience of winning concrete gains, at some points, and of helping others to develop a sense of competence and mastery in their lives. Even when these victories are few and far between, however, many radicals find considerable satisfaction experiencing their lives as consistent with what they believe to be the larger thrust of world history. We cannot overlook the pleasure that comes from experiencing one's life as increasingly committed to a more humanized world and from winning victories toward that end.

Finally, as we become more involved in radical politics, we may discover that our notion of what a risk is changes. The rewards and career development that we may have wanted for ourselves may seem considerably less important to us as we become more involved in radical work. This is not to say that we will become more adept at self-denial. It is to say, as an example, that the joys of being a social work supervisor may seem less like joys, as we experience more fully the cost to us of having to enforce oppressive agency policy or as we come to understand more fully that the power to influence fundamental social dynamics lies, not with the supervisors of the world, but with the rank and file. The goals we had set for ourselves may change so that pursuing a career, in the conventional sense of that term, will seem less important. Obviously as our larger political framework shifts, so too will our inner assessment of our needs and wants.

Whether or not this inner process occurs, it is not necessary for those considering their own political directions to anticipate all of these future possibilities at the outset. Of course some consideration of the question of risk is always appropriate. However it makes a good deal more sense for us to think of a model in which we enter the political arena at some point that feels right to us, experience the pleasures, problems, and dangers that arise, and make judgments, over time and in each case, about what is possible and what is desirable for us. The point of this discussion has been to suggest that we need not be stymied in our efforts to consider the radical alternative by a blanket fear of the dangers that such a course will entail. There will be dangers. At the same time, the sense of danger we experience is likely to be influenced by each of the factors I have discussed. The situations we will face and the ways we experience these situations are not likely to look like we think they might look in anticipation.

Serving Ourselves and Serving Others

Those engaging in radical change efforts and those considering such involvement must accept the fact that the struggle to achieve a Socialist States of North America will be a long-range enterprise. We will be involved with this effort for many years.

Therefore it seems important that we all consider what it will take for us to become involved now, at some level, and what it will take for us to stay involved over the years. What we do today and tomorrow to help build socialism is important. We cannot be complacent about the short run. The world is in too much trouble for complacency, and we ourselves run too much risk of losing sight of more fundamental goals if we wait for some more appropriate future time to engage. At the same time, we must also sustain our energies over the long haul.

Most radicals find that their involvement in organized political work increases and decreases at various points in their lives. There can be no other way for most people. We will experience periods of greater activity and periods when we are forced to retreat. The pressures of the larger society and the demands of our personal lives will dictate that we draw back at some points. Similarly our political commitments will push us forward at other points. We can examine the nature and causes of our retreat when we are in a period of retreat, and we can take steps to move forward again. At the same time, we must not be intolerant of our need to retreat. We can take a longer view of our role, as we take a longer view of the larger process of change. What we do today and tomorrow is important. What we do over five years, ten years, or fifty years is also important. This is not an argument for complacency. It is an effort to develop a perspective on long-term political involvement that will sustain more of us in more aspects of our lives than will a single admonition to all of us to place ourselves on the barricades at each and every moment.

As we must balance short- and long-term involvements, so too must we balance the efforts we make to serve our own immediate needs in the short run and the steps we take to serve ourselves and others through broad-scale social change in the long run. Too often radical people and radical organizations have been, or have seemed to be, opposed to people's efforts to please themselves. They have viewed these efforts as contradictory to radical politics, as though radicals ought not to take care of themselves in ways that they can. However just the opposite is true. Since our political tasks are demanding, we must find ways to take care of ourselves in the short run, as well as find ways to work toward the kind of society in which taking care of ourselves will not pose such a large problem.

This issue often faces people who are radical or who are considering the meaning of a radical commitment in their lives as they face the problem of earning and having money. Very few social service workers are likely to deal with the political dilemmas that would arise from being rich. At the same time, the salaries earned by social service workers allow them to take vacations, buy cars, and so on. Social service workers are experiencing the same financial difficulties as are most working people in this country. However they may well have more money at their disposal than do many other people. It is contradictory to radical political commitments to have enough money to buy amenities and to enjoy these amenities?

Some very important and difficult political questions are involved in this issue. The ways in which any person resolves them may differ from time to time and may differ from the resolution which other people make. In wrestling with this issue, the following distinctions may be useful.

First, it is important to distinguish between having a small surplus to spend on nonessentials and being rich. Of course this is a highly subjective distinction, and each person will make it in a different way. However it seems useful to address the issue in these terms. If being radical involves financial self-sacrifice beyond a given limit, we will not sustain our radical commitments since they will ask too much of us. On the other hand, part of our radicalism reasonably will involve financial support for movement work when that is possible. In part then the political issue is not identical to the monetary issue. It is what we do with the money, and that will vary over time and under various personal and political circumstances.

A second distinction centers on what we do to earn the money we have. Social service workers have what money they do have by virtue of working directly for it. In this way it is legitimate to distinguish our salaries from the profit-making activities of capitalists who make money by virtue of exploiting the labor of others. It can be argued, with some legitimacy, that our salaries are derived from other exploitative relationships, since they are paid from tax monies which are borne disproportionately by lower income people. However this fact seems less compelling than the distinction between earning salaries and making a profit through owning capital.

Similarly a useful distinction can be made between earning a salary as a result of the work we do in welfare settings and going out of our way to take steps to earn more money for the sake of earning more money. It may be that radicals, like nonradicals, will find it necessary to try to earn more money at various points in their lives. At the same time, to the extent that those actions violate our political commitments, they need to be examined carefully. At some points in our lives, for example, it may be possible and desirable for radical social service workers to work directly with and for movement groups and to live on the low pay which movement groups can provide. At other times, we may find that such an arrangement is not possible. Again the judgments are subjective and individual. In making them, we need to balance the personal needs we feel for more immediate material rewards with our willingness and ability to live with less money and to experience the satisfactions of full-time movement work.

It seems reasonable then that we balance our immediate needs for money, and the satisfactions it can allow us to purchase, with the political commitments we have. There are likely to be some conflicts between these impulses. Few people will resolve their conflicts by renouncing their desires for material security. A greater danger is that people will abandon their radical politics because of their guilt at wanting material things. We must expect to live with this contradiction in our lives, just as we live with other contradictions that arise from being radical and continuing to live and work in the existing society. The contradictions will be dealt with in different ways over time, depending on the support we have around us for exploring alternatives. The position likely to serve us least well is a purist position, which would tend to lead us to disengage from radical work. At the same time, the conservative conditioning we have each experienced by virtue of living in this society must be explored, questioned, and challenged.

In addition to dealing with the question of finding satisfaction outside of the context of our political lives, it is important that we give serious attention to the question of finding increasingly more satisfaction through our political work. Our political work needs to be made as satisfying as possible, so that it represents in practice a more fulfilling way of living and supports us in wrestling with the parts of ourselves that are still rooted in capitalist perceptions of "the good life."

We will need to find ways to please ourselves in our work, to reward ourselves for work well done, and to console each other for failures and hardships. We need to develop an appropriate way to enjoy the society we are working to create in the midst of the old society. We can do that through many aspects of our work, including our effort to develop nonhierarchical, nonsexist, and nonracist ways of relating to others. We can invent ways to celebrate the common experiences that nurture our political visions and our deepest human impulses, at one and the same time. In other words, we must find nurturing and playful ways to experience life in the short run as part of our long-term political work.

Radical social work is not a technique or a "practice modality." It is the effort to bring a socialist vision and socialist commitments to bear on our occupational choices as social workers. As such it speaks potentially to every aspect of our lives. No one will be "perfectly radical" all the time. All of us will experience doubts, fears, and confusion. All of us will be torn between the desire to retreat to familiar conventionality and the need to push forward on radical agendas. We can expect to experience these contradictory pulls, and we must be tolerant of our alternative predispositions. We must be tolerant, not in order to condone complacency or conservatism, but in order to allow ourselves to move toward greater consistency with radical views, more clear-minded commitment, and integration of a radical posture.

Radicalism involves various costs, including the risks we take, the potential isolation we feel from what is still the nonradical majority, and the sense of deviancy we may experience and must master. At the same time, radicalism suggests possibilities for changing society in ways that will nurture us more deeply than present society does. It suggests the possibility for greater integration of our lives, for greater integrity, for collectivity, and for movement toward more humane and fulfilling values. I look forward to joining with increasing numbers of social service workers and increasing numbers of others, as well, in working militantly, vigorously, and playfully toward a society that will nurture all of its people, as its first priority.

Index